EVERYMAN HIS OWN POET

Books by A. D. Van Nostrand

THE DENATURED NOVEL

EVERYMAN HIS OWN POET

EVERYMAN HIS OWN POET

Romantic Gospels in American Literature

A. D. Van Nostrand

McGRAW-HILL BOOK COMPANY

New York   Toronto   London   Sydney

for Christie,
Douglas,
Amy,
Jillian,
Kipp

A Note on Texts and Citations

Most of the quotations in this book are from works that are available in reprint editions, sometimes many reprints; and citations of any given edition of these works would not be very useful. I have included the references to these quotations in my text, naming the chapter or other appropriate part of the source from which I am quoting. Any quotation without such a reference or without a footnote is covered by the reference to the previous quotation.

But there are some quotations from works that exist in only one edition or one printed source or one contemporary reprint; and these are footnoted. Chapters 1, 4, 7, and Paradigm Four contain footnote references that cite original sources. The footnotes are at the back of the book.

Where there is a choice of texts because of editorial changes, I have quoted from the so-called standard editions, except for those specified as being more reliable than the standard editions, in the bibliography of Robert Spiller *et al.*, *Literary History of the United States* (1963). Where there is a choice of texts because of an author's revisions, I have quoted from the author's latest revision, except in the case of Walt Whitman, where I have followed the text of the ninth edition of *Leaves of Grass* (1892), the last edition that Whitman supervised, and the 1855 edition of the 1855 Preface, the way Whitman originally wrote it. The other prefaces and essays by Whitman follow the text edited by his literary executors, *The Complete Writings of Walt Whitman* (1902).

Acknowledgments

A longer version of Chapter 4 was originally published as *"The Bridge* and Hart Crane's 'Span of Consciousness,' " in Richard M. Ludwig, ed., *Aspects of American Poetry*, Essays Presented to Howard Mumford Jones (Copyright © 1962 by the Ohio State University Press. All Rights Reserved). This chapter reprints quotations from Brom Weber, ed., *The Letters of Hart Crane: 1916–1932* (New York: Hermitage House, 1952); from Brom Weber, *Hart Crane: A Biographical and Critical Study* (New York: Bodley Press, 1948); and Waldo Frank, ed., *The Complete Poems of Hart Crane* (New York: Copyright © 1933, 1958 by the Liveright Publishing Corp.). I have also quoted from Elizabeth Nowell, ed., *The Letters of Thomas Wolfe* (New York: Charles Scribner's Sons, 1956; from F. O. Mattheissen and Kenneth B. Murdock, eds., *The Notebooks of Henry James* (New York: Oxford University Press, 1947); and from *The Art of the Novel: Critical Prefaces by Henry James* (New York: Charles Scribner's Sons, 1948). I have quoted from William Faulkner's titles: *The Sound and the Fury* (New York: J. Cape and H. Smith, 1929 and Random House, 1946); *Absalom, Absalom!* (New York: Random House, 1936); *Go Down, Moses* (New York: Random House, 1942) and *Intruder in the Dust* (Random House, 1948). I have quoted from William Carlos Williams, *Paterson* (Copyright 1946, 1948, 1949, 1951, 1958 by William Carlos Williams. Reprinted by permission of New Directions Publishing Corp.), and from *The Autobiography of William Carlos Williams* (New York: Random House, 1951. Copyright 1948, 1949, 1951 by William Carlos Williams. Reprinted by permission of New Directions Publishing Corp.). I appreciate the permission to reprint these quotations, and I thank these publishers for their generous assistance.

Contents

Every man with self-respect enough to become effective, if only as a machine, has had to account to himself for himself somehow, and to invent a formula of his own for his universe, if the standard formulas failed.

HENRY ADAMS

Paradigm One

Words are the problem. Not just in the beginning, either, but all the way along. How do you find the words to convey what you cannot comprehend without them? My subject is a group of writings that does not have a name, although it includes some of the most prominent and durable fictions in American literature. There is no generic term for them in critical usage, because they are not generally considered as a group. But if you think of them together, they become a means of understanding and appreciating a great many other writings, both good and poor. This small group of distinctive literary works is the center of my subject; I cannot yet define the perimeter.

Finding a name for them would help to describe what they express in common, which is the attempt, or rather many attempts, to find a vast overview of the universe. The authors of these attempts all struggled to answer the same question, which is this: How do you generate a single theory of all events to explain everything that plagues you? Moreover, how do you make this cosmos of your own conceiving come alive?

Let the perimeter go. It is something to build to. Defining the center of this circle burdens me now. At the center is this group of sprawling fictions that cannot be categorized according to any one literary form. But they do fit certain generalizations. These anomalous writings have the same sort of literary history. Most of them took years to write, and they

were never really finished. Once published, they were regarded as failures, then rediscovered from an academic distance, studied with reverence and ingenuity, and later called
classics. Thoreau's *Walden* and Whitman's *Leaves of Grass*
are among this group; so are Emerson's *Nature*, Poe's *Eureka*, and *The Education of Henry Adams*. Melville's *Moby
Dick*, Hart Crane's *The Bridge*, and Williams' *Paterson* belong with these irregular fictions, along with a lesser work,
the vast, unfinished—and unformed—manuscript of Thomas
Wolfe. These works of art dramatize a characteristic way of
looking at one's self in the world which is generally called
romantic. Together they reveal a persistent overstatement of
a romantic world view, and the overstatement is parochial
and peculiarly American. These fictions manage to sound like
gospels and manuals of instruction at the same time. They
are distinctively evangelical. Even as they conceive of a particular idealism they attempt to make it practical and workable.

How to categorize these writings? They have been variously called novels, romances, essays, poems, free-verse experiments, personal epics, and autobiographies. Each of them
breaks the conventions of the literary form that ostensibly
contains it. Whether in prose or verse or both, each work is
autobiographical, each employs devices of fiction, and each
dramatizes a theory of poetry. They are hybrids, formally
anomalous—no help there for a name. But they do have one
obvious quality in common: they emphasize the dramatic
persona of the author. Although they are vastly discursive,
and despite their disparate subjects, each one expresses its
author's attempt to build a universal system out of words and
make it function in fact. Because they all represent the
struggle to build the one true cosmos, I choose to call them
cosmologies.

This philosophical term presents some difficulties and
some possibilities both. "Cosmology" is not a common literary word. It is used in the disciplines of metaphysics and

theology and sometimes in astronomy. But the word is use-fully general. A cosmology is any philosophy of the nature of the universe, any theory of an orderly, all-encompassing sys-tem, such as these literary works present. The important property of the word for my purpose is the sense of whole-ness that it designates.

The main connotations of the term "cosmology" are most likely to be religious and possibly astronomical. Both are congenial to the literary purpose I have in mind. A cosmol-ogy is a large holistic scheme that either explains or dram-atizes a man's relation to his God or gods and therefore to everything else he can perceive. Simple or sophisticated, it is an ancient, elemental expression. Even the most primitive religions have rituals that re-create the world. The worshiper sanctifies a certain place or space and turns back time to make his own symbolic genesis. Thereby he dramatizes his cosmology, his theory of the universe. But the works I speak of go beyond religious liturgy. They do not re-create some given world. They *create* it.

These literary cosmologies are necessarily original. The na-ture of the universe which they separately propose differs rad-ically from any theology of an extrinsic god. They are roman-tic. They either ignore or qualify the notion of a hierarchy of God and man. They deny the traditional concept of the Great Chain of Being, for example, in which God and man remain fixed in a system of separated status. They propose, instead, a conceptual universe in which all being is contin-uous and unseparated, and which can best be described as or-ganic. Such an organic universe is subjective. Each cosmos is the projection of its author's consciousness, and is therefore necessarily original.

My strategy is to discover a more specific meaning for the term cosmology, not for its own sake but to clarify the nature and significance of these literary works. I have in mind a kind of restless play upon the abstract term and on the works themselves. With luck, their meaning will accrete; the abstract term and the particular works will help to clarify each other. Abstract and particulars are not the same, of course. These literary works are not wholly and simply theories of the universe. They are fictions, which is to say they are dramatic. Each of them represents some desperate struggle to *make* a theory of the universe. These writers do not start with one whole viable cosmos; they have to arrive at it. Their unrehearsed ordeals are like going three steps up a ladder and two steps down. The literary work is not only the record of this struggle, it is the very means of it.

Each of these cosmologies is an attempt to express the ineffable universal principle that plagues its author. So he tries to perceive a whole cosmos to explain this principle of being, whatever it is. He stands in particular relation to this cosmos of his own devising. His invention extends him and it also contains him. But when he does manage to express an organic world of the mind, then the ordeal of expression makes the work of art the very cosmos he is trying to explain. Possibly that notion of the cosmology becoming its own cosmos is too abrupt; but it will happen again and again in this study, because the idea keeps recurring in the works themselves.

One question to be answered is why these cosmologies are distinct among fictions. Every fiction, after all, is to some degree a theory of events. Every fiction is (or attempts to be) a closed system of cause and effect. So it is time to come to terms again. These literary cosmologies *are* fictions; that is, they are feigned; they are imagined. They are new orders of being whose parts have been abstracted from the actual world. But I want to use the term cosmology to denote a distinctive insistence on the order they attempt to create. All fictions generate meaning by supposing relationships between one's self and one's circumstance, but the distinction I am trying to make is a matter of degree. These cosmologies all suppose relationships between self and circumstance on the largest possible scale. In their building a theory of events, nothing less than a cosmos will do. This is distinctive among fictions; the author's tenacity and his insistence on making an ultimate and absolute statement produce a characteristic form.

The form is some version of a dialogue between the author (or his persona) and his intractable material. He builds a metaphor of some sort and then returns incessantly to the metaphor in order to expand and develop it. The speaking voice or consciousness explores the possibilities of analogies in whatever things it contemplates. This is what happens in *Nature* and *Eureka*, in *Leaves of Grass* and *Walden*, in *Moby Dick*, in *The Education of Henry Adams* and *The Bridge* and *Paterson*. This consciousness, the persona of the poet, makes a continuous assault on what it visualizes and what it recollects, restlessly turning sensations into metaphors of totality. By a kind of inspired confusion it discovers what it means. Characteristically the author's restless struggle with a governing metaphor accretes a form resembling the universe that he supposes.

One clear example of this reflexive structure is *Moby Dick*, a novel which is also a cosmology. In fact, the book even explains its own form, which is a series of dialogues. The first three paragraphs of "The Spouter-Inn" (Chapter 3) provide a metaphor of the entire novel. They dramatize Ishmael's consciousness at work, trying to decipher an oil painting that turns out to be a graphic record of the dialogues that will follow it. This painting and his attempts to discover its meaning convey a complete analogy to the novel itself. Having just determined to go to sea on a whaler, to sail to perdition if necessary to rediscover himself, Ishmael has arrived in New Bedford on a black New England winter night. Noting the implications of a tavern sign, "The Spouter Inn: Peter Coffin," he enters the tavern and is immediately confronted by the inscrutable painting, "so thoroughly besmoked and every way defaced, in the unequal cross-lights by which you viewed it, it was only by diligent study and a series of systematic visits to it, and careful inquiry of the neighbors, that you could any way arrive at an understanding of its purpose."

As he confronts this painting and tries to discover its meaning, Ishmael's experience is essentially what it will be aboard the *Pequod*. The way Ishmael confronts the painting is also the way that Melville develops his whole cosmology. Ishmael tries to compensate for "the unequal cross-lights" in which it hangs, "by diligent study and a period of systematic visits to it" and "careful inquiry of the neighbors," in order to arrive at some approximation of its purpose. There is something so ambiguous, so sublime about this spectacle on the wall that "you involuntarily took an oath with yourself to find out what that marvelous painting meant." (The pronoun is "you." He has already cast on the reader the onus of discovery.)

Ishmael speculates about this strange painting: "It's the Black Sea in a midnight gale.—It's the unnatural combat of the four primal elements.—It's the blasted heath.—It's a Hyperborean winter scene.—It's the breaking-up of the ice-bound stream of Time." But all these fancies depend on your interpretation of "That one portentous something in the picture's midst. *That* once found out, and all the rest was plain." This "portentous something," it develops, is a great Leviathan. The painting seems to represent a ship with three dismantled masts, half foundered in a hurricane, and "an exasperated whale, purposing to spring clean over the craft, is in the enormous act of impaling himself upon the three mast-heads."

"A boggy, soggy, squichy picture truly"; and Ishmael's manner of getting at it bears repeating:

> . . . by dint of much and earnest contemplation, and oft-repeated ponderings, and especially by throwing open the little window towards the back of the entry, you at last come to the conclusion. . . .

These are the elements of a metaphor that represents the entire book: the painting in the Spouter-Inn, Ishmael's attempt to discover what it is, and the "unequal crosslights" in which he tries to carry out his search. Metaphor and book alike dramatize the mind perceiving. The act is not described; it simply happens and incessantly recurs: the leap from fact to speculation.

Ishmael's dilemma is a paradigm of *Moby Dick*; it is a skeletal pattern of the whole book. The strategy of the paradigm intrigues me: the use of a model to convey the whole subject in all its complexity. The basic configurations of the subject are inherent in the paradigm, but they are not all at once apparent, except in retrospect; this is the problem. So the strategy is to present this skeletal pattern in different postures: successive paradigms to discover and reveal whatever is there in the subject. This group of cosmologies is my subject; and this paradigm is a way of exemplifying them, of reflecting the way they mean and the significance of the kind of experience they dramatize. Paradigms of cosmologies is my design. But because they are hybrids no one method of literary analysis will suffice. Each of these poets understands his own meaning by exploring what he says as he says it. So their strategy determines mine. Possibly, I can discover the literary and historical significance of these cosmologies by discovering a kind of critical syntax as I go.

So our agenda will be a series of journeys and returns, journeys into these fictional worlds and returns to a paradigm, to the idea of a cosmology. In this way, the parts and the whole idea can work to clarify each other.

I have mentioned some of the distinguishing characteristics of these fictions which I call cosmologies. They all have a doctrine; they all pose some version of an ideal, organic cosmos, a universe of the mind in which all being is continuous and unseparated. It is a religious vision. But the vision is only a fraction of their meaning. These cosmologies are not about any given vision so much as they are about the attempt to express it: the attempt to bring it into being and indoctrinate us all. The dramatic value of these works (and the excitement for the reader) is each author's attempt to express himself, to find a language to convey what he cannot even comprehend without a language.

The crisis of expression obsesses them all, so the first journey in this critical study involves some of the works of Thomas Wolfe and William Carlos Williams. Wolfe never finished the world he tried to build, but the anguish of his struggle is the real story that he had to tell. Williams stated the ideal that Wolfe could scarcely utter. In fact, Williams could state it so easily that he scoffed at it. Wolfe and Williams differently dramatize the search that burdens every one of these cosmologists: the search for a language.

Merely naming an absolute is not enough; and having ignored or qualified traditional metaphors of a God-centered universe they must build a new system of metaphors to convey their own concepts. All these poets were preoccupied with language, not as tracts but as attempts to verbalize the ineffable continuity of all being. In the act of expression the religious vision and the language to convey it are mutually dependent. These writers could achieve a systematic arrangement of concepts (a syntax in the larger sense) only by achieving a systematic arrangement of words. In these cosmologies a philosophy of God and a philosophy of composition are inseparable. If truth could be absolutely named they would never have been written.

CHAPTER ONE

The Mystique of Expression

Thomas Wolfe and William Carlos Williams were both pre-occupied with words. As their fictions testify, each writer was searching for a language to convey what he could not comprehend without it. Wolfe wrote an unwitting and interminable overstatement of his search, and Williams began his with a caricature. Both works are self-conscious, and both are about the problem of expressing a concept called America. Williams' fiction, called *The Great American Novel* (1923), begins as a parody of that legendary work of art, such as Wolfe was seriously trying to write, and Williams turned his parody into a quixotic experiment on the properties of words. Wolfe also experimented with language, but he saw nothing to parody.

Wolfe passionately believed that the great America deserves the great paean, but he was somehow trapped by the idea that until the paean exists, America does not. So he challenged himself to create the one by expressing the other. His fiction is the immense manuscript that he left for his publisher a few months before he died. It is a long and anguished celebration of limitless achievement. Wolfe had worked on it ceaselessly for eight years, for what remained of his life after he published *Look Homeward, Angel* (1929). His colossal monument to America contained dozens of fragments and millions of words on thousands of manuscript pages laid in packing boxes.

Wolfe's second novel, *Of Time and the River* (1935), more than nine hundred pages long, was originally only a

9

part of a part of this manuscript. The massive fiction incorporates fragments that belong in general to two cycles of the
saga Wolfe was trying to tell. The first, from which *Of Time
and the River* was taken, was to be called "The October
Fair." The second, which incorporated the unpublished parts
of the first and nearly all of his writing after 1935, was to be
called "The Vision of Spangler's Paul." Wolfe's final act of
authorship was to organize a table of contents to explain it
all. Significantly, it was a scheme intended to isolate and
specify what still had to be written. After eight years of writing he made an agenda of unfinished business. Using this
agenda, after Wolfe's death, his publisher extracted two
novels: *The Web and the Rock* (1939) and *You Can't Go
Home Again* (1940); and a series of related episodes, *The
Hills Beyond* (1941). Some fragments are still unpublished.

Wolfe's relation to this continuous fiction is really the subject of the fiction. He wrote about writing in his letters and
in his long, autobiographical essay, *The Story of a Novel*
(1936). Fiction and actuality were terribly inseparable to
Wolfe. *The Story of a Novel* is one record of his desperate
struggle with what he called the crisis of "Amount and
Number." He saw himself as the Ancient Mariner, bound to
tell his awful tale in order to be free of it. The thousands of
letters that Wolfe wrote, many of which he never even
mailed, are an encyclopaedic record of this struggle. The
comprehensive selection edited by Elizabeth Nowell, *The
Letters of Thomas Wolfe* (1956), sounds like Wolfe's novels, intoning his voracity and his despair at trying to compress
fact into fiction. He remarked that the outline of his first
book was itself very nearly the length of an average novel. He
was writing three thousand words a day and hoping to increase it. Quantity was a continuous problem. "The business
of selection and revision is simply hell for me—my efforts to
cut out 50,000 words may sometimes result in my adding
75,000." [1] And he despaired over the manuscript of his sec-

ond novel: "Not because I could not write it, but because I could do nothing else but write it.

> The plan and the material, every incident of it, had been clear in my mind for months and months; I saw the whole thing through to its end, down to the minutest detail, and the more I thought about it, the longer it got." [2]

Burdened by almost total recall and by a frightening stamina that allowed him to get it all down, Wolfe tried to rationalize his obsession for totality into a theory of autobiographical fiction. His correspondence over the years suggests a romantic legend growing around these facts. He saw himself as an outcast from the world and yet committed to it, needing desperately to explain himself and his novels to all the people who misunderstood him, and wanting desperately to lead them out of what he supposed to be their own disillusions.

Wolfe's letters tended to be defensive. He would divulge plans for a new book with wild enjoinders to his correspondent to keep silent about them. Invariably it would be the greatest book he had yet written. He would be excited, exhilarated; or else in despair, promising never to write again. ". . . forgive me for talking about myself and my book," he would say, and then start off again about himself and his book. In fact, Wolfe's letters are often more convincing than his novels.

Size was inherently part of Wolfe's subject. Even his final table of contents (which appears as an appendix in Richard S. Kennedy's *The Window of Memory*, 1962) runs to fourteen pages. To Wolfe, the essence of any situation meant the totality of all things inherent in that situation. But size alone could not measure Wolfe's sense of totality. Time and timelessness were other qualities of the dynamic wholeness of all being. Like so many other poets, he was struck by the continuous change of all things and the realization that change is itself a permanent condition. Time meant both flux and

duration, and in *The Story of a Novel* he worked out a nomen-
clature of time in order to talk about totality. In the mind
of his fictional narrator or hero the concepts of past, present,
immutable time, and cyclic change all constitute a nervous,
omnipresent tense.

Wolfe's fiction is also autobiographical in a more obvious
sense. As they were edited and published the novels form a
chronology of his own life. But this is only part of their incessant story, for they repeat and amplify the same events.
The narrative of *Look Homeward, Angel*, begins in 1900,
and the book chronicles the first nineteen years in the life of
Eugene Gant, Wolfe's first projection of himself—the
youngest child of a large family in the hill country of North
Carolina. *Of Time and the River* chronicles events based on
the next four years in Wolfe's life. This second novel is
longer and more discursive than the first, although its narrative time is only one-fifth as long. Then the subject of his fiction began to include his previous writing. The editing of
both novels, under the direction of Maxwell Perkins at Scribner's, left enormous fragments of unpublished manuscript.
Wolfe continued to add to these, and to begin new episodes
as well.

From this gross accumulation, after Wolfe's death, his
second editor, Edward Aswell at Harper's, selected the episodes that continue this saga with a hero named George
Webber. *The Web and the Rock* continues the narrative
present from 1924 to 1928, but it is not merely a sequel. It
telescopes the events of the first two novels, returning to the
narrative time of *Look Homeward, Angel*, and presenting
another version of Wolfe's life to date. *You Can't Go Home
Again* continues the chronicle of George Webber from 1929
to 1937, but in the same reflexive way it retraces events already included in previous novels, in addition to fictionalizing
the whole episode of the publication of Wolfe's first novel.
The effect of all this is a bewildering confusion of fiction and
actuality.

Even so, these fictional installments of Wolfe's life are more ordered than the chaotic manuscript from which Wolfe's editors extracted them. By selecting what would be published, Maxwell Perkins and, later, Edward Aswell, created a proportion that never did exist in the manuscript. Under Perkins' direction *Of Time and the River* was extracted from an enormous saga of Wolfe's European travels and impressions ("The October Fair"). Then, trying to stitch and cut the extracted sections into a whole unit, Wolfe began to add to the beginning, which was his famous account of a long train ride. But the train itself became a focus for Wolfe's description of the lives of the passengers, breeding another autonomous fragment, some 200,000 words long, which he called "K-19." Both "K-19" and the enormous remnant of "The October Fair" were set aside. Perkins advised Wolfe to write some short pieces. Some of these grew into a cluster of episodes about the North Carolina hill country and its past, the so-called Pentland episodes, and these, too, had to be set aside.

The crises of abandoning each of these manuscripts became thematically a part of the fiction that Wolfe continuously wrote. Disenchanted, for six bitter months in 1936 Wolfe carped at Perkins and finally found another publisher. Harper's accepted him, Aswell became his new editor, and Wolfe began to construct his immense scheme to accommodate the myriad of unpublished fragments—all unrelated except for the fact that they were parts of his Gargantuan recollections. The scheme that he left for Aswell included "The October Fair" remnant, "The K-19" fragment, and the Pentland episodes, as well as unused fragments from *Of Time and the River*, and even from *Look Homeward, Angel*.

Wolfe also added more fiction in 1937 that was predictably autobiographical; it was essentially about Wolfe's publishing career and his estrangement from Perkins. This shattering separation provided the theme for the final part of the manuscript which later became *You Can't Go Home Again*. To the very last Wolfe used his own life as a scheme to convey his torrent of impressions. He used his own personal conflicts to dramatize his search for symptoms of his belonging to something larger than himself. In his fiction, as in fact, it was a despairing search.

The idea of a search was all that ever gathered the loose ends in Wolfe's life. As a young man he wrote a letter to his philosophy professor at college, troubled over what it was he must search for. "Your words keep haunting me almost even in my dreams: 'How can there be unity in the midst of ever-lasting change?' In a system where things forever pass and decay, what is there fixed, real, eternal? I search for an answer, but it must be demonstrated to me." [3] His first book, *Look Homeward, Angel,* is all about a bewildered search for the fixed reality. The hero finally makes the stunning discovery that the only fixed reality is within himself. What is real is his own consciousness. This satisfies the hero, but it never satisfied Wolfe. He continued to dramatize himself in his fiction, still searching for some large scheme to which he could belong. He decided that this scheme was America.

After his home town had disinherited him for writing his first book—or so he thought—he had gone to Paris to live, and his letters home were lonely and hurting. He apparently had to define the essence of his entire culture in order to become inseparably one with it. *The Story of a Novel* describes his mission to put America into words, into "A language that would tell its shape, its color, the way we have all known and felt and seen it." He conceived of his life work as building a language to convey the essence of the wholeness of America.

> And when I understood this thing, I saw that I must find for myself the tongue to utter what I knew but could not say. And from the moment of that discovery, the line and the purpose of my life was shaped. [4]

His letters echo this yearning. "Mr. Perkins, no one has ever written a book about America—no one has ever put into it the things I know and the things everyone knows. It may be grandiose, pompous, for me to think I can, but for God's sake let me try." [5] Wolfe sensed some imminent mystical communion of himself and his America, and he needed the words to say it. "I know past all denial," he wrote to Perkins, "what being an American or being anything means; it is not a government, or the Revolutionary War, or the Monroe Doctrine—

> it is the ten million seconds and moments of your life, the shapes you see, the sounds you hear, the food you eat, the colour and texture of the earth you live on. I tell you *this* is what it is, and this is what homesickness is, and by God I'm the world's champion authority on the subject at present." [6]

This letter contains a catalogue of sounds and smells and sights in his America as lyrical as if Hart Crane had written it, or Walt Whitman in a rapturous moment. But most of all it sounds like Wolfe's own fiction.

Book V, *Of Time and the River*, comes closest to rendering the voracity and the despair of Wolfe's search for a language. Entitled "Jason's Voyage," this section contains a writer's diary, which interrupts the narrative with twenty pages of sensations, "splintered flashes without order or coherence." Wolfe called it a random record of the ferment of ten thousand pages and a million words. He railed at "the futility of his insane efforts to memorize every stone and paving brick in Paris, to burn the vision through walls and straight into the lives and hearts of a million people, to read all the books, to eat all the food, and drink all the wine,

> to hold the whole gigantic panorama of the universe within his memory, and somehow make 'one small globe of all his being,' to compact the accumulated experience of eternity into the little prism of his flesh, the small tenement of his brain, and somehow to use it all for one final, perfect, all-and-inclusive work—his life's purpose, his heart's last pulse and anguish, and his soul's desire." [7]

The journal is a record of incessant burden. "Never has the many-ness and the much-ness of things caused me so much trouble," he wrote. "I must mix it all with myself and with America. But infinitely the greater part is in the wash of my brain and blood."

"Jason's Voyage" is a caricature of Wolfe's fiction as a whole. Most of the time Wolfe is indistinguishable from his hero, whether Gant or Webber. He is so intensely close to what he sees and smells and feels that the real conflict in his fiction is his own struggle to order his own material. As the years passed, Wolfe could reflect more philosophically about it, but the consuming nature of his fiction was still a fact. He later wrote to Sherwood Anderson:

> I realize myself through a process of torrential production. . . . As for the rest of it—my death-defying duel with the universe—the business of living which I make so damned hard . . . I think it is pretty closely bound up with my work. In fact, living and working are so close together for me that it seems to me they are damned near the same thing.[8]

Almost everything Wolfe wrote was a tortured record of his struggle to comprehend America. His relativity to the world which he sought to clarify in the first place was indefinable.

The concept of a total expression that inspired Wolfe's fiction also paralyzed it. He could see that somehow language was his problem and his only possibility, but he could not see that his own mystique of an actualizing language was as visionary as the world he sought to represent. Precisely otherwise, William Carlos Williams had his suspicions from the start. He recognized the limiting imprecision of language after he had scarcely begun his first novel, and in this fiction he proceeded to deliberate the poet's possibilities inherent in his problem.

Williams' caricature of the myth, *The Great American Novel*, begins with an uncertain tone of whimsy and sarcasm.

It presents a series of impressionistic episodes that are ostensibly about a little Ford car. But his parody of the consummate fiction must have bored him, for the book abandons this subject after a few chapters, and begins to ponder the relation between words and things. After a false start *The Great American Novel* becomes an author's workbook, serving him the way a series of sketches might serve a painter before he begins a large canvas. These sketches pan across the New World, lingering on past and present scenes that reveal a falseness in the ideal of a consummate fiction. The falseness, he says, comes from a fault in the language, a dishonest relation between words and things. No wonder, the impossibility of The Great American Novel; it may or may not be ineffable, but it is certainly unspeakable.

Language is the subject of *The Great American Novel*; Williams' sketchbook is about words and essence. He proposes that words *make* facts, and he scrutinizes and discusses the words that incidentally convey the episodes of his book. Talking to himself in monologues and dialogues, Williams keeps returning to the idea that word and thing might just be one and the same. He carries on a poet's quarrel with his subject, punctuating his remarks with random catalogues of America, the New World.

Williams' attitude toward this workbook was later vague and noncommittal. He referred to it in his *Autobiography* (1951) as if it had been a wayward indulgence, somewhat embarrassing and best forgotten. In the light of his work as a whole, however, it is anything but wayward. This formless, indulgent series of episodes about the self and words and the world at large was in fact a sketch for the extraordinary work of art about America that he finally did write. His cosmology called *Paterson* takes up the subject of words and things (and the "thingness" of words) where his early workbook left off. Williams came to scoff and stayed to labor. It took another twenty years of writing verse and prose before he could even begin *Paterson*. His superb cosmology reflected a life's work, and it is all about language. *Paterson* begins with a series of epithets that indicate what the whole poem will be. One epithet promises "a plan for action to supplant a plan for action," which is a way of saying that *Paterson* is about how to express what has not yet been said.

In separate ways Wolfe and Williams dramatized the cosmologist's crisis over language. Williams went right to the problem of exploring the limitations and possibilities of words, but Wolfe was forever beginning. "I saw that I must find for myself the tongue to utter what I could not say," he wrote in *The Story of a Novel*. A few months before he died, Wolfe wrote a letter to Max Perkins, triumphantly announcing his newest work-in-progress. It was one of the saddest valedictories of his life. "I am going to write my own 'Ulysses.' I have at last discovered my own America, I believe I have found my language, I think I know my way.

> And I shall wreak out my vision of this life, this way, this world and this America, to the top of my bent, to the height of my ability, but with an unswerving devotion, integrity and purity of purpose that shall not be menaced, altered or weakened by anyone." [9]

And so he finally built a massive table of contents.

Paradigm Two

Back to this word cosmology, and more than a word, really. I have opted for a metaphor to represent several things at once: a group of writings, a kind of fiction, a philosophy of composition, and a key to understanding and appreciating many more writings than the ones I am talking about. But the metaphor has its hazards. I remember one of the countless times Robert Frost was asked "Why do you write poetry?" and he answered, as though he had just thought of it, "Well, I go into a metaphor to see if I can get out of it." Getting out of it is the whole game.

So here is this metaphor, cosmology. To be a useful metaphor it has to convey a precise meaning which is also capable of suggesting other related meanings. One hazard of the cosmology is that it is so general. What I insist on calling cosmologies, for example, all happen to have been written by Americans. Yet these writers have no monopoly on the idea, nor did they invent it. Building a cosmology to account for the experience of being human is as old as fiction.

What about Dante or Milton or Goethe or, for that matter, Homer? They all invented worlds, and there is a definitive sense and majesty about their man-made worlds that these particular American writings never achieve. In fact, the American writings are parochial by comparison, full of special pleading, doubt, and bravado. The reason for this distinction, it seems to me, makes the metaphor of a cosmology more precise. The invented worlds of Homer and

Dante and Milton and Goethe all dramatized a theology that already existed, an orthodox theology. Although different, these theologies all presuppose a God-centered world of which the human being is a part. The writers that I mention as examples did marvelously invent their fictions, but they did not invent a theory of the universe. These American cosmologies, on the other hand, are attempts to build an original cosmos.

The American cosmologists literally conceived of the worlds that they were trying to express. Each work begins with nothing but an individual point of view which then builds an original system in the process of trying to express what it visualizes. In the history of ideas, the notion of building an original, individual universe is romantic. The Americans I speak of inherited this notion and put it to particular use. They have domesticated a romantic world view to suit their own civilization. The domestication is what is particularly American; it is often a high-handed appropriation of literary forms and conventions for new and functional purposes.

The domestication of ideas that I speak of makes these cosmologies self-conscious and evangelical. In accommodating the old notion of an invented universe to a society that seemed distinctively new, these writers have striven to make their doctrines practical and workable. The authors of the next three cosmologies in this critical study chant with the same evangelical zeal. Emerson's *Nature,* Whitman's *Leaves of Grass,* and Hart Crane's *The Bridge* treat us like proselytes. They proclaim a new world in the manner of a gospel and a handbook all at once. They have the same characteristic tone of voice. In this peculiar domesticated romanticism, doctrine takes precedence over theology. The writers preach a gospel for a cosmos that does not exist until the gospel can be preached, and yet they suppose (we infer from the tone) that preaching the doctrine does, in fact, decree that doctrine.

Public evangelism is part of the quality of these works but they are also peculiarly intimate. They do strive to serve some day-to-day function, but even more, each poet conveys the idea that he himself must somehow *live* his organic concept into being. Poetry and autobiography fuse in this attempt to accommodate the vision of an ideal world to the actual, factual circumstances of his life.

These poets all bore an awkward burden of expression. Given their zeal, the burden can be explained by the nature of the ideas they inherited and worked with. Most of these ideas are ancient, and were developed again by writers in the European Renaissance; borrowed and reworked, they are all inherent in the romantic world view that these American poets inherited. One idea is the notion of an organic, unseparated world; another is a theory of metaphor; and another is a singular notion of what poetry is and does. The relation of these ideas to one another gets complicated, as the poets themselves discovered when they tried to express such a relationship; but separately the ideas are all understandable, even familiar.

The most comprehensive of these several ideas concerns what poetry is and does. The cosmologists assumed the ancient and familiar sense of the word in Greek, whereby the poet is the "maker." They passionately believed that poetry *makes* an order of its own and brings it into being. Making is a *process*. To make an order or system in this way is to express whatever one perceives, so it is not surprising that the romantic cosmology is emphatically about the *process* of expressing what its maker perceives. The principal events in each cosmology are the actions of the poet's mind. The cosmologies are generically poems. Whether they were written in prose or verse is irrelevant.

These were all inherited ideas that the romantic poets combined. Even in describing them I am using the words "poetry" and "poem" in the same sense that Renaissance critics used them to interpret classical theories, notably Aristotle's *Poetics*. For example, the idea that poetry and verse are different. One of the most comprehensive statements of poetic theory in the Renaissance, Sir Philip Sidney's *The Apologie for Poetrie* (1595), carefully distinguished between poetry and verse. Sidney argued that poetry is "a representing, counterfeiting, or figuring forth."

Poetry, he said, is an instrument of teaching ("This purifying of wit, this enriching of memory, enabling of judgment, and enlarging of conceit, which we commonly call learning, under what name soever it come forth, or to what immediate end soever it be erected"); and he cautioned that poetry must not be confused with verse ("verse being but an ornament, and no cause to poetry, since there have been most excellent poets that never versified"). The singular characteristic of poetry as an instrument of teaching, Sidney said, is the way it combines different kinds of knowledge: the poet "coupleth the general notion with the particular example."

With this last statement Sidney described exactly what a metaphor is and does: it couples the general notion with the particular example. In this same sense the romantic cosmologies are poems. They are metaphorical. But their emphasis differs from Sidney's. During the two hundred years that followed his work, the defense of poetry was conducted less on moral and didactic grounds and more on epistemological grounds. By the end of the eighteenth century, European critics were discussing poetry primarily in terms of the nature of knowledge and the processes of knowing. Reflecting this newer emphasis, the romantic cosmologies are more insistently about the *process* of making a metaphor than the fact of one. The speaker's subject is really his own attempt to construct a metaphorical system. He has an order or syntax of some sort in mind, and he is preoccupied with extending it as comprehensively as he can. He appropriates some particular knowledge or empirical evidence from which to build (and by which to rationalize) his system. The cosmology, which is a poem, is therefore necessarily autobiographical. This is so, no matter what form it happens to assume, whether it is a philosophical discourse, or a history, or a narrative, or a voyage, or a series of lyrics.

There is a good summary statement of the drama of the consciousness in a poem by Wallace Stevens: "The poem of the mind in the act of finding what will suffice." This first line of Stevens' poem, "Of Modern Poetry" (1940), precisely describes the romantic cosmology. Stevens was describing the process of a poem, but poem and cosmology are alike in kind. The search for analogy, for a metaphor to control one's material, is the process of a lyric poem; and this same process of search and discovery is what the romantic cosmology is, but on an immense scale.

The scheme of a mind building a scheme is a good way to describe a romantic poem. Form and idea duplicate each other; the poem is about itself and how it happened into being. According to this kind of scheme, religion, aesthetics, and ethics are all mutually relevant. The religion happens to be a belief in an organic, unseparated world. Romantic aesthetics and romantic ethics are simply other aspects of this religious belief.

These are large generalizations, I know. They can all be qualified. For example, I have been talking as though there were one single and official romantic philosophy of art. So far as I know, there is not. I am simply abstracting the elements of a theory from many different writings. A theory is a stratagem, a way of explaining and predicting the relation of many different things we observe to occur. It is a way of knowing more. Abstracting and theorizing are ways of opening up the whole view of a subject; and forming a whole view is a way of ordering whatever we know, a way of relating ourselves to our circumstances. As long as we realize that any large statement can be qualified and revised—will be, inevitably—it does not much matter whether a theory is right or wrong. How reliable is it? How much does it explain? These are more useful questions.

One of the elements of this theory of cosmologies is the migration of romantic ideas. How they got from Europe to America is another subject, but what I want to suggest is that romanticism (by which I mean a distinct group of related ideas about the union of God and man) did not happen all at once. Symptoms from a romantic philosophy are apparent in European works of art as early as the fifteenth century, but it was not until the end of the eighteenth century in Europe and in England that the concept of a continuous, unseparated world began to be intellectualized and set down as theory. Romantic predilections prevailed in the fiction of European writers through at least the first third of the nineteenth century; and these predilections—as expressed particularly in Germany and in England—were domesticated in America.

The most eloquent evangelist of romantic idealism in America was Emerson. He domesticated the religion of Transcendentalism from the German romantics and from Carlyle and Coleridge; he gave it a practical turn; and he proselytized his program. Emerson believed that any person's ideal vision of the world should be put to work for mankind's well-being. From inherited ideas and with arguments that he borrowed from other metaphysical systems, he devised a cosmology to rationalize and explain his deep faith in the individual man.

Emerson's essay, *Nature* (1836), is the archetype of the American romantic cosmologies. It is an inspired fiction. It is also marvelously mixed up and confused. After he wrote it he had to revise it. For the next twenty-five years he ingeniously kept his system in repair, amending it drastically in order to accommodate his experience of the actual world to his conviction that the individual man is the aim and the end of the universe. He never changed his conviction. Every borrowed idea, every circular argument, and virtually every confusion in his system helped him to explain his constant belief in the efficacy of the individual.

I hope the next three chapters—about Emerson, Whitman, and Crane—will demonstrate some of the consequences of Emerson's ideas. Not all of them, for they are still happening. Several ideas should recur from one chapter to another. These are inherent and related in romantic philosophy. One is the concept of idealism. Another is the concept of organicism, which is a particular development of idealism. Still another is specifically literary: the idea of a literary form that exists to express a given literary theory. These ideas can be briefly described, although it is somewhat like describing a circular staircase.

Emerson's system in general was an idealism. But he was fascinated with one particular idea, the concept of organicism. He wanted to make his idealistic system incorporate the world and the individual into some entity that would be convincing. He had to devise a continuous, unseparated cosmos. This idea of an organic world is a particular development of idealism.

The first and most common characteristic of all idealistic philosophies is the premise that reality is a form of mind or spirit. For the romantic artist, accordingly, the *perception* of anything constitutes its existence. "To be is to be perceived." G. E. Moore's famous essay, "The Refutation of Idealism" (1903), for example, attacked precisely this concept, this idea of the oneness of the knower and the known, as the premise of all idealisms. The romantic cosmology begins with this notion that the knower and the known share some sort of identity, and the cosmology attempts to develop a system of order in which one's self exists in a continuous, inseparable union with all life in all forms. Divinity is assumed to be inherent in this totality, and therefore in the self. This is what Emerson was trying to work out over the years: the idea of organicism, the idea of a continuous, inseparable being.

Abstracted from its biological meaning, the term "organic" itself becomes metaphorical. Similarly an organic world is a metaphor of the mind. It is also a logical contradiction which goes something like this: an organic world is a whole entity comprised of a continuity of its parts; part and whole are one; and nothing is separable from the whole entity without destroying both the entity and the separated part. The concept presents the same affront to logic as, say, the concept of the Christian trinity; it is not rational but intuitive. In any given person organicism might be only a felt conviction, imperfectly understood. But organicism is nevertheless the principal condition that these cosmologies insist on.

It must appear from all this that the cosmologists were continually wrestling with theories. So they were, particularly with a theory of expression. The cosmologies are versions of an ancient and continuing literary form known as the *ars poetica*, which is an explanation and a rationale of poetry. The generic name is borrowed from the title of Horace's poem about poetry. Ever since the Renaissance, essays such as Sidney's, usually called "A Defense of Poetry," have appeared in all European literatures. The singular quality of the romantic cosmologies in connection with this genre is that they dramatize a theory of poetry by emphasizing the *process* of the poet working out his rationale; and they involve the reader firsthand in this process.

It is a process of *expression*. There is no reality for the poet until he can express it, so he has to develop a theory of expressing it. For example, Emerson's *Nature*. This treatise proposes the theory of an organic cosmos, and its form *is* the attempt to arrive at such a theory. Emerson had to use the language of idealism to get *beyond* idealism to the concept of organic being, and this theorizing is exactly what he proposed a poem ought to be: the *act* of expressing the wholeness of the whole.

I have been talking about ideas which the American cosmologists borrowed, in order to show what they did with these ideas: what they emphasized and refashioned for themselves. One emphasis in their writings is the persistence of an almost unbelievable faith in the efficacy of the individual consciousness. The assumption that the artist can convincingly create a discrete and sufficient world began somewhere in the European origins of romantic fiction. But the American versions of the cosmology insist on the special and often naïve conviction that a new and subjective order of the mind is not merely provisional but a workable fact, to be imposed on the now and here.

CHAPTER TWO

Emerson's Strategic Retreat

Emerson's cosmology was *Nature* (1836). In this poetic essay he worked out the essentials of an ideal system to explain the unseparated continuity of one's self with the material world and God. According to this idealism the totality of all things exists in one's perception of totality. Emerson worked out the terms of his organic system as he went along, developing a form and a language to express it. But *Nature* was neither final nor sufficient; his theoretical system did not square with human experience. In later essays he amplified different aspects of his ideal cosmos, and by means of these essays he began to modify his cosmology. With "Fate" (1860) he thoroughly revised it. He still insisted on a dynamic continuity of self and circumstance in the largest sense, but in order to preserve this organic relationship and to make it consistent with experience, Emerson made a strategic retreat from an idealism to a determinism.

At every stage of repair over the years Emerson's cosmology conveyed the idea that a religion and an aesthetic and an ethic are one and the same. With a borrowed rhetoric and borrowed concepts of idealism he conveyed his own notion of an organic cosmos. His enormous borrowings and the contradictions that resulted grew out of his assumption that a theory of God and a theory of composition and a theory of behavior are simply aspects of the principle of the unity of one's self and all being. Emerson's development of the idea of revelation by poetry is my principal subject. *Na-*

ture (1836), his original system, "The Poet" (1844), one of its amplifications, and "Fate" (1860), its later revision, show how Emerson's religion continued to be also a theory of fiction, even though he exchanged his idealism for a particular determinism.

Nature is a romantic *ars poetica* that argues in the form of a sermon. Its doctrine is that natural and material substances have no significance apart from the totality of all being. Totality is an idea; it is the mind's transfiguration of all natural substances into the concept of a whole entity. Moreover, this idea is the essence of God. It follows, therefore, that God is revealed to exist in whatever mind happens to perceive the totality of all things. The significance of Emerson's cosmology consists largely in the way he presented it; that is, his rhetoric is the organic model of his doctrine. The form of argument that he borrowed and modified is therefore important. His purpose was evangelical, and he used the rhetoric of the sermon form that he had learned and preached as a Unitarian minister.

Emerson's view of God and man was heretical to the Harvard Unitarians, let alone the Calvinists, but the rhetoric by which he argued his view was characteristic of a Puritan sermon. This form of sermon is a series of assertions documented many times from different parts of the Bible. Citations from the Bible are used to justify the "Doctrine," which is the preacher's interpretation of a given Scriptural passage. With superficial logic he uses the Scriptures to prove the Scriptures. This is the method of the Puritan sermon; its sequence and its order serve a circular reasoning for the purpose of repeating itself. Borrowing the rhetoric of the Puritan sermon made it possible for Emerson to reason in circles for his own purpose. But this form also got Emerson into difficulty over the question of what constitutes truth or reality.

The premise of any Puritan sermon is that truth is the word of God, which always has existed and always will exist; truth is contained in the Scriptures; and the function of the sermon is to discover truth, to "raise" the word of God from the Scriptures, to clarify it, to reduce it to a given significance, and to exhort a course of action. The Puritan preacher understood his sermon to be nothing less than the codification of truth; form and content were indistinguishable.

Nature is likewise the paradigm of its own theory; but its theory is that the individual mind creates truth or reality, that the act of perceiving is a fresh and firsthand experience, and that reality is subjective. He appropriated the sermon form to argue a doctrine contradictory to what the sermon form usually supports, and his basic dilemma was simply this: How can the act of perceiving create what already exists? If truth is a single principle then it cannot be both subjective and objective. So the form of *Nature*, which reflects the form of the Puritan sermon, also reflects Emerson's own confusion.

The essay proceeds like a three-part sermon; it states a "Doctrine," then the "Reasons" for the doctrine, and finally the "Uses" of the doctrine. Emerson's particular doctrine is that the true "Nature" is one's consciousness of all separate natural substances. "We mean the integrity of impression made by manifold natural objects." And this, he says, is the "most poetical sense" of the word "Nature." The material world serves the individual man by offering discrete parts that he reconstitutes into a single, unified impression of all being. The world becomes organic through his consciousness of it.

Nature is a tautology, repeating itself in many various ways. The "reasons" for the doctrine, which are the bulk of the essay, are necessarily true by the way they are stated. In fact, the so-called "reason" is often a restatement of the doctrine that it purports to explain. Thus, one "reason" for the totality of all being is that the natural world implies "Beauty," which is the idea of the totality of all being. Another "reason" for the doctrine is that the natural world affords "Discipline" to the mind by presenting these parts for the mind's conception of the whole. These are scarcely reasons in a causal sense, but they give the author occasions to vary what he repeats, which is one way to develop an idea.

Another restatement of the totality of all being occurs in a "reason" called "Language." Herein Emerson explains how poetry reveals God. The oneness of all things, he says, inherently exists in symbolic language; and poetry is the epitome of symbolic language. Emerson makes a paradigm of how poetry reveals God. "Words are signs of natural facts"; and furthermore "particular natural facts are symbols of particular spiritual facts." It follows, therefore, that a word incorporates the spirit by naming a thing. This is the way any metaphor works, of course, but Emerson had in mind no ordinary metaphor. "Parts of speech are metaphors," he says, "because the whole of nature is a metaphor of the human mind."

The world, therefore, is a spectacle in both senses: something to see, and something to see through. Consciousness integrates all visible things into a single subjective impression. In the "reason" called "Idealism" Emerson describes how the poet creates the world: "By a few strokes he delineates, as on air, the sun, the mountain, the camp, the city, the hero, the maiden, not different from what we know them, but only lifted from the ground and afloat before the eye.

> He unfixes the land and the sea, makes them revolve around the axis of his primary thought, and disposes them anew."

This was Emerson's dearest vision. Reality is a metaphor created by the consciousness, dependent on the consciousness for meaning, and serving its point of view. Realizing the divinity of himself, the poet thereby creates a world. "He unfixes the land and the sea, makes them revolve around the axis of his primary thought, and disposes them anew."

According to this particular idealism, the "poet animates nature with his own thoughts." But Platonic idealism was only a step in the right direction; it proposed that the idea is real and that matter is merely a phenomenon. This was not enough for Emerson; it was only a kind of introduction to world building. "It leaves God out of me," he says, in a section called "Spirit." "It leaves me in the splendid labyrinth of my perceptions, to wander without end." Emerson insisted on a causal relation between the seer and the seen: the mind generates the meaning of whatever it contemplates.

But Emerson was supremely careless about ontological niceties. Having raised the question of whether nature is a material or a subjective reality, he states six times (in the section "Idealism") that the question is irrelevant, and he concludes: "Whether nature enjoy a substantial existence without, or is only in the apocalypse of the mind, it is alike useful and alike venerable to me. Be it what it may, it is ideal to me so long as I cannot try the accuracy of my senses."

Nature in the sense of matter exists in order to serve his realization of it. "All the uses of nature admit of being summed in one, which yields the activity of man an infinite scope." This is the burden of his conclusion (or the "Uses," of his doctrine, according to the form of the Puritan sermon). He exhorts his reader to realize the divinity within himself and so to complete the world. It is the same call to duty which also concludes *The American Scholar,* "The Divinity School Address," "Self-Reliance," "The Poet," and most of his other essays.

Nature has an *ad hoc* style. It is impromptu. Emerson experimented as he went along. He had to find a way to express organicism even as he was trying to understand the idea itself. As a result *Nature* expounds an approximate cosmos. He had to use the available terms of idealism in order to say finally that mere idealism is not enough to convey a truly organic world. This is why the sermon form served him so well. It forced him to repeat himself, and thereby enabled him to discover new ways of saying what he was trying to say.

Each new way is a new analogy. He thought in terms of analogy, in terms of metaphor. His essays are full of assertions; but exact statement is rare, because the assertions are metaphorical. An analogy between two things usually suggests more than it says; an analogy, to Emerson, invariably suggested another analogy, another metaphor by which to explain the first. His *ad hoc* style indicates that Emerson saw individual things as metaphors and then inferred a system from the metaphors that he saw.

Emerson's habit of metaphorical inference was a way of accommodating a great many ideas which were mutually relevant but also different and sometimes even contradictory. The sources of these ideas are well known. He began his career as a Unitarian minister, as a legatee of orthodox Protestant Christianity in its most rational and ethical form. Resigning from this discipline, he traveled to England, met Carlyle and Coleridge, and absorbed, at first through them, the tenets of German idealism. The writings of Kant and Hegel renewed Emerson's interest in the study of Plato's theory of ideal reality and also in Neoplatonic mysticism. And there were other influences: the Protestant philosophers of the Jena group; Eastern mysticism, retrieved through their scholarship; and also the teachings of Emanuel Swedenborg. From these various idealisms and mystical concepts and from the rational, ethical emphasis of his own Unitarian religious training Emerson inferred a singular notion of a dynamic idealism with a practical purpose. He assimilated many doctrines, imperfectly and by analogy.

Metaphors were Emerson's means of discovery. He continually evolved new figurations out of the same thread of thought. His theory of art, or of ethics, or of God—they are virtually the same—imply the same syllogism: the sense of a divine unity of things can be achieved through self-realization; poetry is the means of self-realization; therefore poetry is the means of divine revelation. This syllogism holds true for many of his essays. So Emerson's *ad hoc* style illustrates its own argument, namely, that the significance of all things is in the totality that one perceives in all things. Each new metaphor, as he argues, clarifies the others before it, so that meaning is cumulative and continually evolving. At its best the style *is* the argument. Each new metaphor recalls the turn of thought and surprises it into new possibilities, and the writer's new awareness thereby causes another analogy. This is not always so. In Emerson's poorer prose, his more didactic talk, we get the impression of a man picturesquely explaining what he has already decided. But when his style does work we get the impression of a growing idea that is never quite complete.

Whatever Emerson's subject, it usually involves the drama of the author wrestling with his idea. For example, he often talked about motion. He characteristically used metaphors of motion, of ocean and air, connoting flux and flow; he was intrigued with a mystical notion of the emanations of God flowing forth to the mind in its state of contemplation; and he was also a devout believer in movement as progress. Sometimes these various expressions of movement and motion flow comfortably together, and sometimes not, but they usually reveal a kind of dialogue between the writer and his material. The contagion of a metaphor usually lies in the process of perceiving it, of working it out. Not the fact of the analogy but the *act* of making it. According to Emerson's theory of poetry, a poem is precisely this process of discovery.

A curious fact, however, is that Emerson's poems by and large contradict his own theory of what a poem should be. What Wallace Stevens described as "the mind finding what will suffice" is in general the process of a poem as Emerson understood it; except that "what would suffice" for Emerson was nothing less than the organic world conceived by the mind. He devised what you might call an aesthetic of revelation. The fictional "I" of the poem—the speaking consciousness—correlates all revelations through its own self-discovery. Whether one writes in verse or in prose is really irrelevant to Emerson's concept of what a poem ought to be. His own essays defy restatement precisely because they are structured like poetry; which is to say, because they are systems of metaphors. But

Emerson's verse, on the other hand, is likely to yield a much more rational statement, and most of his verse is poor poetry.

Most of Emerson's verse is didactic. It contains large measures of explicit statement that remain unassimilated by the dramatic situation that has supposedly evoked it. The editorial content of most of Emerson's verse is at odds with his metaphors. Insisting on only one significance of a given metaphor reduces the possibilities of suggestion to mere matter of opinion. It is striking that Emerson's most familiar poems, the ones most often reprinted in anthologies, are also the most explicit and didactic. The doctrine takes over the poem because he would not let a metaphor have its own way. Emerson's contradiction of his own poetic theory is the more startling because it is really an overstatement of the theory itself. The evangelical zeal is inherent in his mystique of the poet figure. The unfortunate result is an excessive will to teach. But the act of realizing is a dramatic event; it cannot convincingly be talked about. Those few poems of Emerson which *do* persuade—"Bacchus," for example, or "Days," or "The Humble Bee," and four or five others—dramatize the process of the speaker's mind as he apprehends the entire world opening out before him, vitalized by his vision of it. Paraphrase cannot convey these poems. Simply, the experience *is*.

The most convincing illustrations of what Emerson meant a poem to be are not Emerson's poems but Robert Frost's. Frost once said that everything written is only as good as it is dramatic. His poems characteristically dramatize the act of the mind building a metaphorical meaning out of a local instance. A poem by Frost characteristically begins the moment the local scene presents the speaker with an occurrence of some sort; and the world at large is always implied in the analogy that the speaker discovers between himself and what he sees. When the analogy is barely realized, generally, the poem stops; the experience is complete, or as complete as it can be without being damaged by explicit statement. Here is the drama of the Emersonian poem. Frost's poems often achieve what Emerson's rarely do, namely, the representation of a restless mind coming upon some realization about itself and the world. But in Emerson's poems the lyric voice usually becomes prophetic and proprietary; it tends toward pronouncements. What might have been a realization turns out, instead, to have been a fact established before the event; and the reader's response to the experience is limited to agreeing or disagreeing with its doctrine.

Emerson's most orphic poem is "Merlin" (1847), which is also a capable summary of his essay, "The Poet." "Merlin" is a two-part set of instructions for the "kingly bard" : this is what you shall *be*, and this is what you shall *say*. The instructions are directed actually to the poetasters who might wish to achieve this exalted status. This is what you shall be: the voice of "Artful thunder, which conveys / Secrets of the solar track, / Sparks of a supersolar blaze."—the sum of all known expression uninhibited by man-made metrics. What-you-shall-say is the doctrine of the oneness of all opposites, all pairs, all complements that naturally exist; and your saying will thereby accomplish the union of all being. These directions occur in a catalogue that sounds like a passenger list for a cosmic Noah's ark (a possibility that occurred to Emerson in "The Poet"). "Merlin" is an inspired oration whose entire purpose is programmatic. The kingly bard shall say by doing and do by being; it is all set down in a kit of directions. Here is precisely the statement—and the dilemma—of the practical idealist. It not only assumes that the ideal of an organic cosmos is possible in the first place, but more—and this is the point—it fantastically assumes that this cosmos is achievable through proper administration.

The kingly bard is not so much a poet as a program. As a display of Emerson's programmatic zeal "Merlin" caricatures "The Poet." The essay, like the verse, reprimands the poetasters for their mere conformity to the poet's office, and it describes what it asserts to be the true function and process of art. But "Merlin" abridges the excitement of the essay which, in this case, is the true Emersonian poem. The quality of "Merlin" as compared to "The Poet" is significant. The verse merely summarizes the argument of the prose poem while omitting its real subject, which is the speaker's intoxication with the whole strategy of achieving the ideal cosmos. What "The Poet" represents and what "Merlin" omits is the author's incessant attempt to define the organic world in the midst of his rhapsodizing.

"The Poet," which was published six years after *Nature*, amplifies the theory of language in the earlier work; language is the means of the poet's completing a view of the universe. But in so doing the later essay changes the entire epistemology of *Nature*, the entire theory of how we know what we know. It is a subtle change; possibly Emerson was not even aware of it this early. But it is fundamental, and it anticipated the later revision of his entire thinking with reference to mankind, nature, and God. Emerson's revised theory of language and his revised theory of the nature of knowledge proceed together in "The Poet." According to this essay, the poet's overview of the world is just as crucial as ever, but his function is now more prudential, more tenable, and a shade less divine. It is a retreat from organicism toward Platonic idealism. It is less the creation of one's own world and more the perception of the true order that already exists.

We need an interpreter of experience, Emerson says in "The Poet." We need a "Sayer" who perceives and expresses the truth (that has always existed; "for poetry was all written before time was"). And he observes at length how nature has ensured the poet's fidelity to his high office, how "the beauty of things . . . becomes a newer and higher beauty, when expressed." The metaphorical property of language is the important fact. "I find," he says, "that the fascination resides in the symbol." And he offers a catalogue of the common and general use of emblems of all sorts. The natural world furnishes the poet with symbols, and more: "Nature is a symbol, in the whole, and in every part." Emerson hammers at the idea that all things are essentially organic, are inseparable from the whole of nature: "There is no fact in nature which does not carry the whole sense of nature." The poet simply recognizes this. Drawn anywhere from Nature, the symbol conveys the idea of the organic world, and the poet's sensitivity to the symbol is what enables him to speak beyond himself for the whole of creation. ("The world being thus put under the mind for verb and noun, the poet is he who can articulate it.") By seeing the individual thing as symbolic the poet comprehends the whole.

But "The Poet" assumes the existence of a supreme and timeless order that the true poet can possibly train himself to recognize. This is scarcely the doctrine of *Nature*, whereby the ME creates the NOT ME. On the contrary, in "The Poet" Emerson asserts the existence of "the great calm presence of the Creator" that the poet must try to invoke. He must seek the external order of being. Although he has indeed a great "privacy of power" he can realize it only by abandoning himself to

> the nature of things . . . by unlocking . . . his human doors, and suffering the ethereal tides to roll and circulate through him: then he is caught up into the life of the Universe, his speech is thunder, his thought is law, and his words are universally intelligible. . . .

The fact that the infinite order outside him can enter his consciousness is what makes symbolic language so important. Language is the means by which he can outgrow the mere parochial vision. "It is nature the symbol, nature certifying the supernatural" that the poet appropriates. He is "the Namer or Language-maker, naming things sometimes after their appearance, sometimes after their essence." "Appearance" and "essence" have preceded him, but his perceiving "re-attaches things to nature and the Whole." The value of this transaction "is to enhance the great and constant fact of Life, which can dwarf any and every circumstance. . . ." In sum, the poet revitalizes what already is.

"The Poet" is even more lyrical than *Nature* about the possibilities of one's self-realization. But Emerson's restated theory of language makes a smaller claim. It qualifies the earlier function of the poet as creator to the poet as re-creator or discoverer. It marks a phase in Emerson's strategic retreat from an aggressive dynamic idealism, by which the individual conceives a whole world out of himself, to what finally becomes, in his later essays, a complex determinism that forms the individual consciousness. The retreat from idealism was really a matter of devising a larger system in which the attractive quality of idealism could still work for man's well-being. "The Poet" marks one stage of this retreat. Emerson had still further to go, for even this kingly bard, who is so much more plausible than the animating mind of "Nature," does not in fact exist. Even this poet is imaginary; Emerson concludes, "I look in vain for the poet whom I describe."

The governing idea of Emerson's life and work was his celebration of the individual man. This particular enthusiasm explains virtually all his writing, yet his philosophical system is a changing, plastic scheme marked by confusions and inconsistencies. His philosophy was a continual justification of his belief, rationalizing it according to his own experience of the actual world. What explains most of its inconsistencies is the fact that Emerson changed his system to keep it in repair, continually reconciling his constant belief and the intractable circumstances. In "Fate" Emerson finally devised an organic system congenial to the material, positive world, yet it also kept faith with his exalted idea of the individual.

The reciprocity between one's self and one's circumstances is the stabilizing relationship of Emerson's philosophy. The extent to which he redefined this reciprocity is apparent in two comparable statements about this same relationship.

Both are expressed figuratively, even to the same metaphor. The first occurs toward the end of *Nature*.

> Every spirit builds itself a house, and beyond its house a world, and beyond its world a heaven. Know then that the world exists for you.

The other statement occurs in "Fate," which was published twenty-four years later.

> Every spirit makes its house; but afterwards the house confines the spirit.

The egoistic relationship between self and circumstance in the first statement becomes, in the second, a determinism. This is precisely the extent of Emerson's ingenious revision. The organic relation between self and circumstance is true of both statements, but organicism in "Fate" is more complex.

"Fate" is the first of nine essays in *The Conduct of Life* (1860) that began as a series of lectures in 1851; these were extensively revised. As its title indicates, the volume is a statement of ethics. "Fate" reduces an idea to a working proposition, and exhorts the reader to follow it. Emerson defines Fate as limitation. It is any combination of events that restricts the individual; it is the sum of all the genetic processes and the environment. He broadly catalogues the aspects of tyrannous circumstance that he later calls "unpenetrated causes." "Fate then is a name for facts not yet passed under the fire of thought; for causes which are unpenetrated." Mankind's relationship to Fate is antagonistic.

A conflict exists. Fate is opposed by Power, which is the total energy of man's will, his intuition, and his sense of morality. Power is another name for Thought. Emerson catalogues occasions of the efficacy of Power, or Thought, and concludes with his characteristic exhortation to men: in this case, to put Power to use and penetrate, as it were, unpenetrated cause. "History," he says, "is the action and reaction of these two—Nature and Thought."

But this is no simple case of conflict. Fate is the adversary of mankind, but it is also the organic system that contains both adversaries. Fate is both the whole and a part of the whole. Emerson believed so devoutly in the self-expression of the individual that he constructed a dialectical system that makes self-expression a necessary achievement. According to this dialectic, Fate (the system) necessarily evokes from man (one of its parts) the reaction which annuls Fate (the adversary). Emerson argued it this way. "If you please to plant yourself on the side of Fate and say, Fate is all; then we say, a part of Fate is the freedom of man.

> Forever wells up the impulse of choosing and acting in the soul. Intellect annuls Fate. So far as a man thinks, he is free."

Duality is a familiar device in Emerson's attempt to build a monism. From first to last he labored to explain a continuity of spirit and matter, but always necessarily beginning with the separation of spirit and matter, such as man and nature, or the ME and the NOT ME. From one essay to another each new version of this duality has different synonyms. In this case it is Power and Fate. The idea in each essay is to show how these given opposites compensate or complement each other, or how they are part of some larger synthesis. The rhetoric consists of building images of an organic whole. "Wonderful intricacy in the web," Emerson exclaims.

The governing metaphor of Power and Fate is conflict. Man and nature are not only separate but they are antagonistic— precisely the opposite from what Emerson argued in *Nature*. Moreover, nature now contains the man—which is also precisely the opposite from what he argued in the first essay. Circumstance is Nature, he now says; and circumstance is a limitation; and limitation is Fate, which contains the man. Emerson finally arrived at a position 180 degrees from where he started. He finally argued his case right into a determinism. "A man's power is hooped in by a necessity," he says in "Fate." "The limitation is impassable by any insight of man.

In its last and loftiest ascensions, insight itself and the freedom of will is one of its obedient members."

But this is Emerson's own brand of determinism. It is a stratagem. As he used idealism in *Nature* and in "The Poet" so he used determinism in "Fate" to enforce the idea of the man fulfilling himself. And this determinism accomplishes for Emerson what idealism could not, because it imparts a sense of authority that idealism does not. The conclusion of "Fate" (restating "Uses" of the "Doctrine") is more convincing than the conclusion of any of Emerson's other essays, because the whole system of "Fate" *necessitates* a man's self-fulfillment. What Emerson finally accomplished was a brilliant retreat.

In the context of this determinism even hyperbole makes sense. Opposed to the limiting Fate, man is "a stupendous antagonism, a dragging together of the poles of the Universe." This sounds like Ahab speaking. But Herman Melville was not Ahab, and Emerson spoke for himself; there is the difference. To Emerson the dialectical system of man struggling with unpenetrated cause was reason for optimism. "Fate involves the melioration. No statement of the Universe can have any soundness which does not admit its ascending effort." This optimism has been a cause for caveat ever since among American writers. Nevertheless, Emerson laid down the terms of the argument: in the scheme of things there is a *necessary* reciprocity between the man and his circumstance. "The secret of the world is the tie between person and event. Person makes event, and event person." Henry James built his fiction on this premise; so did William Faulkner. Specifically, the tie that Emerson speaks of is moral choice. "Forever wells up the impulse of choosing and acting in the soul."

Emerson's housebuilding metaphor marks the development of his thought. He retreated from the doctrine that the spirit builds a house and a world and a heaven, which it owns, to the doctrine that the spirit builds a house which then confines it. Thereby he grounded his idealism to an ethical necessity. We can allow the limitation, he said, because of the growth it necessitates within us.

> We stand against Fate, as children stand up against the wall in their father's house and notch their height from year to year. But when the boy grows to man, and is master of the house, he pulls down that wall and builds a new and bigger.

Man's building up the new and bigger wall around himself is necessity, the categorical imperative of the system called Fate. Emerson was a practical idealist. This has been his legacy to writers ever since, the all-important reciprocity of a man and his circumstance as he ponders unpenetrated cause.

Emerson's theoretical system is the archetype of all these cosmologies, not of all their doctrines but of their dynamic development of any given doctrine. The necessary unity in his system is the idea that thought is action. At every stage in Emerson's evolving philosophy the action of thought establishes the continuity of mind and matter. By developing the idea of this continuity as an ethical necessity Emerson finally explained the process of poetry as every man's struggle to understand the world around him. In doing so he also anticipated the singular and ethical evangelism of all these cosmologies.

CHAPTER THREE

The Drift of Whitman

Walt Whitman's ideal cosmos was a "Democratic" America, meaning an America that radiated his own presence and thereby incorporated all human relationships. The expression of his cosmos was equally political, religious, and literary, although it took him more than thirty years to explain this singular equation. His life work is mostly recorded in nine editions of *Leaves of Grass*, from 1855 to his death in 1892, a continuously growing and changing scripture of his "kosmos"; and a tenth edition (1897) includes posthumous additions. This book of poems is the most lavish autobiography in the "national American literature"—a phrase which Whitman admired—yet even this record was not enough. Whitman also attempted at length to explain, refine, and summarize it. In his valedictory essay, "A Backward Glance O'er Travel'd Roads" (1888), he insisted once more that *Leaves* had been essentially an extension of himself:

> an attempt, from first to last, to put *a Person*, a human being (myself, in the latter half of the Nineteenth Century, in America,) freely, fully, and truly on record.

The urge to put one's self wholly on record makes the book greater than the sum of its parts. These parts can all be analyzed as individual lyric poems, even the sections of the integral "Song of Myself," and there are more assertive poor poems than persuasive good ones. But what counts in *Leaves* is the overriding idea that they unevenly express. They are all

44

variations of Whitman's incessant attempts to convey the equivocal nature of one's self and therefore of the universe.

He was excited by the concept of one's simultaneous identity as a discrete self and yet part and parcel of all humanity. The famous lines which he later put at the beginning of *Leaves of Grass* state his proposition of the equivocal self:

> One's-Self I sing, a simple separate person,
> Yet utter the word Democratic, the word En-Masse.

Whitman's stimulation from this idea generated his poetry; simply trying to express it could ravish him. It was the idea of ambivalence, of being separate and central all at once. "This is the thought of identity—yours for you, whoever you are, and mine for me"; yet "significant only because of the Me in the centre." This paradox entranced him. "Miracle of miracles, beyond statement, most spiritual and vaguest of earth's dreams, yet hardest basic fact, and only entrance to all facts."

This notion about his own equivocal self inspired Whitman to propose that there is necessarily an organic cosmos (called "America") with the same equivocal nature. His struggle to state this elusive doctrine is the dramatic subject of *Leaves of Grass*. The continuity of self and cosmos was also the basis of his theory of a national literature. Time and again Whitman shouted impassioned generalities about the true relation of the people and the literature of the people, or between the poet and the cosmos. In the course of his long endeavor to define this true relation he managed to rationalize his particular mysticism into a theory of "Democratic" literature which would be political and religious and ethical at the same time.

Whitman believed in a "Democratic" literature to serve a democratic nation. The 1855 Preface to *Leaves of Grass* is a lyrical celebration of this convention. In "Democratic Vistas" (1871) he specified in political terms what he had instinctively celebrated in the Preface, and he later invoked these political terms more specifically in his 1876 Preface to

Leaves. Whitman's political rationale for an American literature was ingenious; it reinforced the idea of the equivocal self, and it showed cause for the ethical function that he believed literature must serve.

But in the process of defining his organic scheme, over the years, Whitman changed some of his assumptions. He assumed at the beginning that the equivocal self was peculiarly American, and he later abolished this restriction and included all humanity. He assumed at the beginning that the reciprocity of the poet and the people comprised the cosmos, and he later enlarged this cosmos to include a God. Like Emerson retreating from *Nature* to "Fate," Whitman retreated to a larger synthesis in order to continue celebrating the individual.

A comparison of two of Whitman's poems reveals the bard's expanding vision: "Song of the Open Road" (1856) and "Passage to India" (1872). Both poems proselytize a doctrine about the self and the world at large, but not the same doctrine. Whitman's revised cosmos, in "Passage to India," was not so convincing. He invoked an extrinsic God, but he did not really relinquish the idea of the self-sufficient poet. He still believed that literature must be an act of worship, but his amended cosmos was unclear about the relation of man and God, and "Passage to India" reveals a metaphorical confusion.

These two poems also illustrate the more elemental fact that Whitman regarded a poem as an *action.* No matter what the doctrine of a poem, Whitman consistently mistook exhortation for revelation. For him poetry was a way of converting a concept to an act of belief. "And what I assume you shall assume," the poet says at the beginning of "Song of Myself." The function of poetry was to evangelize. His conviction that a poem is essentially an action goes back to his 1855 Preface.

In the beginning was the Preface. The Biblical analogy is inevitable. Whitman was in the Preface, and Whitman *was* the Preface. It is the first and most formidable statement of Whitman's cosmos, as much a part of *Leaves of Grass* as any poem in any edition; it is also an *ars poetica*. It asserts over and over again that the poet represents the world; he is its emblem in person, and he correlates it by what he does. This Preface is a roving and profuse, inspired statement of superlatives. It looks at first like notes for an essay, hanging together by the unlikely device of ellipses; but the uneven punctuation represents no omission, it signals an impetuous tone to Whitman's words. This prose makes a noisy page. The argument contradicts itself in momentary fits of emphasis. It confirms Emerson's argument in "The Poet" in one breathy sentence. "He is a seer . . . . he is individual . . . he is complete in himself . . . . the others are as good as he, only he sees it and they do not."

The Preface is inconsistent about motive and vague about function. It is confusing about the locus of the poem. Its logic is that anything equals everything. But it obviously argues on the assumption that the poet's point of view is sacerdotal. "His brain is the ultimate brain. He is no arguer . . . he is judgment. He judges not as the judge judges but as the sun falling around a helpless thing." Even more: his supreme interpretation of things engenders their meaning. "If he breathes into any thing that was before thought small it dilates with the grandeur and life of the universe."

The argument is this: America is the poem and the poet is its Answerer. It is an overstatement of what Emerson had said in "The Poet." And the rhetoric of the Preface echoes its overstatement. It is antiphonal, repeating the argument over and over with different sets of particulars. A catalogue of snapshot images illustrates some given quality of the people, and the assertion follows that the poet "answers" this quality. Thus, the people are free of constraint (as a catalogue illustrates); and the poet is free of constraint. The people have simplicity and proportion (according to a series of examples); and so does the poet. The people have the virtue of candor (according to his inventory); and the poet "answers" this. The people believe in political liberty; the poet incarnates it. In this antiphony the Answerer expresses the people.

The rhetoric of the Preface anticipates the balanced half lines of his poems—the sort that begin "Song of Myself" (1855), ("And what I assume you shall assume, / For every atom belonging to me as good belongs to you").

The balanced half lines convey the same argument in "Crossing Brooklyn Ferry" (1856): "Just as you feel . . . so I felt"; "Just as you are refresh'd . . . I was refresh'd"; "Just as you stand and lean on the rail, yet hurry . . . I stood yet was hurried." The Preface urges the same antiphony with whole catalogues of abstract qualities in the people, balanced by the matching assertion about the poet; and the Preface ends with a coda about the new and superior breed of poet-priests, the "gangs of kosmos."

In its restless straining against this confining antiphonal form the Preface conveys excitement. Whitman later borrowed chunks and paragraphs from it, converted them into regular lines, and entitled them "By Blue Ontario's Shores" (1856); and the excitement vanished. The result was like a catechism learned by rote. The doctrine had taken over. Whitman later edited the Preface for the seventh edition of *Leaves of Grass* (1882). Having already borrowed many of its catalogues for his poems, he also suppressed other passages. The later version, shorter by a third, is a genteel distortion of his original exuberant declaration.

The presence of the poet in his poems was Whitman's major strategy. And the better poems, like the Preface, have somehow managed to dramatize this presence. But this is no one-for-one biographical equation. Given Whitman's concept of the poem no mere biographical speaker would do. Identity was *the* equivocal word. When the poet says, "One's-Self I sing, a simple separate person, Yet utter the word Democratic, the word En-Masse," he has to be taken metaphorically. The essence of this double identity is the consciousness of the two selves: one's separate self and the self that is part of a continuum. Of course, no actual person continuously expresses this consciousness of plurality. Since the Preface depends on the intensity with which the "I" feels equivocal, therefore, the "I" is necessarily a metaphor.

The Chant, as Whitman called the poem, is the Answerer's self-expression; but this exists everywhere: within the poet, within the listener, within the people on the landscape. The Answerer is a fiction, a legendary projection of this particular author named Whitman. The actual Walt Whitman projected a fictional Walt Whitman to chant his poems. The Answerer is the legend which Whitman created about himself, the witness-singer, seeking and assimilating all experience. This is the "I," the visionary pronoun, that chants "Song of Myself"; and the vitality of these lyrics is the Answerer's incessant return to himself as *the* metaphor of the cosmos. This incessant return to the metaphorical self generates *Leaves of Grass*.

The fictional speaker is the first property of Whitman's poems—or the persuasive ones, at least. Their second property is the way the speaker conducts himself, the way he expresses his mystical doctrine. Whitman discovered a metaphor for this, too. He called it the "drift" of his book: the drift of a poem or a book or a man. In an early poem, a six-line lyric called "Shut Not Your Doors," he talks about *Leaves of Grass*. Although the book (like the poet) is a separate entity, its real substance is all the "untold latencies": not the separateness of things but the way they are all one, that is, the drift of them.

> . . . a book I have made,
> The words of my book nothing, the drift of it
>   everything. . . .

The "drift" of his poems is remarkably consistent. It is the illusion of movement by which the point of view continually dilates. (The Preface says of the greatest poet, "If he breathes into anything that was before thought small it dilates with the grandeur and life of the universe.") The verb "to dilate" can be both transitive and intransitive. As the speaker names his subject both the speaker and his subject grow. What Whitman often attempted and occasionally achieved was the sense of a great swelling omnipresence. As the poet says in Section 6 of "Song of Myself" (1855), "all goes onward and outward, nothing collapses. . . ."

Whitman's metaphor of "drift" also indicates how he expressed this doctrine that all goes onward and outward. How he says it constitutes what he says. Whitman repeats the same grammatical elements in successive sentences with lengthening intervals in between these elements to convey a sense of movement. The words assert that there is an outward movement, and the increasing intervals between the same grammatical elements in successive sentences impart an apparent movement to reinforce it. The drift of these poems is the way the point of view apparently dilates, encompassing what it sees. This happens in the doctrinal poem, "There Was a Child Went Forth," that begins:

> There was a child went forth every day,
> And the first object he look'd upon, that object he became,
> And that object became part of him for the day or a
>   certain part of the day,
> Or for many years or stretching cycles of years.

The grammar then begins to correlate these assertions. In the sequence of subject and verb ("The early lilacs became part of this child"), the subject begins to compound and grow in successive repetitions, pushing the verb further and further away to make the ear listen longer for it.

> The early lilacs became part of this child,
> And grass and white and red morning-glories, and white
>   and red clover, and the song of the phoebe-bird,
> And the Third-month lambs and the sow's pink-faint litter,
>   and the mare's foal and the cow's calf,

And the noisy brood of the barnyard or by the mire of
    the pondside,
And the fish suspending themselves so curiously below
    there, and the beautiful curious liquid,
And the water-plants with their graceful flat heads, all
    became part of him.

As the pattern is repeated and varied in the poem the proposition itself assumes a new value. Each item of the grammatical subject assumes the same value as the first item
stated.

When the point of view—the "I"—is the subject of this
expanding sentence sequence it assumes a dramatic value as
well. This is what happens in "Crossing Brooklyn Ferry," one
of Whitman's most complex poems. Section 2 of the poem
states a proposition:

The simple, compact well-join'd scheme, myself dis-
    integrated, every one disintegrated yet part
    of the scheme. . . .

And a single sentence twenty-two lines long, in the next
section dramatizes it. The first line contains the whole sequence of subject-verb-object ("I too many and many a time
cross'd the river of old"). But the next eleven lines, in appo-
sition, contain only the verb and the object, beginning with
the verb.

Watched the Twelfth-month sea-gulls, saw them high
    in the air floating with motionless wings,
    oscillating their bodies,
Saw how the glistening yellow lit up parts of their
    bodies and left the rest in strong shadow,
Saw the slow-wheeling circles and the gradual edging
    toward the south, . . .

and so on for eight more lines. The next seven lines omit the
verb and begin with the grammatical objects:

The sailors at work in the rigging or out astride
    the spars,

> The round masts, the swinging motion of the hulls,
>   the slender serpentine pennants,
> The large and small steamers in motion, the pilots
>   in their pilot-houses, . . .

and so on; and the final three lines contain not even the objects, but clauses modifying the objects.

This is an ingenious rhetoric. As the grammatical "I" that sees it all disappears from the sentence, the visionary eye is apparently assimilated by the images it sees, thereby dramatizing "The simple, compact, well-join'd scheme, myself disintegrated, every one disintegrated yet part of the scheme. . . ." As this process evolves, one of the lines within the sequence simultaneously sums up the "well-join'd scheme" with a static symbol of the poet looking down at his own image, "at the fine centrifugal spokes of light round the shape of my head in the sunlit water."

The "drift" of a poem is what justifies Whitman's logic that anything equals everything. The sense of a radiating ego dramatizes this argument. But Whitman's cosmos involves no passive merger. His "well-join'd scheme" is ethical; it presupposes a human action. Whitman proselytized a conscious and willful union of all selves. As long as Whitman could keep this idea metaphorical he was all right. But he was always on the verge of exhorting his listener, thereby implying some course of action. But *what* action? One way or another he must answer this or beg the question. "Song of the Open Road" illustrates this whole situation: the illusion of union through movement, and the poet's public invitation to participate, thereby raising and begging the question of how to participate in what.

The "Open Road" symbolizes the continuous movement of the speaker's consciousness ("You express me better than I can express myself"). The poem recounts how this realization occurs to the speaker and how he responds to it. He takes to the open road, describing the continuous, changing scene as he walks along. The panorama excites his speculations, and he begins to identify the open road with his own limitless imaginings. He promises to free himself from all constraints; he will touch upon everything as the road does, blessing those who accept his route, unmindful of those who disagree.

This poem observes the conventional form of the pastoral lyric: the poet on the landscape describing what he sees and then speculating about what he describes, but the prominent quality of this pastoral is the nature of the poet's realization. He becomes aware of idealism. He apprehends that it is not the physical road or the countryside but his *idea* of the road that is real. Moreover, this subjective reality is what constitutes all things and all experience. He discerns that by traveling an uncharted route he will meet *within himself* the essence of whatever he has previously encountered outside himself. "Here is realization!" "Here is the efflux of the soul," he says, "here is happiness." Then he musters all his listeners. "*Allons!*" everybody; "*Allons!* the road is before us!"; sufficiency is in the great companionship of "superior journeys"; "My call is the call of battle, I nourish active rebellion," he shouts. "*Allons!*" The rhetoric of the poem anticipates what he later wrote in "Passage to India," in support of a different doctrine. But both poems beg the same question.

Whitman never finished his cosmos. By its nature it was illimitable. He spent years trying to specify and explain his massive generalities. The Civil War was the obvious detour in Whitman's "Open Road." His earlier poems, published before 1861, had epitomized what he thought was a national willingness to believe in the individual, and more than that: a willingness to believe that the strength and stature of the nation lay precisely in the individual's union with all men. "En-Masse" and "the simple separate person" together constituted Democracy—or Brotherhood or "Kosmos." But the war shattered all this. It was a conflict of interests growing out of the very brotherhood of separate selves that Whitman had championed; a mortal, devastating, military conflict. The human wrecks he had volunteered to nurse were deathly testimonies to this whole terrible contradiction.

Death as a metaphor had been prominent in the third edition of *Leaves* (1860), as a symbol of the union of all men, but now it had an awesome irony. In *Drum-Taps* (1865) Whitman recorded, as he said, the "passing and rapid but actual glimpses of the great struggle between the nation and the slave-power"; and the short, stunned lines of *Drum-Taps* seem scarcely to have been written by the same author of the ebullient claims in his earlier verse. These war poems were incorporated into *Leaves of Grass*. Speaking of this merger in his 1876 Preface, Whitman described the importance of the war and of his poems about it in the whole development of *Leaves*: "the whole book, indeed, revolves around that four years' war, which, as I was in the midst of it, becomes, in 'Drum-Taps,' pivotal to the rest entire. . . ."

His wholesale revision of his earlier poems, beginning in the 1867 edition had already indicated this importance. He had spoken of the "drift" of his poems, meaning the dynamic merger of the self with all things; it conveyed an indiscriminate pantheism. But now he needed, or felt he needed, to reconstrue his cosmos all over again, to interpret it, and thereby to reorient himself to his whole original conception of an organic world. And so the "drift" of Whitman's poems took on extended meaning, beyond what he had originally intended.

The most sustained definition and interpretation of Whitman's cosmos is "Democratic Vistas" (1871). This essay is a didactic revision of the 1855 Preface. Both works proclaim a national American literature; both associate it with political and religious ideas, and celebrate the poet as a secular priest of the commonwealth. Both are effusive, digressing from one aspect of the subject to another, but "Democratic Vistas" attempts to *define* the lyrical equations of the Preface, and therein lies the difference and the change. In the Preface,

"Democracy" means the equality of all things; it is used in a religious sense. "Nationalism" means something more like internationalism. The entire extent of the poet's politics in the Preface is "to cheer slaves and horrify despots." And "Chant," the synonym for poem, is the correlative of all human experience. In its easy, lyrical equations the Preface is indistinguishable from Whitman's early poems. But "Democratic Vistas" attempts to systematize this parochial vocabulary. It is a dissertation on the political justification for a national literature which shall also be religious.

"Democratic Vistas" belongs to the genre known as "The Defense of Poetry," and it begins like dozens of other American domestications of this genre in the nineteenth century. Like the ancient republics—so the argument goes—the new nation needs a literature to express it and to record its achievement. There is a wealth of subject matter, requiring only the artist's faith in its validity and in himself. The best American expressions of this apology (William Cullen Bryant's lectures, for example, or William Ellery Channing's "Remarks on National Literature," or James Russell Lowell's "The Function of the Poet"), all subsume the traditional argument to some personal conviction about the nature of art or the nature of man or the nature of this republic; and so does "Democratic Vistas," which defines the nature of this singular democracy.

Whitman's essay argues that the art inherited from feudal societies is inappropriate to the New World; it reflects merely an aristocratic caste and cannot fulfill the proper function of literature in this particular democracy. Whitman insisted, as James Fenimore Cooper had insisted, that the essence of a national literature is in its political awareness; and Whitman worked it out even more explicitly. The essence of this democratic culture is exactly in its equivocal nature, or what Whitman called "ensemble-individuality."

This peculiar phrase is an apt statement of this nation's political strategy, and of a system of government intended to countenance majority rule and individual privilege at the same time. Logically these two concepts are mutually exclusive, but in the government of the United States, nevertheless, they have always been interdependent. A balance of majority rule and minority rights is the governing political principle of this republic. The system is purposely equivocal, and it happens to resemble the precarious extension of the equivocal self that Whitman celebrated. He did not envisage the intricate system of concessions and compromises that does exist. He did not discuss the expedient ways and means of a two-party system, or the nature of a political party that necessarily exists by reciprocity and contrivance. But he repeatedly acknowledged that the democratic system is a risky investment in the human instincts which cause fraud and insolence and corruption. And he believed that the risk is worth it.

Although the ways and means of reconciliation were beyond him, Whitman insisted that the paradoxical harmony of opposites is precisely the democratic system. As he said, the unyielding principle of "the average" and the unyielding principle of individuality enable each other.

> For to democracy, the leveler, the unyielding principle of the average, is surely join'd another principle, equally unyielding . . . indispensable to it, opposite, (as the sexes are opposite,) . . . yet neither of highest avail without the other. . . . This second principle is individuality, the pride and centripetal isolation of a human being in himself— identity—personalism. . . . It forms . . . the compensating balance-wheel of the successful working machinery of aggregate America.

He argued that the political system based on these compensating opposites was still embryonic, and that a national literature must have a supreme and formative function in preserving both the aggregate of people and the sacred self. The American literature must explain this harmony of opposites in the provisional way that any literature explains its subject.

Even the Puritan ministers had no more functional idea of a literature than Whitman had.

But this is as far as Whitman could get. When it came to specifying such a literature, he asserted that what we need are national archetypes; and he fell back on the catalogue, the most persuasive device he knew by which to convey the unutterable. He took inventory of the people who had arrived on these shores and who belonged to their new regions. He spread upon the page a catalogue of American personalities. Having theorized beyond the early Preface, however, he could not really specify what he meant; he returned, instead, to mystical effusion: to the poet, "the divine literatus," and his art.

> Can there be any doubt who the leader ought to be? Bear in mind, though, that nothing less than the mightiest original non-subordinated SOUL has ever really, gloriously led, or ever can lead. (This SOUL—its other name, in these Vistas, is LITERATURE.)

Leaves of Grass was to be this "SOUL" of the nation, nothing less than the animation of the body politic. He worked out his literary theory more specifically in a new Preface to the sixth edition of *Leaves* (1876), according to which the vital political mission of the United States is to reconcile the conflict of federal authority and states' rights. The civil expression of universal suffrage is "unspeakably important"; but even so, the surest expression of a growing, changing democracy, far more than civil expression, will be artistic and religious: "the true growth-characteristics of the democracy of the New World are henceforth to radiate in superior literary, artistic, and religious expressions, far more than in its republican forms. . . ." Religious and artistic expressions are necessarily political, and they are formative as well as reflective.

Whitman continued to write postscripts to his theory of a literature endemic to an organic, growing entity called Amer-

ica. "Behind all else," he later wrote in "A Backward
Glance," "I consider 'Leaves of Grass' and its theory experimental—as, in the deepest sense, I consider our American republic itself to be, with its theory." The prominent characteristic of these postscripts is rationalization. In retrospect
Whitman was enlarging the scheme by which to explain all
his writing.

In this expanded cosmic theory, religion became his pre-
dominant subject. He had already emphasized the affinity of
political and religious expression. "Democratic Vistas" concludes that the political and social state is a beginning by
which to discover "the deepest basic elements and loftiest
final meanings, of history and man. . . ." This conclusion repeats a long footnote in the essay, explaining that "The altitude of literature and poetry has always been religion—and
always will be." The culmination of all literary expression is
"in metaphysics, including the mysteries of the spiritual
world, the soul itself, and the question of the immortal con-
tinuation of our identity." This bears an unmistakable new
emphasis on futurity.

In the fifth edition of *Leaves* (1872), to which Whitman
appended "Passage to India," his Preface emphasizes the
restless, experimental nature of the book ("the earnest trial
and persistent exploration"). He makes the point that one
purpose has governed all the others, "and that has been the
religious purpose. Amid many changes, and a formulation
taking far different shape from what I at first supposed, this
basic purpose has never been departed from in the composition of my verses.

> Not of course to exhibit itself in the old ways, as in writing
> hymns or psalms with an eye to the church-pew, or to ex-
> press conventional pietism, or the sickly yearnings of devo-
> tees, but in new ways, and aiming at the widest sub-bases
> and inclusions of humanity, and tallying the fresh air of sea
> and land.

Later, in the 1876 Preface, Whitman pointedly incorporated politics in "the pensive thought of immortality," saying that in his mind the latter had grown out of the former. His footnotes explaining the affinity of politics and religion are nearly as long as the Preface that contains them. He was anxious to explain how "Passage to India" epitomized all his former implications. "For, in my opinion, it is no less than this idea of immortality, above all other ideas, that is to enter into, and vivify, and give crowning religious stamp, to democracy in the New World." The drift of Whitman was really an approach to a more conventional religious concept of life after death.

The footnote in the 1876 Preface, explaining why "Passage to India" has become his valedictory, incidentally describes the dramatic situation of the poem itself. "As in some ancient legend-play, to close the plot and the hero's career, there is a farewell gathering on ship's deck and on shore, a loosing of hawsers and ties, a spreading of sails to the wind—

> a starting out on unknown seas, to fetch up no one knows whither—to return no more—and the curtain falls, and there is the end of it. . . ."

The poem begins by celebrating the technological achievements which have joined men and continents: the Suez Canal, the first transcontinental railroad, the Atlantic cable —as though Whitman had finally found documentary proof of the "Open Road." The poet sees the evolving wonders of technology and perceives them to be manifestations of divine will. With catalogues of scenic images and ancient voyagers he elaborates his claim that science has been broadening the way for the prophetic poet.

Then the poem becomes imperative. The exploring and expanding soul must make the final and completing journey: "Passage to more than India!"; passage to the revelation of the nature of God and man. The poem proposes a course of action, after first establishing the poet's mandate to act. The summary of scientific exploration and technology necessarily ordains the poet. Here, abstracted from the poem, is the mandate:

> After the great captains and engineers have accomplished their work . . . the poet . . . the true son of God shall come singing his songs. . . . Then . . . all these separations and gaps shall be taken up and hook'd and link'd together. The whole earth, this cold impassive voiceless earth shall be completely justified . . . gloriously accomplished by the true son of God, the poet.

The poet's utterance "shall absolutely fuse" all created parts. The poem concludes with the poet charging his soul to begin the metaphorical journey, the final "passage . . . to primal thought."

Whitman's insistence in his later prefaces indicates how important "Passage to India" had become in his whole scheme of things, and in a later essay ("Poetry To-day in America," 1881) he specified how his vision had broadened with time. "I see that this world of the West, as part of all, fuses inseparably with the East, and with all, as time does— the ever new, yet old, old human race. . . ." His later essays, beginning with "Democratic Vistas," also included science—by which he meant technology—as well as civil government in his idea of religious revelation. And he made it clear that "Passage to India" was the apogee of his whole evolving system.

Ironically this poem *was* the epitome of Whitman's striving self-expression, but not entirely in the way he had intended. What it correlates is Whitman's notion of the poem as an action. "Passage to India" formally repeats "Song of the Open Road." In each of these pastoral lyrics the poet sees the physical aspects of a landscape, thereby conceives of the inseparable wholeness of the world, and realizes that the conception itself is ideal. In the course of his descriptions the poet recognizes the efficacy of his own consciousness, and he attempts to convert his impressions into a course of action. Nothing has changed in this respect.

The "vast Rondure" that the poet celebrates in "Passage to India" is his ideal conception ("my thought begins to span thee"). His realization of his own efficacy then begets self-exhortations. But exhortations to what? What is this metaphorical journey on which he is champing to embark? In the poem's narrative sense it is the final passage of the soul to a God external to one's self, a more or less orthodox journey congenial to the piety of Whitman's later essays. But in the poem's dramatic sense—the poet's realization of his own efficacy—the poet has already completed the very journey he anticipates. The essence of the vast rondure that so excites him has been his own realization of it, but he commits the redundancy of setting out on a journey to accomplish what he has just achieved.

The subjective vision has its own efficacy; beyond this it is ineffable. In this poem God's purpose, allegedly about to be realized, has *just been* realized. There is nothing more to say, but "Passage to India" tries to say it, tries to actuate it. The real revelation, of course, is the consciousness of the poet as he struggles to consummate his own vision, to enact what is already consummate.

Whitman never did put himself "freely, fully, and truly on the record" to his own satisfaction. He never did complete his cosmos to suit himself. Later in his life he had the idea of writing a book of chants, one for each day of the year—a definitive book of a sort; but he never got around to it because he never finished *Leaves of Grass*. The ravening, innocent passion to encompass the world with one's self never could be fulfilled. The doctrinal failure is implicit in the doctrine, but so is the ceaseless attempt to give it form and to communicate it.

Of all the properties of Whitman's visionary world the program which he could never specify became his insistent legacy. Whitman himself suspected as much. "Poets to come!" he says, "you must justify me. . . . I myself but / write one or two indicative words for the future . . . .

> Leaving it to you to prove and define it,
> Expecting the main things from you."

It was a lovely-terrible legacy.

CHAPTER FOUR

Hart Crane's
"Span of Consciousness"

The Bridge (1930) was the end, both the aim and the termination, of Hart Crane's short, violent career as a poet. It took him seven years to render it, from what he first called a "new longish poem" to the final structure of some eighteen hundred lines. Crane composed its parts during brief, intense periods which were separated by long intervals, often months, of obsessive inactivity. He finally achieved a sequence of fifteen poems in eight sections that he stoutly believed to be a single organic structure. Crane was right about the integrity of his poem, although he did not know why. But his critics disagreed with him. *The Bridge* is a major work of art, and part of its historical significance is the widespread misunderstanding it caused among the literary taste makers who were Crane's contemporaries, even those who wanted to be sympathetic. Crane's theory of a poem was out of joint with theirs, and this conflict has left a legacy of confusion.

Among the criticisms of *The Bridge* majority opinion still holds that Crane, a disciple of Walt Whitman, failed to render his intended "American synthesis" because the concept itself was faulty. Moreover, Section 4 ("Cape Hatteras") is usually offered as a symptom of *The Bridge* as a whole—or rather its failure to be a whole: merely a striking series of uneven lyrics shuttling back and forth between high hope and despair. This part-truth has caused most of the confusion over the poem. To make a case against the doctrine of the poem is to miss the point. In fact, the terms in which *The Bridge* was conceived denied at the beginning any chance of its succeeding in a rational or ideological way. Understanding Crane's *attempt* to render a doctrine is crucial to understanding the poem.

These lyrics are a single entity. The subject of *The Bridge* is not its doctrine but its author's struggle to express one. This burden of expression is one of the distinctive characteristics of a romantic cosmology, which *The Bridge* assuredly is. It proposes an organic world of the mind, and it is therefore necessarily autobiographical. Its author's attempt is the poem's subject, so the poem necessarily dramatizes the process of his expression; its rhetoric is the model of the universe it proposes. To view *The Bridge* as a cosmology allows the possibility of appraising the comprehensive whole of it; and Crane did build a whole entity in spite of his doctrine, or rather because of his attempt to express it.

Crane attempted to render continent, community, and individual man into a divine, organic entity simply by subsuming these elements to his own vision. For a long while he believed that he had only to metaphorize this ideal in order to realize it. He explained at the outset that his poem would concern "a mystical synthesis of 'America.' History and fact, location, etc., all have to be transfigured into abstract form that would almost function independently of its subject matter." [1] This oneness of America was his doctrine, but Crane himself believed that a poem renders more than merely a doctrine.

"Poetry," he explained, "is simply the concrete *evidence* of the *experience* of a recognition (*knowledge* if you like)." The poem offers a ratio of experience and fact, he insisted: "it is both perception and thing perceived." [2] He once celebrated the fact that Alfred Stieglitz made the camera into an "instrument of something more especially vital—apprehension." [3] The process of Crane's own apprehending is the vital principle of *The Bridge*. The point is not that it makes the poem succeed; rather, it *makes* the poem.

The Bridge represents Crane's struggle with his own material. It dramatizes his attempts to deputize voices to explain
and rationalize the vision of Brooklyn Bridge that he had in
the first place. These voices reveal Crane's search for evidence to justify the organic unity of the world that the
Bridge first symbolized to him and which he stated in
"Proem" and "Atlantis." Between these two lyrics addressed
to the Bridge itself, at either end of the whole poem, a restless consciousness presides. In the printed sequence the lyrics
reveal an apparent order in this search for the one world: excursions into the past followed by inspections of the present
experience for evidence to support Crane's vision of unity.
But the sequence of their composition is something else
again. This sequence is the really convincing fact of Crane's
own participation. The tortuous record of it lies in his correspondence.

Crane began at the end, with his vision of the Bridge as
the apotheosis of human experience, and then in fits and
starts he constructed the seven preceding parts and a proem,
working backward and forward toward the physical and dramatic center of the poem. As he explained to Otto Kahn, he
got the idea for the poem from his midnight vision of Brooklyn Bridge:

> Strangely enough that final section of the poem has been
> the first to be completed,—yet there's a logic to it, after all;
> it is the mystic consummation toward which all the other
> sections of the poem converge. Their contents are implicit
> in its summary.[4]

The problem was to make these implicit "contents" *explicit.*
The great burden of the poem for Crane was the necessity of
having to specify the circumstances that might have comprised this "mystic consummation," and to re-create a convincing illusion of them.

Crane had substantially finished "Atlantis" by July, 1923,
yet two-and-a-half years later, newly revised, it was still the
only completed section of *The Bridge.* Most of *The Bridge*
was written during the spring and summer of 1926. During

this period of intense writing he set to work on the "Ave Maria" section; he sketched out a sequence for all the lyrics, then composed the "Proem" and "Cutty Sark"; he worked on three parts of "Powhatan's Daughter" and completed "The Tunnel." In the order of composition Crane skipped from Section 8 to Section 1, to the "Proem," to Section 2, to Section 7—always working toward a center of some sort that might finally define the poem's dialectic. But it was more than another year—in the autumn of 1927—before he could finally specify what the center sections of the poem would be; and it was nearly two years after that, in the summer of 1929, that he was finally and feverishly working on these interior parts: "Cape Hatteras," "Quaker Hill," and the last section of "Powhatan's Daughter."

Two related conditions have marked the history of *The Bridge*: Crane's explicit attempts to make the poem work as a doctrine, and a general tendency among critics to take him at his word. He conceived a highly subjective proposition about a monistic world, and declared it to be the subject of *The Bridge*; then he found himself overwhelmed by the burden of defining a concept that did not exist in fact in an idiom that did not exist at all. He had to correlate his own perceiving, or what (in "Cape Hatteras") he called "the span of consciousness." Although his struggle to make this correlation was not his declared intention, it became his preoccupation. His struggle to find a form became the subject of his poem, which makes it a whole and sufficient work of art. His inability to extricate himself from his own poem, moreover, helps to explain its significance among romantic cosmologies.

Crane's first letter to Otto Kahn about *The Bridge* implies his commitment to its doctrine: "aiming as it does to enunciate a new cultural system of values in terms of our America." [5] In the poem this emblematic America has no geographical finitude: it extends from the origins of Columbus in the East to an indefinite West described as Cathay; it has no boundaries at the North or South. It is not a continent but a condition. This America has no political or economic ideology, no concept of the United States, for example. It has virtually no population. Although it is the locus of a great many dramatic situations, they represent merely fragments of persons. The only sustained personage in this America is the speaker of the poem, the voice in its various guises, the consciousness that generates this spiritual New World and then tries to evangelize it.

The poet's sense of mission intensified whenever he was thinking about T. S. Eliot, which was often. Eliot's poetry had a peculiar importance in helping Crane to define his own attitude about the possibilities of mankind. Crane wished to affirm. He decried "the national pessimism of the hour so well established by T. S. Eliot" [6] and blamed Eliot for "the poetic determinism of our age." [7] As Crane explained to Allen Tate, "In his own realm Eliot presents us with an absolute *impasse*. . . . I, for instance, would like to leave a few of his 'negations' behind me, risk the realm of the obvious more, in quest of new sensations, new *humours*." [8] He wrote this in 1922, before he conceived of *The Bridge*. In this letter he was already working out a strategy with reference to Eliot's poetry, "a safe tangent to strike which, if I can possibly explain the position,—goes *through* him toward a *different goal*."

Crane elaborated on this strategy and clarified his own dogma a few months later in a letter to Gorham Munson:

> There is no one writing in English who can command so much respect, to my mind, as Eliot. However, I take Eliot as a point of departure toward an almost complete reverse of direction. His pessimism is amply justified, in his own case. But I would apply as much of his erudition and technique as I can absorb and assemble toward a more positive, or . . . ecstatic goal. . . . I feel that Eliot ignores certain spiritual events and possibilities as real and powerful now as, say, in the time of Blake.[9]

The letters about Eliot consistently indicate Crane's belief in a certain editorial affirmation that he thought his own poem must have. He not only anticipated its criticism on these grounds, he invited it. Throughout the long years of its composition, Crane had confided his plans for *The Bridge* to a few literary colleagues whose approbation he very much wanted. When *The Bridge* was first published two of these colleagues, Gorham Munson and Waldo Frank, were silent; three others wrote reviews—Malcolm Cowley, Allen Tate, and Yvor Winters—which in sum ranged from equivocal praise to outright deprecation. The crux of each review was the allegedly faulty doctrine of the poem. Together they indicate the range of attitudes in the criticism of *The Bridge* ever since.

As tactfully as possible, Cowley acknowledged Crane's "attempt to create the myth of America": "We might well conclude that such an attempt was foredoomed to failure." [10] Then having raised the question he diplomatically begged it. The poem had succeeded "to an impressive degree," he said, "in its presumptuous effort"—not wholly, of course, "for its faults are obvious." Cowley pointedly declined to specify these faults, but Allen Tate and Yvor Winters were both explicit about the poem's doctrinal failure.

Tate perceived that the poem "lacks an objective pattern of ideas elaborate enough to carry it through an epic or heroic work." [11] "If we subtract from Crane's idea what he has to say about it, we have left only the static abstraction, 'the grandeur of America,' which is not only incapable of further elucidation on the logical plane, but actually obstructs it."

Yvor Winters also acknowledged Crane's "endeavor to create and embody a national myth," and he agreed that Whitman had been an accessory before the fact. But in Winters's singular judgment this amounted to a moral indictment, and he concluded his review of *The Bridge*, triumphantly offering "Crane's wreckage" as evidence of the end of the "Whitmanian tradition."

Winters charged that "The Whitmanian basis of Mr. Crane's book makes a hero . . . impossible." [12] He asserted that there is no hero, no consciousness in the poem that might rescue the abstract doctrine from itself. What Tate said, however, was something else again: "the coherence of the work consists in the personal quality of the writing—in mood, feeling, and tone." To subtract Crane's idea from what he has to say about it "would leave only the static abstraction." The distinction is significant in that Tate did recognize Crane's participation, on stage, as it were, in his own poem. That Crane did not sufficiently preside over his own materials, to the detriment of the poem—as Tate argued—is subsequent to his premise, at least, that Crane *did* participate.

Crane was unable to discover precisely what it was he wanted to say. As Tate pointed out, "The poet has not observed the distinction between a metaphor and a philosophical idea." [13] Crane's "mystical synthesis of America" is a metaphor, but he kept trying to define it. Crane considered himself a mystic, but one sure characteristic of the mystical experience is its ineffability. As William James explained it, the essence of this experience is nontransferable; it cannot even be accurately described, since words are derived from the sensory-intellectual consciousness whose range the mystical experience escapes. This does not deny the validity of the experience itself. The efficacy of such an experience in most cases, James said, is "to add a supersensitive meaning to the outward data of consciousness." [14] But this supersensitive meaning is not transferable. The feeling Crane wanted to formalize was beyond the capacity of discursive language to convey. By testimony of mystics for centuries, the essence of the mystical experience is apparently its transport beyond any concept whatever. It is the achievement of a supersensuous, superrational consciousness, by its nature devoid of idea.

If the mystical experience was ineffable, then the next best thing would be an approximation of some sort, such as the *idea* of mysticism, some extrapolation from the mystical experience itself. Crane's "mystical synthesis of America" was just such a derivative. But Crane also had an acute awareness of his own identity. His excitement with himself was what he really could be sure of. The "supersensitive meaning" that Crane derived from mystical experience was evidently and peculiarly a new self-consciousness; and this really engaged him.

Crane's famous letter to Gorham Munson, describing his ecstatic experience while under anesthesia in the dentist's chair, for example, emphasizes a distinct self in a dramatic situation. Although his mind "spiraled to a kind of seventh heaven of consciousness," Crane could still recall performing an "egoistic dance among the seven spheres" and listening to the words of another, discrete presence: ". . . something like an objective voice kept saying to me, 'you have the higher consciousness—you have the higher consciousness. This is something that very few have. This is what is called genius.'" Crane went on to say, "I felt the two worlds. And at once." [15] On another occasion Crane explained to Waldo Frank the ecstasy of walking hand in hand with a lover across the Brooklyn Bridge—"the cables enclosing us and pulling us upwards in such a dance as I have never walked and never can walk with another"—in terms that came closer to the undifferentiated oneness of mystical experience—"I have seen the Word made Flesh"—yet his description still emphasized the sublimation of the discrete self. [16]

By whatever means, Crane derived a concept of the mystical experience; and his distinctive self seems always to have been at the center of it. Although this present self—and self-awareness—contradicted the mystical experience, it nevertheless provided Crane's only continuity from the experience to the images and sensuous associations by which every poet communicates. He employed himself—or some version of himself—as a kind of continuous bridge between two kinds of consciousness. This self generates the intensity of the whole poem.

Crane searched long and hard for some relevant form, some way of controlling the images he visualized. The subject continually recurs in his letters. Although he was not always aware of it, this search for a form was the means of organizing a poem around his own presence. He explored various possibilities, always looking for that organizing metaphor and remarking excitedly whenever one seemed to present itself; for example, his frequent musical analogies. He wanted to devise a language in which sound might escape verbal limitations to a kind of music, in the manner of the Symbolists, whose legacy he readily acknowledged. ". . . observe the water-swell rhythm that persists until the Palos reference . . ." he wrote of the "Ave Maria" lyric, "Then the more absolute and marked imitation of the great *Te Deum* of the court, later held,—here in terms of C[olumbus]'s own cosmography." [17] He enthused over the jazz rhythm at the beginning of "The River" and its modulation to a slow regularity approximating the gait of the hoboes along the railroad track. "Cutty Sark" was a fugue. But "Atlantis" in particular was to be the great "symphonic" composition.

He was always searching for a form. "Let us invent an idiom for the proper transposition of jazz into words! Something clean, sparkling, elusive!" [18] unconstrained by any rhyme scheme. He wanted what he called "an 'interior' form, a form that is so thorough and intense as to dye the words themselves with a peculiarity of meaning, slightly different maybe from the ordering definition of them separate from the poem." [19]

Crane's theorizing about the aims and obligations of the poet helps to explain his urgent search for an "interior form." In his essay, "Modern Poetry," he insisted that the poet's concern "must be, as always, self-discipline toward a formal integration of experience," and that modern poetry must now "absorb the machine, i.e., *acclimatize* it," as it has done with "all other human associations of the past." [20] This task would impose immense responsibility on the poet. In order to assimilate all dogma (of the "Machine Age" in this case) the modern poet must develop "an extraordinary capacity for surrender, at least temporarily, to the sensations of urban life." This opinion he had already stated earlier. "What I am after is an assimilation of this experience," Crane explained in his first synopsis of *The Bridge*, "a more organic panorama, showing the continuous and living evidence of the past in the inmost vital substance of the present." [21] But "assimilation," to Crane, meant a special kind of participation in the poem. The "interior form" he sought was really some way of dramatizing his own presence; but he did not clearly see this. Whatever part of *The Bridge* happened to engage him at the moment he considered the "real center" of the poem— ironically, since the poem had no center at all for many years, other than his search for it.

The first and principal metaphor of his monism, the bridge, had its own sufficiency; it did not require any development. The connotation of "Atlantis," his paean to the Bridge, conveys the sense of wholeness. Rhetorically, this apostrophe to the Bridge is one long-suspended period. Although grammatically there are many verbs in its ninety-six lines, the only verb that governs the rhetorical apostrophe ("O arching strands of song . . . hold thy floating singer late") occurs nearly seventy lines after its subject. There is no motion in this state of sufficiency. "Atlantis" is all noun. How could he make it dynamic? He despaired of doing so. He saw that he was trying to write shorthand about an endless subject. "Emotionally I should like to write *The Bridge*; intellectually judged the whole theme and project seems more and more absurd." The metaphors of past and present, by which he had hoped to represent an organic world, suddenly would not work. "By which I mean that however great their subjective significance to me . . . these forms, materials, dynamics are simply nonexistent in the world." And he added, "I am only evading recognition and playing Don Quixote in an immorally conscious way." [22]

Soon after Crane had posted this letter to Waldo Frank he wrote again, ecstatically celebrating his reunion with the whole project. He had just finished "Proem to Brooklyn Bridge," and was ready to take on the whole monistic world again.

> Hail Brother! I feel an absolute music in the air again, and some tremendous rondure floating somewhere—perhaps my little dedication ["To Brooklyn Bridge"] is going to swing me back to San Cristobal again. . . . That little prelude, by the way, I think to be almost the best thing I've ever written, something steady and uncompromising about it.[23]

The irony of Crane's regeneration is unmistakable. For all it renewed his faith, his new proem represented no advance whatever into the dialectic of *The Bridge*. It is an exciting invocation, but it merely calls upon the Bridge to "lend a myth to God," that is, to become the symbol that Crane had already made of it three years before. He had merely recalled the Bridge to mind and literally invoked its presence again. And so it went for years. He had already begun at that "real center" for which he was still looking.

Crane's struggle to order his material was his surest subject. The illusion of a wild and restless consciousness governs the poem: a lyric voice, scantily disguised as other voices. In "Atlantis," the voice that deifies the Bridge is scarcely aware of itself, but in the interior sections, "Indiana," "Cape Hatteras," and "Quaker Hill," precisely the ones he put off writing, the voice becomes self-conscious, public, and editorial. The dramatic difference between the concluding lyric that Crane wrote first and those interior sections that Crane wrote last marks the extent of his struggle to idealize a world. Crane's technical problem was to organize these echoing voices. But the problem was immense, because in the saga of composing his poem he himself had become personally and actually the hero.

His letters make this clear. Crane dramatized himself as a voice in the wilderness with an urgent need to explain, to confess all. He was set apart from his community, and painfully aware of this fact. He was at odds with his parents; he could make love to no woman; and he compulsively put off his friends when he most needed them. Crane railed at his poverty, at having to take jobs that prostituted him; yet when some benefactor paid his debts, he would suffer in abject luxury, awed by his obligation to write poetry in return for the subsidy. Always tending toward extremes, he wanted to confess and yet to justify himself at the same time. He wanted to assimilate, to devour whole experiences, and he despaired because he could not. He wanted to settle down, but he was rarely at home wherever he was, always moving from city to town and back again, always looking for an exit. No wonder his fascination—in *The Bridge*—with the notion of journeying, the restlessness, and the sense of urgency. The voice in *The Bridge* speaks for a questing, hungering evangelist. In fact, it becomes the voice of a symbolic poet.

The scenery and the situations in *The Bridge* are symbolic because he sees them so. In this way the fifteen lyrics do become a whole poem. The organizing speaker repeats his quest for unity in a series of apostrophes: monologues addressed to real or imagined listeners, called up or recalled for each occasion; and these apostrophes invoke the presence of things, of legends, of poets and explorers and pioneers. Ghosts and shades and spirits are invoked. Columbus calls upon two faithful peers who merge into a third partisan, in the poet's mind; then, dehumanized, they represent the spirit of exploration and search. The poet addresses an emblematic lover and then Van Winkle, who becomes a metaphor of the bewildering orientation of one's self to everything else. Again, the poet invokes Pocahontas as the fertile earth incarnate, but interrupts the incantation with an address to the

Indian chief who first possessed the symbolic Pocahontas. Later, Walt Whitman becomes the apocalyptic singer; and Poe, an emblem of disembodied horror. Finally, in the poet's mind, the Bridge becomes the revelation of God.

The lyric voice idealizes each occasion, generating what it names into some iconic significance. The metaphorical "Tunnel" becomes a sort of anti-Bridge—however illogically —and Quaker Hill symbolizes the desecrated "Promised Land." Three Songs variously epitomize womankind: the Southern Cross, disappearing over the horizon, incarnates a "nameless" ideal; the stripteaser becomes the definitive "burlesque of our lust—and faith"; and "Virginia" palely idealizes the playmate and companion. With every new lyric the poet's voice summons up a world that is literally immaterial, in a consciousness that has its own sufficiency.

This consciousness repeatedly embarks on metaphorical journeys. In the printed order of its parts *The Bridge* is a sequence of explorations: first, into the historical or legendary past, to discover some grand holistic scheme; then into a various present, searching for evidence to test this scheme. In these excursions the seeking consciousness exchanges metaphors of space and time: voyaging at once westward and into the past, or along city streets to pluperfect recollections, or up the Hudson to primal spring. Time and space become relative to the observer, and this witness celebrates a plenitude that absorbs all movement into a continuum.

These are symbolic journeys. Crane also tried to say all this editorially. Midway in the whole sequence, in "Cape Hatteras," the lyric voice invokes both past and present in order to establish—by assertion—the organic unity of all experience. But this was virtually Crane's last journey in the composition of *The Bridge*. Viewed in the order of their composition, which was so different from their printed sequence, these journeys indicate a kind of therapeutic itinerary of Crane's, attempting to arrive—in "Cape Hatteras"—at some final definition of his visionary idea.

This is the part of *The Bridge*, according to most commentary, where Crane's "doctrinal failure" damages the poetry. Brom Weber summed up the critical consensus in an unequivocal statement: "This section is a complete failure, both as a complete poem and as a contributory part of *The Bridge*": except for scattered lines and stanzas, an abysmal descent from Crane's usual level of writing.[24] The symbolism of the earlier sections, Weber wrote, has been dissipated in mere virtuosity. Karl Shapiro's extended analysis of the "Cape Hatteras" manuscript makes the point that the fault in the poetry is precisely that failure to assimilate the machine images which Crane had said the modern poet must accomplish. The fault, said Shapiro—echoing Winters—lies in the false image of life that Crane appropriated from Whitman.

To insist on such a literal reading of "Cape Hatteras" is to make a small point by missing the large one, since the subject of this poem *is* the struggle—as Shapiro so well put it—of "a demonic poet who has lost his way." [25] Working backward and forward through his material, Crane finally arrived at the point where empirical knowledge obviously contradicted his visionary order, at the point where the contradiction must somehow be resolved into a state of belief, into a commitment of some sort. At this point Crane had to make a stand. This was the denouement of his drama.

Crane himself signaled the importance of "Cape Hatteras" to *The Bridge*. In the first synopsis that he sent to Otto Kahn a projected episode about Whitman was to be one of the center sections of the poem; and more than four years later, even with an entirely new version of his homage to Whitman, he reminded Caresse Crosby, ". . . according to *my* ideas of *The Bridge* this edition wouldn't be complete or even representative without it." [26]

The function of "Cape Hatteras" was to invoke Whitman's vision of an organic cosmos to "prove" that the human epoch with its shallow past is truly joined to the ages of geological time. Mankind is now superimposed on the earth ("Those continental folded aeons, surcharged / With sweetness below derricks, chimneys, tunnels—"); [27] but the poet wants to show that it is only transient imposition. "Cape Hatteras" begins as though it might test Whitman's vision of unity against the uncongenial evidence of a mechanized society. Then the lyric becomes an impassioned defense of Whitman's precept in spite of the evidence.

The argument is as circular as any essay of Emerson's or any Puritan sermon, and with cause. Its premise is that truth already exists; it is not to be reasoned out but simply discovered. Long before he wrote "Cape Hatteras," Crane had decided that Whitman, better than any other, had been able to order the world into a personal vision. But "Cape Hatteras" follows more than just the inherited premise about the pre-existence of truth. Its sequence stylizes the whole doctrine-reasons-uses order of sermon argument.

The poem's first four stanzas state the doctrine of the futility of mankind's tenancy on earth without revelation. Six more stanzas amplify the "reasons" of this doctrine, imaging first the bright, brainless speed of mechanical parts, and then the short, fatal flight of a warplane. In this elaboration of the "reasons," fourteen lines of metaphors—in stanza five— reduce the energy of dynamos ("The nasal whine of power") to a drunken parody of parts in motion. The dizzy, gyrating hardware, on bearings confined "in oilrinsed circles of blind ecstasy," relentlessly and ridiculously transforms energy to no consequence:

> Power's script,—wound, bobbin-bound, refined—
> Is stropped to the slap of belts on booming spools, spurred
> Into bulging bouillon, harnessed jelly of the stars.
> Towards what?

Then five more stanzas launch a warplane and shoot it down—"down whizzing zodiacs . . . into smashed and shapeless debris. . . ."

After these two caricatures of mankind's futility, the dynamos and the plane, the poet apostrophizes Whitman, and the tone of this sermon-like lyric changes. These last seven stanzas present the program, the "uses" of the doctrine. This is the longest part of the poem's argument beginning with

> The stars have grooved our eyes with old persuasions
> Of love and hatred, birth,—surcease of nations
> But who has held the heights more sure than thou, O Walt?

It is also the most programmatic. The poet declares that he will reinstate the "span of consciousness" which Whitman celebrated; and herein lies the "use" of Whitman's vision and its beatific consequence. The engines return, but now their images connote rebirth, vitality.

> And now, as launched in abysmal cupolas of space,
> Toward endless terminals, Easters of speeding light—
> Vast engines outward veering with seraphic grace
> On Clarion cylinders pass out of sight
> To course that span of consciousness thou'st named
> The Open Road—thy vision is reclaimed!
> What heritage thou'st signalled to our hands!

This is a prospectus for a better world, which depends on the realization that creates it. "The Open Road" is one of two allusions in "Cape Hatteras" to poems of Whitman that assume this premise. The other, quoted in the epigram ("The seas all cross'd, weathered the capes, the voyage done . . .") is "Passage to India." Each of Whitman's poems anticipates the programmatic "Cape Hatteras"; each defines subjective realization as the life-giving process and then attempts to put it to work. In Whitman's "Passage to India" the poet realizes that his own consciousness will accomplish the final assimilation of all experience. In the course of celebrating "the vast rondure of the world," Whitman perceives that it is the reality of his own consciousness. "Now first it seems my thought begins to span thee."

But having already perceived an organic world, he proceeds

to invoke an extrinsic God. He sets out on a metaphorical journey to a destination at which he has already arrived before he starts. Crane's "Cape Hatteras" commits the same redundancy, and so does the whole saga of *The Bridge*. The subjective vision has its own efficacy; beyond this it is ineffable. The attempt to make a doctrine of it causes a dramatic crisis, which becomes a subject in itself.

To recall where I began this discussion, Hart Crane's prodigious attempt to write a "synthesis of America" was beyond the critical theories that were used to appraise it. *The Bridge* transcends Yvor Winters's ethical insistence and his attempt to take the poet's doctrine literally. It also transcends the limits of the early New Criticism. The assumptions that a work of art is a complete and distinct entity, that this discrete experience is the principal subject for literary analysis, and that its meaning inheres exclusively in the relationships between its parts are all useful, but by themselves they fail to explain *The Bridge*. This whole poem records the poet's struggle to express a world. In fact, his spastic dialogue with his material is form and subject both. Crane's attitude toward his struggle is intrinsic and not extrinsic to *The Bridge*, and any appraisal which separates this poem from the poet is bound to be limited.

Crane himself contributed to the misunderstanding of his poem by the way he talked about it. Certainly the antipathy he encountered had its snobbish aspects. He not only publicly disagreed with T. S. Eliot, which was a formidable trespass on literary vogue, but he announced ahead of time, even shouted, what his poem was about, thus depriving anyone else of the privilege. Finding fault with Eliot, however, was only incidental to Crane's purpose, which was to attack the concept of an impersonal poem. In view of all this, it is curious that the New Criticism, deriving as it did from Coleridge's philosophy of art, should have been so inadequate to a poem that derived from the same source. The form of a poem Coleridge considered to be the physical correlation of the soul within it. Accordingly, the poem is not a cunning construction of parts but a growth from a central, vital principle. Crane's letters made it abundantly clear that the central, living principle in *The Bridge* is the on-stage consciousness, contemplating the Bridge and trying to generate a new significance about it. Without this vital presence the Bridge would have no nature apart from its mere actuality as a magnificent engineering structure.

But Crane had to make this generating presence dramatically convincing. In organizing the various voices that would speak the poem, Crane was limited by the fact that he was really the subject of his own fiction. He must displace himself; yet to what extent? His editorializing in "Quaker Hill" is too arbitrary to allow the reader to share any illusion beyond that of Crane speaking. But Crane also lacked the sense of humor, the ironic awareness, that is apparently necessary in creating a deliberately different speaker. The mother who intones in "Indiana" is utterly unconvincing. Given her past and her present circumstance, she simply would not speak the way Crane made her speak. His intellectualizing overwhelmed the disguise he contrived for it. *The Bridge* is compelling, however, when the speaking voice remains personal yet without insistent personification. Thus: in "Ave Maria" Columbus becomes less the human figure and more the spirit of search; in "Cutty Sark"—and to a degree in "The Tunnel"—the fugue of disembodied voices registers upon a present consciousness; and thus, the speaker in "The River" and "The Dance"—and especially in "Cape Hatteras." These episodes all accomplish illusions of a consciousness becoming charged by the impressions it receives, to a point almost beyond endurance.

By this extremity, by its desperate excitement, *The Bridge* is an overstatement of what has always been a preoccupation in this national literature. It is an emphatic document in the American domestication of romanticism. It presumes to correct an inherited assumption about the human condition, namely, that the glory of the past and the hope for the future are at odds with the dreary present. The author, of course, appropriates a subjective reordering of the world; but more than that, he does so on the singular assumption of his ability to do something about it. The visionary world is more than a condition; it is a great power to be harnessed and put to work for mankind's well-being—through the alembic of the poet.

Paradigm Three

From the writings of Emerson, Whitman, and Crane we can infer the main characteristics of the romantic cosmology. Each cosmology is a distinct and singular version of organic idealism. Each is a parochial scheme of the universe, compounded of autobiography, fiction, and art theory that demonstrate the unseparated wholeness of all being according to the single vision of its author. But the subject of these works is not their idealistic doctrines so much as the author's struggle with the material evidence of the intractable world in his effort to express his doctrine. The author assumes that the reality of his own subjective vision can be validly extended beyond himself, and he assimilates or rationalizes empirical knowledge and previously formulated theory wherever such knowledge or theory might confirm his subjective vision.

By illustrating the characteristics of these particular writings I have been trying to emphasize how to read them and others like them. Using these same characteristics, I have also been trying to formulate the metaphor of a cosmology which you can use as a kind of tool. My purpose is practical, and probably evangelical, too. I think that the characteristics of the romantic cosmology suggest a strategy for reading other fictions that are not so obviously cosmologies, but in which the same characteristics are latent. Poetry offers one kind of knowledge of the world, and since this knowledge cannot be come by in any other way, it is worth the effort to formulate some comprehensive theory of reading fiction—or

83

poetry. Expressing such a theory is exactly my purpose. What I want to be able to say is that knowing how a poem is constructed helps in understanding all kinds of fiction.

The words "poetry" and "fiction" have a peculiar historical relationship. Any comprehensive theory of fiction really concerns what historically has been called poetry. I am referring to the generic process of constructing a system of metaphors to explore the relation between one's self and everything else.

Literary theory is full of terms that are imprecise because they have been differently used at different times. They have a broad range of related but separate meanings. Common and familiar terms—like poetry and fiction—offer a convenient approximation up to a point; then they must be defined. We can identify the generic process easily enough, but the trouble in naming it is that contemporary usage has shrunk the word "poetry" and assigned several different meanings to "fiction." Generally "poetry" now has an academic odor, and "fiction" smells commercial. To accommodate this change in usage we have tolerated dreadful euphemisms in college catalogues and book-review pages, like "creative writing" and "works of the imagination" to say nothing of "*belles lettres.*"

Some definition is necessary, so I will start with an artifact and call it a fictional construction. We can name it later. A fictional construction is a particular order of events that does not exist anywhere else. Probably each of these events is partly remembered and partly imagined, but their sequence and their consequence are new. The author has built this order of events for the purpose of clarifying, primarily to himself, the nature of his own experience and the actual experience of others that he knows of. This construction may be called either a poem or a fiction, although further definition would necessarily distinguish between the two. Even so, what I have called cosmologies would accommodate both terms. Cosmologies are fictions because they are discrete, imagined orders of events. They are also poems because of the characteristic way in which they are constructed, because of the distinctive behavior of the point of view, the persona, which builds a metaphor as it goes. A poem reveals its meaning by the way it proceeds. This distinctive way of proceeding is what is poetic about a poem.

This poetic quality of the cosmologies can also form and shape a fiction of narrative construction, particularly a novel. The next cluster of chapters, about *Walden* and *Moby Dick*, should develop this idea. The first step will be to show how the narrative *Walden* is both a fiction and a poem. The next step will be to show how the novel *Moby Dick* duplicates itself by its poetic construction. Together they should illustrate what I am about to explain, namely, that the novel form can readily accommodate the poetic characteristics of the cosmology.

The novel has length, a narrative, a conflict, and a point of view; and this combination of characteristics is amenable to the expression of a cosmology. Point of view (that is, the consciousness whose presence forms the rhetoric) is the most important link between these two forms of fiction; but it is really the combination of characteristics that makes the novel a good vehicle for a cosmology. The epic poem offers an apt comparison; it has these same characteristics as the novel form, but the combination of them in the epic makes it a public document in the sense that no cosmology is. The scope of the cosmology is not measured by the panorama of human events but by the individual consciousness that tells the story. Cause and effect in the epic is a divine and superhuman affair, but the whole psychology of the romantic cosmos is different. The cosmology is about the self that utters it; and the novel can emphasize this self-concern. Unburdened by conventions about its subject, least of all the acts of the gods, the novel can dramatize the point of view, the particular consciousness that is trying to build the largest possible metaphor of itself.

The combination of the length and the narrative and the

conflict is what develops the point of view in the novel. The point of view tells its story in many different ways, more or less at the same time. It reveals itself by the way it repeats the conflict; it can relate a conflict in different situations, in different time spans, through different characters and different metaphors—successively or in conjunction with one another. The novel form allows an author to accrete a meaning by a *progressive and qualifying repetition,* like a gunner trying to straddle a target that he cannot locate.

Suppose the conflict should happen to involve the point of view (which is disguised, say, as the person telling the story). Suppose this conflict should happen to be his struggle to build and decree a new and original world out of his own vision, in the face of evidence that contradicts it. This is the kind of confrontation that involved Emerson and Whitman and Crane—and Wolfe. And these poets expressed the same proposition: the artist needs to state an essence of all the particulars he apprehends. The more he struggles to order them into some unified idea, the more he is committed to his own vision. The more he is committed, the greater the tension and excitement his striving necessarily conveys.

The vital confrontation of the writer and his material is true of every novel, and so is his struggle, to some degree. But the cosmology is such an extreme and persistent statement of this struggle that a reader, once aware of it, has an insight into every novel he encounters.

The past few paragraphs have led me into a more elaborate statement of what I started to say at the beginning of this paradigm, namely, that knowing how a poem is constructed helps in understanding fiction. Perhaps I can repeat this proposition in another way, by putting it into some historical perspective. The epoch I have in mind is roughly the first half of the nineteenth century, which marked the first development (although not the first essays) of literary theory in America. The development, of course, was a process of domesticating many existing literary theories.

In the domestication of romantic aesthetics, American writers and critics became particularly aware of the convention of the point of view—not in connection with the novel, to begin with, but rather with poetry. In fact, the early history of the novel in America reveals no literary criticism of any consequence. Novels were popular, but they were not esteemed. There was no considered analysis of the form before the 1820s, and with the exception of a few writers there was only a narrow and prudential theory of the novel for many years after. If the protests of Cooper and Longfellow and John Neal and W. G. Simms and Henry Timrod were at all indicative, their readers considered the novel to be a form of amusement rather than a form of art. This form of amusement was so often censured by book reviewers and religious spokesmen, who considered it to be frivolous and wasteful and even dangerous, that theorizing about the novel was primarily confined to defending it against censure. The defense usually rested on the old Renaissance notion of poetry (now extended to all fiction) as a sugar-coated pill, the idea being to please in order to instruct. The prefaces to hundreds of American novels throughout the nineteenth century show how long this idea lingered.

It was the domestication of romantic theories of poetry that developed the convention of the point of view. The principal influence in the development was probably Samuel Taylor Coleridge. The vitality of the imagination is the crux of Coleridge's theory of art. (In the writer's diary in his novel *Of Time and the River* Thomas Wolfe celebrated Coleridge, saying "Coleridge is not one of the great English poets. He is The Poet.") Coleridge immensely developed the concept of the imagination, but he did not invent it. The idea of the vital imagination evolved from eighteenth-century aesthetics, and it was Coleridge who most comprehensively stated it. For him it was a way of explaining the function of art.

Coleridge's essay "On Poesy or Art" (1818) is a broad statement of the purpose in many of his writings. He argued that art reconciles nature and man; it mediates them. It "humanizes" nature in the sense of making nature realizable to human feeling. Art represents the essence of nature, and this essence is the union of the universal and all particulars. Art represents nature by symbols, and symbols necessarily resolve "multiplicity into unity" and reduce "the many into one." He explained this mediating function of art through his definition of the term "Imagination." He considered the imagination not as a property of the mind so much as the *energy* that coalesces all of a man's faculties: as a process of realization, of the fusion of all mental and sensory responses into a single awareness. In this sense the imagination generates a correspondence to the union, in nature, of the universal and all particulars. It was, he said, "the completing power."

Coleridge's theorizing was piecemeal. His remarks on the imagination were scattered and discursive and often unclear; but by and large he was trying to extend the inherited idea that art is the imitation of nature. Broadly viewed, his theory of the imagination is a long series of spasmodic attempts to harmonize the neoclassical aesthetics, the rationalism and the facultative psychology still current in the eighteenth century, with the idea of vitalism, the belief in some moving, energizing presence within the mind.

Neoclassical critics had already anticipated Coleridge's emphasis on the vitality of the artistic process. Samuel Johnson abhorred mere imitation; Addison and Hume and Young and Burke had already invested the words "fancy" and "imagination" with the notion of human pleasure. Sir Joshua Reynolds developed the idea, arguing that what is pleasurable to the mind is exactly the distortion and rearrangement of natural impressions. Later this notion of the dynamism of the mind fascinated Hazlitt. He associated the imagination with the passions. And Shelley proclaimed that the passions are inherently moral.

Vitalism was enormously appealing. The investment of the imagination with this vitality as a general tendency by the middle of the nineteenth century is faithfully reflected in J. R. Lowell's two essays, "The Imagination" and "The Function of the Poet," both published in 1855 (the year of Whitman's first Preface). These essays show how thoroughly the notion of the dynamic imagination was understood and put to use in American criticism. Lowell was arguing that the distinctive and timeless function of the poetic imagination had been displaced in America by the intellect alone. The practical had usurped the domain of the ideal, he said; creative thought had been appropriated by technology. And Lowell invoked the imagination and summoned the poet to rediscover significance in a material world. Lowell's faith in the poetic imagination was no more extraordinary than Emerson's or Whitman's or, for that matter, Hart Crane's. In fact, Crane's cosmology tries to state and execute exactly this governing vision of the material world that Lowell called for.

A superb explanation of Coleridge's theory of vitalism in art was written by E. P. Whipple, a New Englander and a distinguished literary critic, lecturer, and newspaper editor. His five volumes of criticism, particularly his two-volume *Essays and Reviews* (1848), were major statements of literary theory in America in the nineteenth century. Whipple was a disciple of Coleridge, and his essay, "Coleridge as a Philosophical Critic," is reflected in the second volume of *Essays and Reviews*.

The premise that Whipple appropriated from Coleridge is simply that every work of art, every poem, has its own "principle of vitality." Since the whole poem is an expression of its "vital principle," the first task of the literary critic in each case is to discover and state this principle. The second task is to discover the degree to which the work conforms to its own principle of being. Whipple emphasized Coleridge's distinction "between *mechanical regularity* and *organic form*."

> The form or body of a work of genius, [Coleridge] considered as physiognomical of the soul within; that it was not a

collection of parts, cunningly put together but a growth
from a central principle of life; and that every production
of the mind, which was animated with life, was to be
judged by its *organic* laws.

The first thing to settle about a poem, Whipple insisted, is
its vitality. "Has it life? Did it grow to its present shape, or
was it merely put together?" In the latter case the poem is
only a corpse, he said, and why criticize a corpse? But "if a
poem have life, the principle of growth and assimilation,
then criticism should first develop from within the laws of its
being." He insisted on the concept of a poem as an organism
"developed from its central principle of vitality—and the ac-
cretions which may have stuck to it."

Whipple's argument and his language connoting animate
life indicate the nature of this vital principle. It is some projection of the author himself; it is his point of view. Whipple used the term himself. "By assuming the writer's own
point of view," he argued, a just criticism could discern the
distance between the law of a given work and its embodi-
ment therein.

The *sine qua non* of poetry, for Whipple, was the presence
of the poet in his poem. This premise seems obvious once it
is stated, but no more obvious than it was to Emerson or
Whitman. The poet is special, Emerson said. "He unfixes
the land and the sea, makes them revolve around the axis of
his primary thought, and disposes them anew." Whitman declared of the poet, "His brain is the ultimate brain. . . . He
judges . . . as the sun falling around a helpless thing. . . .
If he breathes into anything that was before thought small it
dilates with the grandeur of life and the universe." But the
poet-expressing-himself is a *fictional* presence in the work of
art. Emerson's poet, as he pointed out, is an ideal poet. In
Whitman's poem the child that went forth and became
whatever he saw is a deliberately symbolic figure. According
to both these poets, the self-expressing fictional presence is
what makes the work of art cohere.

It seems to me that the point of view of a narrative cosmology is substantially what Whipple called the vital principle of a poem, and that *Walden* and *Moby Dick* bear this out. Although *Walden* is not a novel, because it does not dramatize a conflict, the point of view of each fiction nevertheless accretes its meaning in the same way. *Walden's* episodes dramatize the same consciousness discovering new analogies between itself and the physical world, and discovering them repeatedly in the same self-conscious way. Walden Pond is a mirror of this searching mind whose subject is itself. *Moby Dick* is about the conflict between Ahab and the whale, but it is "about" it in a particular way. It is about the witnessing of the conflict and the perceiving of its significance. The repeated attempts to assess the conflict occur mostly in the consciousness of Ishmael, who is thereby engaged in discovering the nature of himself and the world.

I think it is more than coincidence that Theoreau's narrator and Melville's Ishmael think alike. They are two of a kind. They do not happen to arrive at the same conclusion, but the more you listen to these two minds the more alike they sound. Their intense cerebrations serve the same strategy of discovery.

CHAPTER FIVE

Thoreau Beside Himself

The subject of Henry Thoreau's writing is primarily Henry Thoreau. Autobiography was his life work. Although he lived to publish only two books, some twenty titles since edited and brought to print, including his journal, confirm his preoccupation with defining himself and his world. He worked at it, revising continually and constructing a language as tough and sinewy as his complex subject. And he worked with dedication. "Sentences . . . which suggest far more than they say, which have an atmosphere about them, which do not merely report an old, but make a new, impression," he wrote in his journal (August 22, 1851), "sentences which suggest as many things and are as durable as a Roman aqueduct; to frame these, that is the *art* of writing.

> Sentences which are expensive, towards which so many volumes, so much life, went; which lie like boulders on the page, up and down or across; which contain the seed of other sentences, not mere repetition, but creation; which a man might sell his grounds and castles to build."

His composition of his two books is indicative. They are successive installments of a continuing work-in-progress. *A Week on the Concord and Merrimack Rivers* (1849) describes a journey that he had made to the White Mountains in New Hampshire ten years earlier. His second book, *Walden; or, Life in the Woods* (1854), dramatizes his residence in the countryside beyond the village of Concord, Massachusetts, from the summer of 1845 through the summer of 1847. Thoreau worked on both books during his two years at Walden Pond, and he returned to Concord with a draft of each. The two books recount journeys of different proportions. In each work Thoreau interpolated entries from his journals written before and after the nominal event. His idea in each case was that the actual journey should correlate a figurative voyaging in ideas; and he repeatedly worked over this scheme.

By the time *A Week* was published in 1849 Thoreau had already completed three versions of what was later to be *Walden*. Partly because of the poor sale of the first book he chose to continue rewriting the second. This process took another five years and four more versions of his work. What he finally published as *Walden* in 1854 was a printer's copy based on seven separate versions of manuscript that had been written during a period of seven or eight years. James Shanley's significant discovery and analysis of this process, in *The Making of Walden* (1957), emphasize that *Walden* grew as a living organism grows, by accreting new tissue around its basic structure. Shanley explains that the published book, twice as long as the first version, was the result of stages of growth: of additions from Thoreau's journals, of cancellations and reordering and revision by which Thoreau gradually re-created his experience. In the process, of course, the final *Walden* had become a new experience of its own.

Walden was Thoreau's definitive work. Its complexity defies any summary précis. Any faithful description of it is necessarily equivocal. *Walden* is a discursive autobiography in which certain fictional techniques have been highly developed. The work is even more equivocal than this, for insofar as it is fiction *Walden* is what Thoreau understood poetry to be. *Walden* is about a way of perceiving; in fact, it dramatizes perceiving, even as it feigns innocence of what it is really about. It is a difficult book, and although it is self-sufficient and explains itself, its complexities nevertheless become clearer in terms of Thoreau's other writings.

What *Walden* means and the way it means become more quickly apparent in light of the earlier autobiographical narrative, *A Week*, in which Thoreau began to work out his method. Because *A Week* contains many of the conclusions Thoreau allegedly perceives in *Walden*, it is an invaluable commentary on *Walden* and on Thoreau's philosophy of art in a self-centered world. Among the other writings that cast light on the ideas and the images and the rhetoric of *Walden*, one was Thoreau's first major essay, "A Natural History of Massachusetts" (1842), his review of a volume of botanical and zoological reports published by the state legislature. Another is "Walking," one of his later lectures, posthumously published (1862). Together these writings reveal the stamina of a few perceptions and the extraordinary permutations by which he developed them. What *Walden* alone achieved, however, was the dramatization of the mind perceiving.

Thoreau tells us in the second paragraph of *Walden* that his subject will be himself. "In most books, the *I*, or first person, is omitted; in this it will be retained; that, in respect to egotism, is the main difference." After explaining that a book always speaks in the first person no matter what the pronoun, he adds, "I should not talk so much about myself if there were anybody else whom I knew as well. Unfortunately, I am confined to this theme by the narrowness of my experience." But this statement is disarming. What Thoreau acknowledges to be his subject is in fact an ambivalent "I"; it is a double consciousness, as he later defines it in the fifth chapter, called "Solitude." It is a consciousness of separate selves, a point of view that witnesses its other self in the process of perceiving.

The author explains his strategy in terms of one's own double nature. "With thinking we may be beside ourselves in a sane sense." We can consciously stand apart from the events that involve us, he says. "I only know myself as a human entity; the scene, so to speak, of thoughts and affections; and am sensible of a certain doubleness by which I can stand as remote from myself as from another.

> However intense my experience I am conscious of the presence and criticism of a part of me, which, as it were, is not a part of me, but a spectator, sharing no experience, but taking note of it, and that is no more I than it is you."

According to Thoreau, therefore, there is an active self and a spectator self, and the latter witnesses the former. But Thoreau goes beyond this; he says that in his case the active self is fictional. He draws the analogy of a spectator who has witnessed a stage play. This play has been a drama about one's (active) self, in which this self has been feigned. "It was a kind of fiction, a work of the imagination only," Thoreau says. But there is even more to it; *Walden* is even more extensively and completely a fiction. Although Thoreau does not spell it out, the narrator of *Walden* does. By remembering and expressing what he has witnessed about his active self (which is a fiction) the narrator (or spectator self) is also a fiction.

In sum, the narrator or persona (or spectator self) selects and orders events about a naturalist (his active self) who went to Walden Pond. What the narrator selects to tell us and how he orders it have the effect of dramatizing this active self. Furthermore, what the narrator makes of his drama repeatedly reveals his own nature, which is emphatically symbolic. The events all demonstrate that the narrator is an absolute analogy to the natural world.

This fictional point of view (or the persona remembering his past) presents all of *Walden* except the first three chapters and the last one. In the first and last chapters Thoreau presents his conclusions in person, particularly in the first chapter, "Economy," in which he preaches the virtue of limiting our wants to our animal necessities, of abandoning our social, superficial wishes, the better to discover and make peace with ourselves. "Economy" insists and exhorts as much as any Puritan sermon ever did, with its doctrine just as clearly reduced to an ethic. The second, third, and final chapters are also preachments. But in the fourteen interior chapters about the experience at Walden Pond, Thoreau deputized a persona, the first-person singular in the act of self-realization. These chapters invoke the sounds and sights of the landscape, the animals and the solitude that kept him company, his building a house around himself, his planting and harvesting, the geography of the clearing in the woods and even of the village beyond; in sum, the aspects of a living physical world in ceaseless change.

This fictional narrator and conversationalist shapes the enormous resources of "the great outdoors," as he calls it, into analogies to himself. In general he recognizes himself as a part of the natural world. In particular he employs the natural world in all its parts as a mirror. What this fictional naturalist describes invariably becomes analogous to his own consciousness. What he says of Walden Pond really does epitomize his attitude toward all the natural phenomena. "A lake is the landscape's most beautiful and expressive feature," he says in a chapter called "The Ponds." "It is the earth's eye; looking into which the beholder measures the depth of his own nature." The metaphor is striking: earth's eye is the self's mirror. This is no stylistic ornament. It is essential to *Walden*; it is a way of looking at things and a way of understanding.

The interior chapters develop by means of the fictional narrator evaluating his own past. The narrator is a narrow and well-defined persona. He is deliberate and self-conscious; he is speculative and intellectual; his manner is ingeniously innocent. He candidly shares the excitement of discovery. But for all his candor there are no shared intimacies. On the contrary, he is clinical. He remains aloof. Despite the deeply personal nature of his subject he has the detached aspect of a teacher or an elder friend. He invites and shares and yet puts you off; he turns the subject back at you. Although the subject is himself, although he is bent on revealing it as precisely as possible, this self is no less than human consciousness. The universality of this self, in his view, explains some of the intensity of the writing.

But this symbolic projection of himself was a matter of development. Thoreau had not yet achieved it, although he was apparently working at something of the sort, in *A Week on the Concord and Merrimack Rivers.* The river journey was to be a convenient means of correlating the speculations taken from his journal, about history and religion and genius and friendship and literary style, and about local geography and antiquarianism and the function of art. It is an intriguing treasury of opinion, and the narrative ostensibly provides occasions for these excursions into ideas; yet no principle governs them.

A Week is told to us by a narrator who has two separate and successive points of view. One symptom of this condition lies in the past tense of the narrative and the present tense of the editorial speculations. Another symptom is the pronoun "we," which sometimes means Thoreau and his brother, who also made the journey, and sometimes Thoreau and the reader. No dramatic necessity relates the two uses of "we." The work trades on the pretense that the events produce the opinions, but it remains pretense, rarely becoming an achieved illusion. There are a few occasions where Thoreau's habit of reasoning by analogy makes swift conversions from the current of the river to the current of his thought; but Thoreau remains himself in fact, now as a voyager and now as spokesman. In both aspects he is insistently didactic.

The change from *A Week* to *Walden* is in Thoreau's use of the point of view. In *A Week* he remained the actual author assuming different roles. What he later achieved in *Walden,* in the course of many revisions, was a single point of view within the narrative, dramatically responding to the events. To this extent he developed a fiction about himself.

The physical world in *Walden* serves as a metaphor of the self. This is the strategy of the book—or to use E. P. Whipple's term, its "vital principle." Thoreau was an immense egoist; he would hibernate, he would withdraw to order the things he saw into realizations about himself. There are passages in *A Week* that explain this strategy of retreating in order to keep a poet's vigil. "The poet is he that hath fat enough, like bears and marmots, to suck his claws all winter. He hibernates in this world, and feeds on his own marrow." This particular poet calls himself a natural historian, and "the fruit of the naturalist's observations is not in the new genera or species, but in new contemplations still. . . ." Science, he says, is only a more contemplative man's recreation.

The metaphor of withdrawal in the world—not *from* the world but *within* it—largely explains the strategy of *Walden*. This deliberate metaphor gets at the center of the Walden experience (and it is literally at the center of the book). This fixed center of *Walden* is the book's shortest chapter. It is called, of all things, "The Village" (not "The Pond" or "The Woods" but "The Village"), and this discrepancy is no coincidence. The chapter is about the paradoxical idea of having to get lost in order to find one's self. The persona speaks of going to Concord from time to time, and of his visitors from that village, and he gradually establishes the village and the woods as poles of experience. He repeats episodes of travelers who have become lost along the familiar route, of persons who, taking the accustomed path, could no longer find their way; and his point is to suggest the virtue of deliberately getting lost. He himself has done it often. "Not till we are lost, in other words not till we have lost the world, do we begin to find ourselves, and realize where we are and the infinite extent of our relations."

Thoreau stoutly insisted that the way to achieve personal

freedom is through a kind of disassociation. His early book review, "A Natural History of Massachusetts," observes that the night fisherman "may have to steer his way home through the dark by the north star, and he will feel himself some degrees nearer to it for having lost his way on the earth." A *Week* several times celebrates the true fisherman who gives himself up to the elements, not to catch fish but to find himself through contemplation. The roving, contemplative mind begets the paradox, in "Civil Disobedience" (1849), of a man being truly free while locked in jail. The idea of ignoring one's place to discover one's self is the organizing idea of the compendious lecture, "Walking." In *Walden* it is not only the subject of Thoreau's preachment in the first chapter but a governing metaphor of the whole book.

Thoreau's insight was metaphorical. "He referred every minute fact to cosmical laws," Emerson said of him. "The depth of his perception found likeness of law throughout Nature, and I know not any genius who so swiftly inferred universal law from the single fact." This was part of Emerson's address on the occasion of Thoreau's funeral. He celebrated Thoreau's independence of mind, his rare knowledge of the natural world, and above all his faculty for turning this knowledge into a "religious synthesis." Thoreau's "excellent wisdom . . . showed him the material world as a means and a symbol." Thus it was, said Emerson, that "The pond was a small ocean; the Atlantic, a large Walden Pond. He referred every minute fact to cosmical laws."

Walden reveals a symbolic man in terms of the natural world. This man exploits reflection in both senses of the word. He reflects upon everything he sees until it reflects him. One of the presiding metaphors of the book, which I have mentioned, is the image of hibernating in this world, of losing one's bearings in order to find one's self. Another governing metaphor is the image of reflection. Walden Pond itself is the principal object in this recurring metaphor. "It is earth's eye; looking into which the beholder measures the depth of his own nature."

Thoreau continually reworks this idea. At one point in "The Pond in Winter" he has set about mapping the Pond and defining its contours. He has just deduced an accurate way of plotting its maximum depth from its surface measurements ("the line of greatest length intersected the line of greatest breadth *exactly* at the point of greatest depth"); and he proves out his method in Walden's coves and in nearby White Pond until he is sure that he has a natural fact. "If we knew all the laws of Nature, we should need only one fact, or the description of one actual phenomenon, to infer all the particular results at that point." Then straightway to the analogy. "What I have observed of the pond is no less true in ethics," he says: "draw lines through the length and breadth of the aggregate of a man's particular daily behaviors and waves of life into his coves and inlets, and where they intersect will be the height or depth of his character." Perhaps we can infer a man's depth from the way his shores—that is, his circumstances—tend. "If he is surrounded by mountainous circumstances, an Achillean shore, whose peaks overshadow and are reflected in his bosom, they suggest a corresponding depth in him. But a low and smooth shore proves him shallow on that side."

From here Thoreau goes on to develop the analogy of the bar or reef across the mouth of every cove, sometimes raised by storms and currents until it rises above the surface; and the water within, cut off from the rest, chemically changes and becomes a new entity. By a similar process in human growth, Thoreau says, circumstances shape and determine a new idea in one's mind. "At the advent of each individual into this life, may we not suppose that such a bar has risen to the surface somewhere?" And suddenly he completes the analogy: an ethical judgment, rendered out of the measurement of a pond.

It is true, we are such poor navigators that our thoughts, for the most part, stand off and on upon a harborless coast, are conversant only with the bights of the bays of poesy, or steer for the public ports of entry, and go into the dry docks of science, where they merely refit for this world, and no natural currents concur to individualize them.

This ethical appraisal of our common lack of individuality—the referent of his metaphor—proceeds from the original analogy of pond and man by the same increments as the underwater reef that rises to the surface. It *grows* out of itself. Because the judgment proceeds organically from the illustrating fact, it has an authority about it, a sense of inevitability and rightness. It is not merely the quantitative increments that accomplish this sense of authority, but the illusion of the process happening in our presence. It is dramatic. The final judgment turns back upon the fact which begat it. We apparently see it happening. There is an illusion of the consciousness at work, of a restless straining at the fact once the fact is stated.

Sometimes the development of a fact is so rapid, the consciousness so instinctively alert, that we apparently witness Thoreau witnessing an epiphany. Here is such a case. In order to drink from the Pond on a winter morning he has cut through a foot of snow and a foot of ice, as he says, to open a window under his feet.

> I look down into the quiet parlor of the fishes, pervaded by a softened light as through ground glass, with its bright sanded floor the same as in summer; there a perennial waveless serenity reigns as in the amber twilight sky, corresponding to the cool and even temperament of the inhabitants. Heaven is under our feet as well as over our heads.

That last sentence is a sudden revelation. "Heaven is under our feet as well as over our heads." It surprises us into acceptance before we have had a chance to realize that it is not quite like the statements of fact that have preceded it, or that even these statements about a hole in the ice are more equivocal than they first appear to be.

All of these metaphors develop in a way that illustrates Emerson's celebration of Thoreau: his knowledge of Nature as a "religious synthesis"; his swift inference of universal law from the single fact. The proposition about the depth of Walden Pond, for example, outgrows the fact almost before the fact is stated. "This is a remarkable depth for so small an area," he says, having just discovered that it is 107 feet deep, "yet not an inch of it can be spared by the imagination." And thereby Thoreau comments on his own image-making. "What if all ponds were shallow? Would it not react on the minds of men? I am thankful that this pond was made deep and pure for a symbol."

These passages convey the illusion of the mind discovering affinities; but this illusion was a matter of development by trial and error. He began, in A *Week*, by using narrative sequence to correlate the progressive speculations of his mind. The purpose was to give dramatic immediacy to the significant statement or conclusion, whatever that statement might be. What he often achieved was a kind of lamination of ideas: layers of speculation built up from some passing fact or impression. As often as not these observations turned out to be merely random, without necessity, offering only a tentative, patent probing of an idea to see what might come of it.

One such laminated episode in A *Week* presents Thoreau's speculations about a fisherman. It is Saturday (the account of the journey is divided by days), somewhere on the river between Ball's Hill and Carlisle Bridge. The brothers have just rowed past a man fishing from the shore with a long birch pole, and Thoreau begins to contemplate the solitary figure in retrospect, attempting by stages to generate him into a symbol. This fisherman is a judge arbitrating the case "between muckworm and shiner, amid the fragrance of water-lilies, mint and pontederia, leading his life many rods from the dry land, within a pole's length of where the larger fishes swim." Then the man on the shore reminds Thoreau of another fisherman, an old brown-coated man from Northumberland, who seemed to wear the aspect of a priest in the sacrament of withdrawal. Following this is a sober account of the fisherman as a natural historian and of the true harvest of the contemplative man—"not in new genera or species, but in new contemplations still." Finally Thoreau belabors the obvious with a wondering statement about the ubiquity of fish upon the earth and about how alike they all are. But it does not work. Despite the labored similes along the way no gathering metaphor has developed, and Thoreau breaks it off. "That was a long pull from Ball's Hill to Carlisle Bridge," he remarks wryly.

He tries again. The next day Thoreau begins to contemplate the image of some trees reflected in the water, as though pondering what he might make of it:

> For every oak and birch, too, growing on the hilltop, as well as for these elms and willows, we knew that there was a graceful, ethereal and ideal tree making down from the roots, and sometimes Nature in high tides brings her mirror to its foot and makes it visible.

This was the familiar image of reflection that later dominated a whole system of metaphors so splendidly in *Walden*. But on this occasion Thoreau had his troubles. The impression of a correspondence between these material trees, in Thoreau's treatment of it, resists any further metaphorical significance. He first observes how the clear air gives the landscape a sense of remoteness, as a glass does to the picture behind it; then he wishes that such distinct delineations of objects might exist in our own lives; and finally he says that true character, whether in persons or in things, does indeed stand forth from trivial objects. These pronouncements are more trite than obvious because they are so labored. A *Week* contains many more of such laminated sequences—and more successful ones. In method, in the progress of observations from the literal to the connotative, they are characteristic of the thought sequences that he perfected in *Walden*.

One of the most exciting passages in *Walden* is the well-known one in "Spring," which completes a cycle of seasons in the interior chapters of the book. Spring, he says, "is like the creation of Cosmos out of Chaos." The ice on the ponds has broken up and disappeared. On the bank of a railroad cut the frost coming out of the ground sends wet fingers of sand out through the snow and down the incline, between the leaflike channels of water running to the bottom. This interlaced sand debris is "a sort of hybrid product, which obeys half way the law of currents, and half way that of vegetation." And with this sentence the literal pattern of sand on the snow engenders yet another hybrid product of impressions by which the channeled veins and leaves of sand become by turns the excrement of the earth, animal viscera, the primal form of outward foliage, indeed of "vaster leaves whose pulp is intervening earth, and towns and cities are the ova of insects in their axils."

This whole passage is a metaphorical statement of organicism, of a belief in the coherence of all changing and evolving forms of life. It is the concept that Emerson was attempting to work out in *Nature*. In that essay Emerson was fashioning a language to convey an idea whose fragments he was still trying to resolve for himself. But Emerson's impromptu associations, his sudden assertions of correspondences, were far different from Thoreau's ordered explorations of an organic whole. Thus, from the lowest to the highest forms of life the sand traceries reveal their vital affinities —to the blood system even, which releases still another rushing channel of impressions ("What is man but a mass of thawing clay?"). "Thus it seemed that this one hillside illustrated the principle of all the operations of Nature." And still the subject opens up before his eyes: "There is no end to the heaps of liver, lights, and bowels, as if the globe were turned wrong side outward," Thoreau says; and this suggests the coherence of all things.

"There is nothing inorganic," Thoreau says—and observes. Even as he watches, it seems, the earth pours out in sand the forms of all the life it bears; and comparably the idea has grown in the impressed observer: the creation of cosmos out of chaos. "This is the frost coming out of the ground; this is Spring. It precedes the green and flowery spring, as mythology precedes regular poetry."

This whole development of an idea, including the final proposition about mythology begetting poetry, grew out of a brief observation in the first version of *Walden*—a scant nine lines of fragments, as James Shanley has printed it—in which Thoreau observes that the sand, like lava, has streamed into forms resembling vegetation. The idea obviously attracted Thoreau: the affinity of vegetation and a moving stream was "unaccountably interesting and beautiful"; and after six more versions of *Walden* what he finally made of his affinity is nothing less than the organic wholeness of all creation, suggesting, as it does, the growth of a man and of all mankind.

Emerson was acutely right about Thoreau's swift inference of "universal law from single fact." Thoreau himself often proclaimed this purpose, albeit metaphorically. He provided his own directions for what he wrote. "I am convinced that my genius dates from an older era than the agricultural," Thoreau says (in "Sunday") in *A Week*. "What have I to do with plows? I cut another furrow than you see.

> Where the off ox treads, there it is not, it is further off; where the nigh ox walks, it will not be, it is nigher still. If corn fails, my crop fails not, and what are drought and rain to me?"

The furrows he speaks of are figurative. They are impressions on the consciousness. ("The fact you tell is of no value, but only the impression," Emerson said, explaining Thoreau.) These furrows are Thoreau's expanded inferences from limited facts, so juxtaposed sometimes that suggestion fairly leaps at you from the page.

The chapter called "The Bean-Field" in *Walden* is all about these furrows. It is one of the most sustained developments of an idea in the book; and this idea is really a commentary on the purpose and method of *Walden* as a whole. Close by his shack near Walden Pond, according to his account, Thoreau has planted two-and-a-half acres of beans. The upland was originally cleared some fifteen years before, and the weeds and grass are rampant. This chapter recounts his attempts, as he says, to make the earth say beans instead of grass. "What shall I learn of beans or beans of me?" he wonders at the beginning, and begins to ponder the labor and the consequences of his two-and-a-half acres of furrows.

He speaks of the literal furrows in the ground, but he has other furrows in mind. ("I cut another furrow than you see," he said in *A Week*.) The occasional military sounds from the village a few miles away spur on this spokesman in his war against the weeds. "That's Roman wormwood,—that's pigweed,—that's sorrel, that's piper-grass—have at him, chop him up, turn his roots upward to the sun, don't let him have a fiber in the shade, if you do he'll turn himself t'other side up and be as green as a leek in two days." It is a hot, tiring, ceaseless battle: "A long war, not with cranes, but with weeds, those Trojans who had sun and rain and dews on their side." Two-and-a-half acres of beans; and for what? "Not that I wanted beans to eat . . . but . . . to serve a parable-maker one day."

To serve a parable-maker. This is one of Thoreau's cryptic revelations about *Walden* itself. This is what the whole book does over and over: it tills beans to serve a parable-maker. The narrator tills beans and measures ponds and builds a house and describes wildlife and listens to sounds and silences and catalogues the symptoms of the seasons—all to serve himself as a parable-maker who has other furrows to plow.

And how does the parable happen? In terms of beans, he tells us: "I gave them no manure, and did not hoe them all once, I hoed them unusually well as far as I went, and was paid well for it in the end,

> 'there being in truth,' as Evelyn says, 'no compost or laetation whatsoever to this continual motion, repastination, and turning of the mould with the spade.' "

The parable is the point. The ruminating consciousness—the "repastination and the turning of the mould"—is what nourishes its growth. Thoreau's paragraph continues with arch innocence about the chemical vitality of newly-spaded earth, but by this time Thoreau has tilled the beans. It turns out that he is a poet disguised as a laborer, harvesting parables out of facts.

The theory of poetry engaged Thoreau. During all his writing years he was engrossed in the subject. He wrote about it in his journal, and much of his theory he collated in *A Week* and in "Walking." Both reflect his hortative tone and his insistence on what poetry really is. "Walking" broaches the subject by indicting no less than the entire tradition of English lyric poetry. "It is an essentially tame and civilized literature, reflecting Greece and Rome"; it lacks the fresh, wild strain. "There is plenty of the genial love of Nature, but not so much of Nature herself." Despite the discoveries of science and accumulated learning of mankind, he says, the contemporary poet enjoys no advantages over Homer. And Thoreau's fixed idea of what the poet ought to be recalls the Emersonian ideal. In "Walking" Thoreau says this: "He would be a poet who could impress the winds and streams into his service, to speak for him:

> who nailed words to their primitive senses, as farmers drive down stakes in the spring, which the frost has heaved; who derived his words as often as he used them,—transplanted them to his page with earth adhering to their roots. . . ."

As this passage continues he sounds momentarily like Whitman. He wants a poet beyond the limits of any inherited culture. He wants a mythmaker, who might possibly come from the New World. "Above all we cannot afford not to live in the present." He wants "a newer testament,—the gospel according to this moment."

But this reference to time conveys a special sense. Thoreau was not concerned with the historical present but with psychological immediacy. He was forever celebrating the continuous awareness of the human consciousness—what you might call an ever-present tense. He tried to define poetry in terms of this awareness, while at the same time insisting on its transcendence over any one consciousness. In *A Week* he returns again and again to the subject. "But after all, man is the great poet, and not Homer or Shakespeare," he says. "Poetry is so universally true and independent of experience, that it does not need any particular biography to illustrate it. . . ." Poetry is some vital spirit abroad in the world. For poetry write love, he says, and it will be equally true. Poetry is the original experience, and history is but the prose narrative of poetic deeds. Poetry is not merely the record of an act; it is the very action, the proceeding itself. Moreover, it is not merely a cerebral process but an act of total commitment. Being so, "It is the simplest relation of phenomena"; it is revelation; it is apocalyptic.

Poetry is an action, Thoreau claims. But he saves and savors to the end of his journey the nature of the action. In his record for "Friday," the last day in *A Week*, after dozens of cryptic definitions of poetry and illustrations of what poetry is not, Thoreau finally works his way to this:

> The true poem is not that which the public read. There is always a poem not printed on paper, coincident with the production of this, stereotyped in the poet's life. It is *what he has become through his work*. Not how is the idea expressed in stone, or on canvas or paper, is the question, but how far it has obtained form and expression in the life of

the artist. His true work will not stand in any prince's gallery.

The italics are Thoreau's. "It is *what he has become through his work.*" Poetry is the developed consciousness of one's self and the world. The value of any given poem depends on the extent to which this developed consciousness "has obtained form and expression in the life of the artist." Thoreau has finally defined the action called poetry in terms of the condition it begets. It is still not exact, but the implications are clear. A poem is the act of perceiving or the condition of perceiving or possibly both at once.

The most convincing illustration of Thoreau's definition of poetry is *Walden*. Thoreau's discursive autobiography repeatedly dramatizes the one characteristic action of its speaker: the process of appropriating the details of the natural world to the purpose of revealing the nature of one's self. *Walden* is a poem by Thoreau's terms. Insofar as it renders the process of perceiving the affinities between world and self, insofar as it dramatizes the consciousness of its speaker in the act of finding what will suffice, and insofar as his expression of correspondences develops his self-realization, *Walden* is a poem by Thoreau's terms.

These terms distinguish poetry from verse. Thoreau also wrote verse, but it scarcely lives up to his concept of poetry. It is relevant to this discussion that he wrote most of his verse while still a young man, and gradually abandoned it for prose. Although his own verse copiously illustrates his arguments in *A Week*, he purged most of his verse from *Walden*. Those verses which he did publish separately tend toward the expression of attitudes. They are explicitly biographical in a way that *Walden* is not; they are characteristically about opinions rather than the realizations that precede them. These verses are didactic, which is to say the opinions they express are unassimilated by the dramatic situation from which they ostensibly proceed.

Thoreau's verse is an overstatement of his work as a whole.

It is a reliable indication of the will to teach, which characterizes virtually everything he wrote. With Thoreau the fact must always illustrate a truth. His early review of the Massachusetts botanical and zoological reports excuses their detailed recording of measurements, saying, "Let us not underrate the value of a fact; it will one day flower in a truth." When his own writing fails to persuade it is usually because the truth has not grown from the fact but appears instead to have been grafted onto it. This is what is wrong with those metaphors in *A Week*, which insist on a significance, any significance, without a necessity; and occasionally this happens in *Walden*. They overstate an ethical tendency in Thoreau. The didacticism of such metaphors was partly a hazard of his method of composition, of his piecemeal interpolation of opinions among the impressions of events; and it was partly the result of his conviction that every natural fact must have a corresponding truth.

Walden is just as ethical as any of Thoreau's other writings. Indeed, therein the facts all seem to yield but one, single, corresponding truth: the nature of the world reflects the man. "The universe constantly and obediently answers to our conceptions," he says in *Walden's* second chapter. "Let us spend our lives in conceiving them." And *Walden* has a corresponding doctrine: "Explore thyself." Thoreau saw the limitations in himself, and also the limitations in the extrinsic world around him; but given the choice between limitations, as the more reliable means of apprehending God, he chose himself. An ethic is implicit in the choice. By perceiving the affinities between world and self the poet *performs* the poem.

It *is* a performance. The search for quintessence is the subject of the poem. What we see is a dramatization of Thoreau thinking, a fictional projection of a searching self. *Walden's* persuasion lies less in its preachments and more in the dramatic immediacy of the endeavors of this persona, poring over the world's materials to discover what will satisfy him.

This immediacy is what Thoreau speaks of in his definition of the ideal poet who would derive his words by using them, and transplant them to his page "with earth adhering to their roots."

These earthy roots are the materials that Thoreau worked with and worked against, subsuming them to his conception of himself. These roots and the reefs across the coves and the sandy bottom of the Pond and the colors of the ice and the sounds of the woods and the house that contained him and yet extended him and the furrows in the bean field: these are the substances from which, in *Walden*, he shapes his parables. His prodding of this material to his own purpose, his "continual motion, repastination, and turning of the mould with the spade," are the continual effort and struggle of the book.

Struggle inheres in the search for quintessence, and the struggling search is characteristic of the romantic cosmology. Given the concept of an entire cosmos encompassed by a single vision, the poet is likely to discover sooner or later that the world in fact resists his vision of it. Occasionally in *Walden* and often in *A Week* Thoreau's metaphors fail. They simply do not convey what he wanted them to. But he managed so well, on the whole, because he deliberately dramatized the effort itself; he purposely represented the exertion of the poet shaping substances to a universal parable. To the extent that Thoreau removed himself and preserved the fiction of the searching narrator, to the extent that, to use his word, he was "beside" himself, he controlled his subject.

I have already suggested that *Walden* and *Moby Dick* illuminate each other. In both books the arena in which the action occurs is the consciousness. Thoreau spoke of "a newer testament—the gospel according to this moment," and he dramatized over and over again the process of a new and present realization. To a high degree Thoreau developed a questing persona that repeatedly crowds limited evidence to stunning conclusions about itself and the world. Thoreau's persona and Melville's Ishmael are akin. In *Moby Dick,* however, the questing mind reflects not only on the natural evidence but on the efforts of another questing mind. Melville thereby accomplished countless repetitions of the poet *performing* his poem, *perceiving* into existence a cosmos that would extend and contain him.

CHAPTER SIX

The Linked Analogies
of Moby Dick

Herman Melville's *Moby Dick* (1851) is an exciting and complex fiction in which one cosmology contains another. The novel counterpoints two separate and continuous attempts to perceive an organic cosmos: one is narrative and the other is speculative; one is the basis for the other; and both are dramatic. The narrative concerns Captain Ahab's mortal attempt to destroy the white whale, and thereby to prove his own vision of a cosmos. His affront, both blasphemous and noble, is a tragic action which the affronted universe completes by destroying him, his ship, and his crew, save one. This one is Ishmael, whose speculations on the action generate a cosmos to explain it.

The principal event in *Moby Dick* is the confrontation between the intolerant Ahab and his intolerable circumstances. This event is told through a consciousness, at first called Ishmael, which refracts it into tens and hundreds of events whose essence is the same intolerable conflict. Repetition is one characteristic property of the novel form that Melville stunningly exploited. Virtually every episode and every cluster of events magnify the conflict into a gigantic parable of the human condition. The essence of the action is the contradicting man contradicted by an inscrutable universe. The essential idea is the necessity of universal contradiction. The subject of the narrative is Ahab's pursuit of Moby Dick, but this is always subjectively seen, in turns dispersed and concentrated through a consciousness.

Ahab and the whale are both immense and both equivocal: the heroic man is mad, and the leviathan, inscrutable; but they manifest these qualities because of the mind that reports them. Ahab speaks magnificently for himself, yet even Ahab's tough intelligence is remarkably like the restless consciousness that magnifies his conflict in the telling of it. This consciousness belongs to the ordinary seaman, Ishmael, but it also extends beyond him. Whether or not Ishmael is present, as the narrative proceeds, his habit of thought pervades the book and shapes the questions: What is Moby Dick? What more does it represent than primitive power? What confirms Ahab's conviction that the whale is evil? And from these questions others grow: What is the nature of God? The nature of man? The nature of the universe? The point of view probes every circumstance to such extent that the probing itself becomes the subject of the fiction.

Ishmael's attempt to discover the meaning of the defaced painting in the Spouter Inn, as I have already mentioned, is a paradigm of the novel itself. It is a model of Ishmael's—and Melville's—strategy of perceiving.

Ishmael, like the narrator of *Walden*, is ingeniously innocent; he has a way of detaching himself from a situation that contains him, the better to see its significance. Thoreau speaks of the poet hibernating within this world and nourishing himself on the marrow from his own paws; he speaks of needing to get lost in order to find one's self. And the same with Ishmael, who has been sitting in bed with his new friend, Queequeg, conversing with his eyes shut—"because no man can ever feel his own identity aright except his eyes be closed." Ishmael needs his "self-created darkness."

Ishmael and Thoreau's narrator share the same metaphorical insight: inventing analogies to develop an idea, and always seeing one's self in the event. Each reflects upon circumstance until it reflects him. Thoreau's narrator observes that a lake "is earth's eye; looking into which the beholder measures the depth of his own nature." And Ishmael (in Chapter 1) recalls the myth of Narcissus,

who because he could not grasp the tormenting, mild image
he saw in the fountain, plunged into it and was drowned.
But that same image, we ourselves see in all rivers and
oceans. It is the image of the ungraspable phantom of life;
and this is the key to it all.

Both statements reveal a strategy of seeing, a way of recognizing reflections of self, the better to understand. But there is a
difference, too. Both see the reflecting water, but Ishmael's
glance more obviously encompasses the searching figure looking into it. And he sees a different significance. To him the
reflecting water images something unknown, "the ungraspable phantom of life."

The burden of Ishmael's story is the necessary assault upon
the unknowable, necessarily repulsed. It is what Ahab is
about; and Ishmael, too, except that Ishmael finally perceives, as Ahab never does, the reciprocity between the person and his circumstance. Ishmael and Ahab are both committed to the assault, Ahab relentlessly hunting his whale,
and Ishmael incessantly pursuing this truth or that, time and
again with whatever new fact confronts him. Telling of
Ahab's assault on the unknown commits Ishmael to similar
assaults.

To both minds the whale is a symbol of the wholeness of
things; but these two committed characters differently invoke
it. Ahab knows exactly what he is after, and he chants it out
(in "The Quarter-Deck," Chapter 36): this whale tasks him
with its outrageous strength and inscrutable malice. "That
inscrutable thing is chiefly what I hate; and be the white
whale agent, or be the white whale principal, I will wreak
that hate upon him. Talk not to me of blasphemy, man; I'd
strike the sun if it insulted me." The whale is also a metaphor to Ishmael ("whaleness" and "wholeness" are one to
him); but the whale to Ishmael is a means and not an end.

With a frigate's anchors for my bridle-bitts and fasces of
harpoons for spurs, would I could mount that whale and
leap the topmost skies, to see whether the fabled heavens

with all their countless tents really lie encamped beyond my mortal sight!

Ishmael's statement concludes a chapter that seems on first impression to have a most unlikely title: "Of Whales in Paint; in Teeth; in Wood; in Sheet-iron; in Stone; in Mountains; in Stars." Yet this title—just the sequence of it— summarizes the way he thinks: the climb from mundane paint and wood and iron and stone to a mountaintop of speculation; and then that sudden leap to the stars. Ishmael breeds metaphors. In relating an episode he singles out an item or event and idly ponders it, while seeming merely to describe, until all at once this fact has new, immense significance. Ishmael makes so many of these prodigious leaps to significance that it is something of a problem to isolate a few, in order to explain the pattern of his thought. Five or six examples will have to do, to show two things: the act of the mind discovering, and the mutual relevance of these discoveries.

Ishmael's revelations come like codas at the chapter-ends. The first one occurs in "The Lee Shore" (Chapter 23), as soon as the *Pequod* has cleared Nantucket Harbor. Ishmael comes on deck in a winter gale, sees Bulkington at the helm, and ponders the alternative dangers to the mariner: to be dashed on the treacherous shore of the friendly, beckoning land, or to sail to windward, toward all the unknown perils of the ocean, to seek the sea's "landlessness." To leeward lies certain ignominious ruin; to windward, only unknown dangers. ("this six-inch chapter is the stoneless grave of Bulkington.") And suddenly Bulkington becomes the signal for analogy in Ishmael's mind: these are the same alternatives of the consciousness: the sudden death of wavering, cautious thought, or the desperate "landlessness" of deep committed effort.

> Know ye, now, Bulkington? Glimpses do ye seem to see of that mortally intolerable truth; that all deep, earnest thinking is but the intrepid effort of the soul to keep the open

independence of her sea; while the wildest winds of heaven and earth conspire to cast her on the treacherous, slavish shore?

And then the final leap to significance—to the value of opposite thinking—as he returns to the terms of the metaphor. "But as in landlessness alone resides the highest truth, shoreless, indefinite as God—so, better is it to perish in that howling infinite, than be ingloriously dashed upon the lee, even if that were safety!" Thereby the human being is a demigod. "Up, from the spray of thy ocean-perishing—straight up leaps thy apotheosis!"

"The Lee Shore" exemplifies a pattern of descriptive discourse leading to hypothesis. This pattern resembles the rhetoric of a pastoral poem, in which the poet sees an object on the landscape, ponders his relation to it, and arrives at some truth about God and man and nature. But as Melville handles the pastoral formula the truth arrived at is not a conclusive statement but a startling new idea, the more stunning because we have seen the consciousness in the act of realizing it.

Another example of this pattern occurs in "The Mat-Maker" (Chapter 47), where Ishmael and Queequeg are idly engaged in weaving a sword-mat for a lashing on a whaleboat. Ishmael passes and returns the woof of marline between the long yarns of the warp, using his hand as a shuttle, while Queequeg, standing sideways, careless and unthinking, tamps down the marline woof. Within the space of one startling paragraph Ishmael turns this into a metaphor of the reciprocity between the individual man and all his circumstances. The woven sword-mat seems to him the very "Loom of Time," the plaited pattern of necessity, free will, and chance.

> aye, chance, free will, and necessity—no wise incompatible —all interweavingly working together. The straight warp of necessity, not to be swerved from its ultimate course—its every alternating vibration, indeed, only tending to that;

free will still free to ply her shuttle between given threads;
and chance, though restrained in its play within the right
lines of necessity, and sideways in its motions directed by
free will, though thus prescribed to by both, chance by
turns rules either, and has the last featuring blow at
events.

A third example of this habit of thought occurs in Ishmael's
response to the safety line known as the monkey-rope (in
Chapter 72), which protects the harpooner who is over the
ship's side butchering the whale. Standing awash on the
whale's carcass, the harpooner is tied to a seaman on deck
who must guard his comrade or be pulled over the side himself. Two lives are at stake. Tied as he is to Queequeg over
the side of the ship, Ishmael makes short work of this circumstance, turning it into a metaphor of the human condition. He sees that his individuality has "merged in a joint
stock company of two," that his free will has received a mortal wound, and that someone else's mistake might plunge
him into unmerited disaster and death. "Therefore, I saw
that here was a sort of interregnum in Providence; for its
even-handed equity could never have sanctioned so gross an
injustice." And the realization continues:

> I saw that this situation of mine was the precise situation of
> every mortal that breathes; only, in most cases, he, one way
> or other, has this Siamese connexion with a plurality of
> other mortals. If your banker breaks, you snap; if your
> apothecary by mistake sends you poison in your pills, you
> die.

True, one's caution might have some limited value, but Ishmael's final, sobering realization is that no matter what else
happens he has the management of only one end of the line.

In "The Mast-Head" (Chapter 35) Ishmael once more reveals this pattern of thought. He speaks of the trance-like
state of mind when one is aloft in the crow's-nest, presumably watching for whales.

With the problem of the universe revolving in me, how could I—being left completely to myself at such a thought-engendering altitude,—how could I but lightly hold my obligations to observe all whale-ships' standing orders, "Keep your weather eye open, and sing out every time."

Ishmael likens the masthead lookout to a "young Platonist," lulled into a listless, unconscious reverie, blending the cadence of waves with thoughts, so that "at last he loses his identity" and has almost a mystical experience with the ocean, which is the visible symbol of the bottomless soul of man and nature alike. And then the sudden significance. In this trance, if the Platonist moves one inch and slips, his identity horribly returns. Material reality contradicts his ideal being as he drops into the sea and is no more. "Heed it well, ye Pantheists!"

A fifth example of this swift revelation occurs in "Brit" (Chapter 58). Brit is the name for small, free-swimming organisms on which the right whale feeds. This chapter describes the surface of the ocean covered by the fields of yellow brit, as if it were a vast wheat field. But the benign appearance belies reality. Beneath this lovely and serene aspect is the universal cannibalism of the sea, all creatures preying on one another, "carrying on eternal war since the world began." Then comes the inevitable metaphor of one's self, with a clear warning never to venture beyond the safety of what one can really know.

> For as this appalling ocean surrounds the verdant land, so in the soul of man there lies one insular Tahiti, full of peace and joy, but encompassed by all the horrors of the half-known life. God keep thee! Push not off from that isle, thou canst never return!

These five episodes variously repeat the same speculative soaring beyond empirical fact to swift, apocalyptic realizations about the self and the world. Melville even parodied this pattern in his point of view, in an outrageous overstatement in "The Fountain" (Chapter 85). This chapter discusses the whale's spout, explaining why and how his breathing brings him periodically to the surface during the chase. The discussion pedantically considers the exact nature of the exhalation. Is it water or vapor? This spouting canal in the whale's head is like a gas pipe laid under a city street. Or is it a water pipe? What do you feel from a cascading whale close by? Is it water from the spiracle or is it a condensed vapor on your skin?

Ishmael finally states a tentative conclusion—which, of course, is all about the way he has been proceeding in this chapter—"My hypothesis is this: that the spout is nothing but mist." The reason for this conclusion is that the whale is no shallow being; he is ponderous and profound. "And I am convinced that from the heads of all ponderous profound beings, such as Plato, Pyrrho, the Devil, Jupiter, Dante, and so on, there always goes up a certain semi-visible steam, while in the act of thinking deep thoughts." Ishmael is certain of this because of his own experience. "While composing a little treatise on Eternity, I had the curiosity to place a mirror before me; and ere long saw reflected there a curious involved worming and undulation in the atmosphere over my head." In short, the most intense cerebration produces mist. The statement is definitive. This conclusive evidence, he reports, occurred after six cups of hot tea in a thin-shingled attic on an August noon.

You are the target of these rhetorical thrusts. The ocean under the brit field is your hazard. The monkey-rope dramatizes your helplessness. The mat-maker analogizes your circumstances. The masthead challenges your illusory world. The lee shore in a storm presents you with an awesome choice between destructions. The analogies are all aimed at you.

"The Line" (Chapter 60) describes the hazard of sitting in a whaleboat, grazed by the swift, silent rope as it follows the harpooned whale to the bottom of the ocean. Get caught in it and you are doomed. "But why say more? All men live

enveloped in whale-lines. All are born with halters round
their necks; but it is only when caught in the swift, sudden
turn of death, that mortals realize the silent, subtle, ever-
present perils of life." Whether you are a philosopher in a
whaleboat or sitting at home with a poker instead of a harpoon, the consequence is the same. Ahab's death by means
of the harpoon line fouled around his neck gives a final authority to this analogy.

Melville impales his readers on Ishmael's speculations.
Another metaphor involving you occurs in "Fast-Fish and
Loose-Fish" (Chapter 89), which weighs the legal aspects of
the ownership of a floating carcass. A fast-fish, being fastened
down one way or another, is already owned; and a loose-fish
is fair game for anyone to seize. This observation scarcely justifies all of the legal talk, if this is all he wants to clarify. But
the point, of course, lies elsewhere. "Fast-fish" and "loose-
fish" compend all human situations.

> What are the Rights of Man and the Liberties of the
> World but Loose-Fish? What all men's minds and opinions
> but Loose-Fish? What is the principle of religious belief in
> them but a Loose-Fish? What to the ostentatious smug-
> gling verbalists are the thoughts of thinkers but Loose-Fish?
> What is the great globe itself but a Loose-Fish?

Then, finally, he scores his point about equivocal mankind.
"And what are you, reader, but a Loose-Fish and a Fast-Fish,
too?"

But these episodes also accumulate a mutual significance.
The equivocal nature of human beings is also the nature of
the universe. This is what Ishmael's truths add up to. The
only possible conclusion is that paradox is more authoritative
than any single conviction. By the fact of contradiction Melville correlates this. Contradiction is the sum and total sense
of Ishmael's piecemeal realizations.

Ultimate truth becomes fugitive. These definitive statements so qualify one another that contradiction becomes the

most insistently repeated element in the novel. Take "Lee Shore" and "Brit," for example. At the conclusion of "Brit," having described the docile earth and the cannibalistic depths surrounding it, Ishmael exhorts you never to leave your insular Tahiti—never to exchange whatever idyllic certainty you have—for the horrors of half-known life. But in "Lee Shore" Ishmael scorns the mortal safety of the land and celebrates the landlessness of the mind whose very perishing becomes apotheosis. This contradiction is joined by still another. What is sublime about Ahab, after all, is precisely this landless striving of thought. And what does Ishmael say of this? He says, in "The Chart" (Chapter 44): "God help thee, old man, thy thoughts have created a creature in thee; and he whose intense thinking thus makes him a Prometheus; a vulture feeds upon that heart for ever; that vulture the very creature he creates."

Contradiction becomes the presiding idea in *Moby Dick*. In the space of a few paragraphs "The Mast-Head" emphasizes this. It dramatizes the irreconcilability of the discrete material world and the ideal image of an organic, whole world. The masthead lookout, called a Platonist, cannot live at once in both worlds. Each is valid in its own terms, but each contradicts the other. If he gives himself entirely to an ideal world, then the material world will claim his life. This episode fairly summarizes the way in which irreconcilable doctrines claim equal authority over mankind. By various repetition Melville enlarges the synthesis of contradicting opposites until anomaly becomes the central fact of the human condition.

"The Monkey-Rope" makes the human anomaly explicit in terms of ligatures which bind a man into a "joint stock company" of determining factors. "The Mat-Maker," the most explicit doctrinal chapter in the novel, proposes a pattern to explain discrepancies which are the human lot: thus, every event is woven according to necessity, free will, chance. These are the terms of a man's interaction with circumstance, a reciprocity which is divine, man-made, and qualified by chance. The various patterns of this interaction are what Ishmael continually reveals to himself. He enforces the same sense of reciprocity between the man and the event that Emerson (in "Fate") insists upon, the sense of concurrence and collusion at the same time.

"The Mat-Maker" states what finally becomes Ishmael's theology. But *Moby Dick* is not a tract against Calvinist orthodoxy. It is even more dangerous and more formidable, because it converts into drama the process of discovering that orthodoxy is not enough. Ishmael's sudden, unanticipated flights of mind and the narrative events themselves unevenly enforce a larger synthesis, an ever-broader view of man and God, in order to assimilate the contradictions that exist. Ishmael's realizations overflow the narrative situations that beget them; they occur by a process of association that generates discovery. Simply and merely juxtaposing two ideas breeds yet another. The narrative event provides the elements which, juxtaposed, reveal still new perceptions. This is what happens in the most sustained symbolic episode of Ishmael in the novel, in which he survives a crisis by realizing its implications.

His great crisis occurs in "The Try-Works" (Chapter 96); and it is virtually the last we see of Ishmael in the novel. Ishmael takes his turn at the helm, at night, with the flaming tryworks up on deck ahead of him. The pyre of whale flesh so hypnotizes the helmsman that he loses his bearings, turns away from the compass, and faces aft, nearly causing the ship to capsize. But he recovers the helm at the last instant, and immediately responds to what has happened. "Look not too long in the face of the fire, O Man! Never dream with thy hand on the helm! Turn not thy back to the compass." Tomorrow the natural sun will shine brighter than this flaming artificial glare.

This prudential advice sounds at first like the concept in "The Mast-Head" of the irreconcilability of the world of fact and the ideal world; but Ishmael goes beyond this. He insists that the sun does not hide the untenable, uninhabitable reaches of the world; on the contrary, it illuminates them. One must be true to the comprehensive, contradicting nature of the universe, or else he has only a fragment to believe in; and his fragmentary belief can only distort. That mortal man who has more of joy than sorrow in him must change and become true or remain undeveloped. The same with books, says Ishmael, quoting Solomon: "There is a wisdom that is woe but there is a woe that is madness." An eagle swooping down into the gloom of mountain ravines is nevertheless higher up than the birds flying over the plains, no matter how high they soar.

This is Ishmael's stunning recovery from his crisis. It is a metaphor. Losing sight of the compass, the acknowledged, limited authority, he has intuited a larger concept to contain all contradicting phenomena and all existing guides, including the compass. In this episode Melville dramatized a process of discovering which Henry Thoreau also recommended: a strategy of losing one's way in order to find one's self. In this case, loosed from his compass bearings, Ishmael returns to the compass only to heap up one qualification upon another until he discovers that no single, orthodox authority— not even a compass—suffices for one's self, and that only the broadest world view, containing all possible contradictions, will do. The metaphor is made of layered speculations. The fact that we see it happening is what enforces it.

Ishmael represents a consciousness at work, badgering facts to make them yield up implications and then distending implications to new significance. But Ishmael is less a person than a scheme, a way of getting at the unknown, a pattern of attack. This strategy or scheme or pattern extends beyond the character. It is present with or without Ishmael.

Apocalyptic revelation seems always imminent in *Moby Dick*; the characters think in these terms. It is all we see of some of them: Father Mapple, for example, whose sermon in the whaleman's chapel argues a particular doctrine of God's revelation. Mapple's Calvinism is the major value system in the book; its revelation is a norm for all other doctrines which qualify it. But the prophesying mind becomes extravagant in Gabriel and in Elijah, the self-appointed messengers of doom; it is exaggerated in Fedallah, the phantom boatswain's mate, and in Pip, the Negro cabin boy, both of whom are alleged to be media of occult knowledge. These are caricatures; they overstate an awareness of revelation that everywhere abounds aboard the *Pequod*.

Ahab, "whose intense thinking thus makes a Prometheus," attacks material facts to make them yield up essence. His oration to the sperm whale's head, exhorting it to speak its secrets (in "The Sphinx," Chapter 70), discloses his idea of revelation. Every fact must manifest the wholeness of the whole; yet it cannot. This is what his peroration says:

> "O Nature, and O soul of man! how far beyond all utterance are your linked analogies! not the smallest atom stirs or lives on matter, but has its cunning duplicate in mind."

The linked analogies of fact and essence proceed from Ahab's acute awareness. Ahab's crewmen are like so many chips and shards of similar awareness. They are remarkably alert. "Midnight, Forecastle" (Chapter 40) is a forum of response to Ahab's disclosure of his mission; it ends with Pip's prayer. Even the cabin boy is aware. "Oh, thou big white God aloft there somewhere in yon darkness, have mercy on this small black boy down here; preserve him from all men that have no bowels to feel fear!" Pip unwittingly prophesies his own madness, the responsibility for which is Stubb's, not Ahab's; but this irony exists at all because Pip's sense of imminent consequence is so acute.

Much later, in "The Log and Line" (Chapter 125), with the *Pequod* closer to its doom, still another mind ponders Pip's madness, linking it to Ahab's and to the fact of a rotten log line. The line needs repair, as the old Manx sailor points out to Ahab. The quadrant and the compass have already been destroyed. But Ahab disregards this warning, orders him to heave the line astern and snub it down. The Manxman does; it snaps; Ahab shrugs it off. But not the sailor. "There he goes now; to him nothing's happened; but to me, the skewer seems loosening out of the middle of the world." Pip intrudes; the Manxman scolds him off; but Ahab comforts him and clasps his hand. And the Manxman, holding the parted line, watches them walk away. "There go two daft ones now," he mutters. "One daft with strength, the other daft with weakness. But here's the end of the rotten line—all dripping, too. Mend it, eh? I think we had best have a new line altogether."

A characteristic idiom of thought pervades the *Pequod's* crew. It is a way of seeing evidence, or rather a way of shaping information into evidence beyond the fact. In trying to shut the mouth of a dead shark, Queequeg nearly loses his hand. " 'Queequeg no care what god made him shark,' said the savage, agonizingly lifting his hand up and down; 'wedder Fejee god or Nantucket god; but de god what made shark must be one dam Ingin.' " Even Stubb, the second mate, who views the world with equanimity, is capable of forcing fact to implication. When his harpooner announces that the whale they chased and caught is dead, Stubb answers: " 'Yes; both pipes smoked out!' and withdrawing his own from his mouth, Stubb scattered the dead ashes over the water; and, for a moment, stood thoughtfully eyeing the vast corpse he had made." Juxtaposed details like these are in the point of view. A given system of selection and emphasis common to so many characters goes beyond any one of them, including Ishmael. This is clear, for example, in "The Chart," which describes the obsessed captain in his cabin, poring over calculations of the whale's course. The chapter concludes with Ishmael's realization about Ahab "God help thee, old man, thy thoughts have created a creature in thee."

It is typical of Ishmael's thrusts at final realization, yet by no dramatic probability could Ishmael have been present in Ahab's cabin on this occasion. There is a characteristic point of view at work whether or not its utterance is assigned to any given character.

Sooner or later this novel conveys the illusion of a community of awareness and of a shared process of perceiving; and this fact is related to the properties of the novel form. Among many critical readers of *Moby Dick*, Richard Blackmur has spoken the most precisely about the affinity of the shared awareness and the novel form. He observes that Melville was impatient with the dramatic conventions of the novel form, and consequently careless of them; and that *Moby Dick* succeeds as well as it does because it has—unlike *Pierre*, for example—a cohesive center in the lore and history and romance of its subject. In *The Expense of Greatness* (1940) Blackmur writes that Melville employed only the shells of stock characters, heightened only by the author's eloquent voice, to accompany the development of an idea. This deprived the characters of individuality; and worse: after establishing a single consciousness Melville shifted to other minds without warning, which made them unconvincing.

Blackmur's judgment is that *Moby Dick* suffers by this author-character relationship. On the contrary, I think the book gains far more than it suffers thereby; but my disagreement is incidental to the terms of Blackmur's judgment, which do indicate the nature of the novel. The characters do amplify and resonate the novel's questing point of view. And this point of view patently correlates Melville's restless struggle with religious conviction, his own search for certainty. Educated to the doctrine of Calvinism, Melville was critical of this doctrine, yet he was also dissatisfied with any merely negative state of disbelief. In his long poem, *Clarel*, published twenty-five years after *Moby Dick*, he was still exploring the validity of a world view based on a plurality of convictions.

These characters in *Moby Dick* are echoing voices, and the subject of the novel lies in what these voices echo. The subject is the probing of circumstance for an explanation, the attack upon appearances in order to penetrate appearances. (Emerson's idea of Fate as unpenetrated cause is so relevant here. To him Power is the penetrating thought.) The doctrinal impossibility of ever defining ultimate truth is self-evident. On its own terms such searching can never achieve its goal. But the dramatization of the search itself is another matter: the representation of the struggling consciousness collaborating with its circumstances to rout out meaning, to organize the inexplicable into some system of knowledge, if not belief. *Moby Dick* is the dramatization of this act of mind, over and over. It exploits the fact that a novel is a system of analogies. It echoes and reverberates this act of mind until the act itself becomes the resonant subject.

The repetition in the novel goes beyond the ruminating characters. It also organizes groups of chapters. The train of thought within a chapter—from fact to speculation—is a normal sequence which recurs in different scopes, in various durations, through several chapters in a sequence. Events and consequences cluster in a way that magnifies the searching consciousness. One obvious cluster of chapters (36 through 40) congregates the various responses to Ahab's declaration of his mission, from the captain himself to the cabin boy. The last three chapters comprise another obvious cluster. The confrontation of Ahab and the whale, of course, culminates all that has occurred; and theatrically it concentrates the portents of the ship's disaster which have occurred with growing frequency during the previous sixteen chapters.

Less obviously but often in this novel episodes contain other episodes in such a way as to accumulate analogies. "Stubb Kills a Whale" (Chapter 61) is the narrative core of several related events (Chapters 60 through 70), all of which have implications beyond the killing of a whale. The process of harpooning, metaphorically understood, presents the proposition that all men live enveloped in whale lines. Stubb's supper of whale meat, the cook's sermon to the sharks, and the discussion of the whale as an item of food all develop the proposition that men—like sharks—are cannibals by nature; and the massacre of the sharks raises the question of the creation of sharks—and of men—in the first place. The prospect of the vultures piously dining on the butchered whale amplifies the association of man and shark. The stripped carcass, floating and frightening future navigators because it is uncharted, suggests that the whale's inscrutability survives even the whale. Finally Ahab's oration to the suspended head— about the linked analogies of man and nature which are beyond all utterance—insists on this inscrutability. From the beginning of this episode, ten chapters earlier, in fact, from the discussion of what and how the whale line binds, the linking of analogies of man and nature have been occurring all the while.

There are dozens of clustered chapters. The butchering of the whale and the boiling of the blubber in the night (Chapters 95 through 98) amplify the central episode of Ishmael's crisis at the helm. Earlier, Ishmael's ambition to mount the whale and leap the topmost skies to see if any heaven does exist—this statement—grows from a cluster of chapters (55 through 57) about the various artistic representations of the whale; and the fact that they are all imperfect, that the whale remains beyond them, links these chapters to "Brit," and "Squid," which follow and present the horrifying portent of the faceless whale.

There are so many of these clustered events that beginning and end are often indeterminate. The crucial cluster of "The Chapel," "The Pulpit," and "The Sermon" (Chapters 7 through 9) extends far beyond these chapters. Father Mapple's doctrine is immediately qualified by the fact of Jojo, Queequeg's God, which inspires Ishmael's ecumenical thoughts. Mapple's doctrine is later parodied by Fleece's sermon to the sharks (Chapter 49) and by "Jonah historically regarded" (Chapter 83); and the Calvinistic orthodoxy is further qualified by the metaphor of plural cause, in "The Mat-Maker" (Chapter 47) and in "The Try-Works" (Chapter 96).

The book is grounded to itself. As it proceeds, the clusters implicitly appraise one another. Their mutual existence energizes their suggested meaning. This system of analogies that are only partially insulated from one another can shock at almost any point you touch. Melville's metaphor of this developing realization through the repeated process of cross reference is, of course, the besmoked painting in the Spouter-Inn, and Ishmael's systematic attempts to study it "by dint of much and earnest contemplation, and oft-repeated ponderings" in "the unequal cross-lights" where he happens to find it.

The novel form in general is a system of resonant analogies. The analogies are various repetitions of a central event, which is a conflict. By these repetitions any novel appraises the event. In *Moby Dick* the central narrative event is the confrontation of Ahab and the whale. But any novel must show cause. This particular novel must explain or otherwise reveal the nature of the man and of the whale and of their confrontation. Like any other novel it reveals, intensifies, and amplifies the only way it can, which is to offer versions of its conflict which are mutually relevant.

Unlike most novels, *Moby Dick* presents myriad versions of its conflict, many of them obvious. The final chase presents three explicit confrontations of Ahab and the whale. Four of the ships the *Pequod* meets at sea have already hunted Moby Dick at heavy cost; a fifth, whose captain does not believe in Moby Dick, is laden with the priceless sperm and homeward bound. The ten chapters about the killing of Stubb's whale is yet another version of the confrontation; and before that, "The First Lowering" (Chapter 48), when Starbuck's crew rows up on the whale's back. Still earlier, in "Moby Dick" (Chapter 41), the history of this conflict presents another version of the final confrontation. Each of these is refracted through a point of view whose speculations amplify the conflict.

By means of these uncounted versions of the confrontation the novel does show cause. Ahab and the whale are both immense and both equivocal. The man perceives these qualities in the whale and, maddened by the whale and being human, must try to strike it down; and, being human, must inevitably be destroyed in his attempt. The terror lies in the inevitability of this conflict and its issue—given the nature of the principals. Accordingly, the novel demonstrates repeatedly, it overstates and understates, the nature of the principals.

These statements, about whale and man alike, contradict each other; if not obviously, then in their implications. On the third day, within the final minutes of the chase, the pursued whale turns on his attackers, "to present his blank forehead at bay." He rams the ship with his "predestinating head"—what Starbuck calls "his unappeasable brow"—and to Ahab the *Pequod* becomes a "god-bullied hull." These terms themselves and the concept of faceless, frontless force have been anticipated since the beginning of the voyage. From the first mention of Moby Dick on the quarter-deck the inscrutability of this immense force has been insisted on. The white whale has no color; it reflects all colors. The burden of research, to get beyond this faceless front, is Ishmael's. He makes all sorts of limited, inaccurate statements. Since he can never visualize the whole living whale, he speculates beyond what he can empirically know.

Ishmael sees the whale in parts, and documents what he sees. But this is only classroom knowledge. Having lectured on the subject of "The Tail" (Chapter 86), he must conclude, "Dissect him how I may, then, I but go skin deep; I know him not, and never will. But if I know not even the tail of this whale, how understand his head? much more, how comprehend his face, when face he has none?" Having said this he repeats it in the next two sentences:

> Thou shalt see my back parts, my tail, he seems to say, but
> my face shall not be seen. But I cannot completely make
> out his back parts; and hint what he will about his face, I
> say again he has no face.

Elsewhere, having failed to define and measure the sperm
whale's neck, Ishmael proposes that the head itself (which
seems to Ahab like the Sphinx—"thou vast and venerable
head") must therefore be only a delusion. Ishmael begins his
zoological approach in "Cetology" (Chapter 32): a catalogue
of fourteen whales in three bookish classifications, buttressed
by lesser "chapters." It is a burlesque of pedantry whose long
descriptions yield learned, superficial fragments. But "Cetology" is a paradigm of the novel that contains it.

> God keep me from ever completing anything. This whole
> book is but a draught—nay, but the draught of a draught.

Ishmael confirms his zoological speculations with a survey of
art and artifacts about the whale (in Chapter 66), and he acknowledges that "any way you may look at it, you must
needs conclude that the great Leviathan is that one creature
in the world which must remain unpainted to the last." This
statement about the whale is also about the novel. One portrait might be better than another, he says, but the only way
to get even a tolerable idea of a whale is to go whaling; "but
by so doing, you run no small risk of being eternally stove
and sunk by him."

Ishmael's inventory of the great bulk of historical, Biblical,
and fictional material about the whale in general and Moby
Dick in particular is as inconclusive as his survey of art and
his zoological cataloguing; he can see nothing in this massive
record but diverse meanings ascribed to the whale. No one
document is any more authoritative than any of the opinions
of the crew aboard the *Pequod*. Any given testimony invariably reveals more about the witness than the whale. So Moby
Dick presents no color of his own, reflects all colors cast upon
him. And Melville's metaphor of the painting in the Spouter-

Inn—viewed "in unequal cross-lights"—becomes more relevant. According to Ishmael's final theory that picture represents a half-foundered ship in a hurricane, with an enormous, exasperated whale impaled on its broken mast, and sprawling across the middle of it—something like the whaling lore that sprawls across the middle of the novel and threatens to submerge it.

Part of what Ishmael must fathom, of course, is Ahab. Like the whale, Ahab is immense and equivocal. His stature grows with the narrative; his ambiguity is the first impression that we have. In "The Ship" (Chapter 16) Ishmael wants to meet his captain, and Peleg puts him off. "I don't know exactly what's the matter with him; but he keeps close inside the house; a sort of sick, and yet he don't look so. In fact, he ain't sick; but no, he isn't well either." Peleg tries to sum it up: "he's Ahab, boy; and Ahab of old, thou knowest, was a crowned king!" When Ishmael objects that Ahab was a wicked king, Peleg tries again:

> He's a queer man, Captain Ahab—so some think—but a good one. . . . He is a grand, ungodly, god-like man, Captain Ahab . . . a good man—not a pious, good man but . . . a swearing good man.

Floundering in ambiguity, Peleg asks: Can there be any utter, hopeless harm in Ahab? "No, no, my lad; stricken, blasted if he be, Ahab has his humanities!"

The sum of these statements, if not contradiction, is ambivalence: "stricken, blasted if he be, Ahab has his humanities!" And each successive view of Ahab confirms the ambivalence. He is cut off from the world, finally denying every human tie he can deny, and yet he is the incarnation of every human dignity and self-assertion. On the one hand, he is an isolated, self-consuming man, a Prometheus. Yet he is all humanity incarnate. He is the excess of humanity. Toward the end of the voyage, while his ship is laboring in a typhoon, he grounds himself to the flaming yardarms by a length of chain at the mainmast ("the white flames but light the way to the White Whale!"), and thus he defies supernal force. His testament is in "The Candles" (Chapter 119):

> Oh! thou clear spirit of clear fire . . . I now know thee . . . I now know that thy right worship is defiance. . . . No fearless fool now fronts thee. I own thy speechless, placeless power; but to the last gasp of my earthquake life will dispute its unconditional, unintegral mastery in me.

The ambiguity is superb (I *own* thy speechless, placeless power): in one verb he acknowledges the existence of extrinsic power and claims possession of it. And Ahab claims it in the name of all humanity:

> In the midst of the personified impersonal, a personality stands here. Though but a point at best; whencesoe'er I came; wheresoe'er I go; yet while I earthly live, the queenly personality lives in me and feels her royal rights.

Ahab's excess of humanity cuts him off from other humans. His ambivalent nature is represented as a state of madness. Indeed, he insists that he is madness maddened. In his soliloquy (in "Sunset," Chapter 37) following his challenge on the quarter-deck, he defines his own condition. "They think me mad—Starbuck does; but I'm demoniac, I am madness maddened! That wild madness that's only calm to comprehend itself!" In "The Forge" (Chapter 113) he tells his blacksmith that he is impatient of all misery in others that is not mad. "Thou should'st go mad, blacksmith; say, why dost thou not go mad? How can'st thou endure without being mad? Do the heavens yet hate thee, that thou can'st not go mad?" And he acknowledges his bond with Pip, the mad cabin boy, and takes him to live in the captain's cabin.

Madness is a way of correlating Ahab's ambivalence. Even the madness "that's only calm to comprehend itself" is contradictory. Ahab is mad, and he thinks the white whale evil. Gabriel, the madman who has seen the whale, declares it to

be God. Both are mad, which might explain away the contradiction except that madness cannot be discredited. The madness of Pip (in "The Castaway," Chapter 93) is alleged to be
a state of divine knowledge. Having jumped from Stubb's
whaleboat and been left behind to perish, Pip has undergone
a marvelous transformation. The sea has kept his body up,
but carried down his soul to the depths of "the unwarped
primal world," down to the hoarded treasures of "the miser-
merman Wisdom": "Pip saw the multitudinous, God-omni-
present, coral insects, that out of the firmament of waters
heaved the colossal orbs. He saw God's foot upon the treadle
of the loom, and spoke it; and therefore his shipmates called
him mad.

> So man's insanity is heaven's sense; and wandering from all
> mortal reason, man comes at last to that celestial thought,
> which, to reason, is absurd and frantic; and weal or woe,
> feels then uncompromised, indifferent as his God."

Ahab himself expresses the dilemma. Is it God or is it
Ahab that drives him on? In his final dialogue with Starbuck,
in "The Symphony" (Chapter 132), Ahab comes the closest
to a recognition.

> What is it, what nameless, inscrutable, unearthly thing is it;
> what cozzening, hidden lord and master, and cruel, re-
> morseless emperor commands me; that against all natural
> lovings and longings, I so keep pushing, and crowding, and
> jamming myself on all the time; recklessly making me ready
> to do what in my own proper, natural heart, I durst not so
> much as dare? Is Ahab, Ahab? Is it I, God, or who, that
> lifts this arm?

It must be God. How else can any order be explained?

> But if the great sun move not of himself; but is an errand-
> boy in heaven; nor one single star can revolve, but by some
> invisible power; how then can this one small heart beat; this
> one small brain think thoughts; unless God does that beat-
> ing, does that thinking, does that living, and not I. By

> heaven, man, we are turned round and round in this world, like yonder windlass, and Fate is the handspike.

This idea, in turn, becomes intolerable, for "Who's to doom, when the judge himself is dragged to the bar?" Mortal Ahab never finds his answer. Moreover, who is the judge? Fouled by his own harpoon, Ahab is dragged to the bottom when the whale retreats. In the great and final confrontation the white whale shows his backside.

Ahab and the whale, the principals, remain equivocal. The only constant fact is contradiction. Accordingly, no absolute is safe, including the Calvinistic doctrine that Melville emphatically provided for the judgment of events. One of the most fruitful sources of contradiction, in fact, is the positive sermon of Father Mapple—or rather the analogies between the sermon and the other events of the novel. Just as Jonah's fate, for example, is the opposite of Ahab's, so most of the sermon's analogies involve discrepancy; they are ironic. This is so with the sermon's doctrine which Father Mapple has abstracted from the Book of Jonah: "And if we obey God, we must disobey ourselves; and it is in this disobeying ourselves, wherein the hardness of obeying God consists." From this, according to the sermon form, he derives his "Uses": to repent and do God's bidding.

Mapple has one lesson for his congregation and one lesson for himself. The lesson for his congregation—to repent, recant, rebel against one's own nature—forms one line of reasoning in the novel, and ties together many chapter clusters. According to this reasoning, mankind is animal by nature and will not willingly resign himself to God's order. This proposition is amplified in the only other sermon in the novel, Fleece's sermon to the sharks (in "Stubb's Supper," Chapter 64). Stubb has ordered the old cook to preach to the sharks to stop their racket in their ravage of the whale's corpse. Goaded, he reluctantly proceeds.

> Your woraciousness, fellow-critters, I don't blame ye so much for; dat is natur, and can't be helped; but to gobern

> dat wicked natur, dat is de pint. You is sharks, sartin; but if you gobern de shark in you, why den you be angel; for all angel is not'ing more dan de shark well goberned.

But it is hopeless. The sharks simply will not listen to the old man's impeccable logic.

> No use goin' on; de dam willains will keep a scrougin' and slappin' each oder, Massa Stubb; dey don't hear one word; no use a-preachin' to such dam g'uttons as you call 'em, till dare bellies is full, and dare bellies is bottomless; and when dey do get em full, dey wont hear you den; for den dey sink in de sea, go fast to sleep on de coral, and can't hear not'ing at all, no more, for eber and eber.

The chapter ends with the usual epiphany, this time recalling Ishmael's observations about the cannibalism of mankind. Stubb is more shark "dan Mass Shark hisself," the old man mutters.

This is one line of reasoning, but there is another which runs counter to it. The counter-reasoning urges the imperative need to perceive some order in the universe which one can serve by understanding. The need for order causes the constant pressure and direction of the point of view: those leaps from fact to speculation which characterize the ever-present and presiding consciousness in the novel. And when this consciousness is manifest as Ishmael, the need to perceive becomes his special burden.

The special burden to perceive no less than all the truth —this concept—leads us back to Ishmael, just as the novel leads us back to the evidence that he alone is saved. Why he survives is really a doctrinal question. Dramatically, the epilogue confirms his rescue; but his rescue must confirm the fact of his salvation or else it has no meaning. Any novel must explain itself—dramatically and doctrinally—or fail. Ishmael is saved—to answer this question in terms of doctrine—by the fact that he alone has perceived the multiplicity of contradicting doctrines to explain the world. Contradiction is quintessence: this is his world view. The continuity of his perceptions yields exactly this. Dramatically his crisis and his recognition have occurred in the tryworks episode, when, having turned unwittingly away from the compass, he has denied the devilish, hypnotizing fire in favor of the sun, and then realized that the sun shines indiscriminately on all the contradicting phenomena of the world.

But the question over why Ishmael is saved implies prior questions with similar significance: Why, in the first place, did Ishmael embark on this quest, on this story he must tell with such urgent dedication? Why does he so overstate the case for finding out? As thought is action, why does he so overact? A partial explanation lies in his similarity to Ahab. Ahab and Ishmael are versions of the self-seeking mind that Emerson defined and Thoreau dramatized. Each self-sufficiently generates an order of being. Each relegates events to his peculiar world. Each is driven by an obsession for encounter.

The similarity of Ahab and Ishmael is mutually revealing, but the course of events deprives Ahab of his self-sufficiency —the independence and the self-assurance of this style of poet. He turns to Pip for refuge or renewal in that innocent's vision of truth. These same events only nourish Ishmael more; they confirm him in his search. He is similar to something more than Ahab. The answer to his motive force seems to lie instead in one more linked analogy to Father Mapple's sermon.

The affinity of motives—Ishmael's and Mapple's—is in the second lesson which the preacher draws from his doctrine, "And if we obey God we must disobey ourselves." The second lesson is the lesson to the preacher: "To preach the truth to the face of Falsehood! . . . and woe to that pilot of the living God who slights it." Seven times with seven woes Father Mapple amplifies this warning in his lesson.

> Woe to him whom this world charms from Gospel duty!
> Woe to him who seeks to pour oil upon the waters when

God has brewed them into a gale! Woe to him who seeks to please rather than to appal! Woe to him whose good name is more to him than goodness! Woe to him who, in this world, courts not dishonor! Woe to him who would not be true, even though to be false were salvation! Yea, woe to him who, as the great Pilot Paul has it, while preaching to others is himself a castaway!

In this episode Mapple's passion is about the awesome burden of revelation. In the novel Ishmael bears this sense of mission, too. Both men speak with passion but preach a different doctrine.

They disagree. According to Genesis, in Mapple's parochial authority, Ishmael was a castaway; indeed, according to this Scriptural authority this Ishmael in the congregation must be a heretic. Mapple invokes the sole authority of Calvin's God. Ishmael forthwith leaves the chapel and, by extending Mapple's reasoning about the will of God, he casually turns idolator to Queequeg's pagan idol. Ishmael thereby generates his own ecumenical orthodoxy. Mapple preaches a sermon on Necessity: on the omnipotence of God and the inefficacy of God-determined man. But Ishmael qualifies it. He builds a metaphor out of a sword-mat, by which necessity, free will, and chance become the plaited cause of all events.

It may be remembered that behind Father Mapple's pulpit hangs the painting of a ship. It is a gallant ship, beating along a lee shore against a terrible storm. This picture solves the ship's predicament by representing "high above the flying scud and dark-rolling clouds . . . a little isle of sunlight, from which beamed forth an angel's face"; and Ishmael puts its sentiment in words:

> "Ah, noble ship," the angel seemed to say, "beat on, beat on, thou noble ship, and bear a hardy helm; for lo! the sun is breaking through; the clouds are rolling off—serenest azure is at hand."

Here is Ishmael's version of Mapple's faith. And what of Ishmael's own? The painting in the Spouter-Inn is what engages him. Except for the adversity of the two ships the pictures have nothing else in common. Mapple's fervor has a counterpart in Ishmael's stamina, in the fits and starts of his persistent speculations. But instead of preaching a sermon Ishmael crowds the facts and generates them into metaphors about the inscrutable universe and the impossibility of any doctrine except a plurality of doctrines. The truth, whatever it might be, is in the telling of it. This is the heresy that Melville built, and *Moby Dick* is its gospel, the record of its revelation.

Paradigm Four

If I could diagram my subject I would draw a series of concentric circles and call the center of them "the drama of the author's consciousness." Let each circle mark the relative distance of a work of fiction from this center, and let the radius of each represent the extent to which the author had removed himself from the drama. This would be a descriptive figure measuring what is known in literary criticism as "aesthetic distance," that is, the author's apparent objectivity. The circles of shorter radius in this diagram would mark the romantic cosmologies that emphasize the drama of the author in his own person. Successively wider circles would mark those fictions that transfer to a persona and then to characters the attempt to build a cosmology.

Labeling each circle would be a game of individual judgment. The circle of Thomas Wolfe's fiction, for example, would be close to the center. The cosmologies would fall into some sort of progression with *Moby Dick* having the longest radius. This cosmology about a cosmology presents two versions of the Emersonian poet: Ahab and Ishmael; and largely through Ishmael's point of view the author appraises Ahab's struggle to enforce a personal monism on the world.

Successively wider circles on the diagram would mark the fictions of Henry James and some of the fictions of William Faulkner, which are subjects of the next two chapters in this study. James's fictions dramatize a character's attempt to enforce an ideal world on the intractable circumstances in

141

which he lives. The necessity of idealism and its necessary limits constitute James's subject. His intense characters discover themselves by discovering this circumscribing environment. Some of Faulkner's fictions—particularly *The Sound and the Fury, Light in August, Absalom, Absalom!* and "The Bear"—similarly dramatize the mind struggling with its environment (which happens to be a hazardous combination of fact and hearsay evidence) to try to find a complete system of cause and effect. Beyond these fictions of James and Faulkner there would be many more circles, stretching way off the page.

This marvelous diagram would settle a great many questions of literary form, if it could ever be drawn. But of course it could not. Aesthetic distance is only apparent distance, an illusion of objectivity that the writer tries to create in order to separate his conflict from himself and bring it closer to his reader. There is no way to measure the distance and fix the radius of any such circle, so the diagram will not work. It is merely one conceit of a whole view of all fiction. Except for approximate relationships, such as the relativity of James's fiction and Faulkner's fiction to the cosmologies, the diagram will have to be abandoned. The only part we are left with is the center, which is the drama of the author's consciousness. But this is worth the whole conceit, as long as it emphasizes the kind of energy that generates a fiction.

The reason I keep returning to the idea of the author's problem is that I think reading fiction effectively depends on the reader's awareness of the real task the writer has set for himself: what he *must* do, no matter what he appears to be doing. With one strategy or another he must make the actual chaos of the material world that he has experienced reveal some ordered, comprehensive view of life. To need to know *why* is, of course, a universal necessity, but the actual world does not usually offer a satisfactory answer. The human mind must build some scheme of cause and effect to contain itself, to insulate itself from chaos. The more chaos one tries to subsume to an ordered vision, the greater the struggle and the greater the odds against achieving any doctrinal or ideological success—and occasionally the greater the achievement.

So the writer builds a scheme to explain *why*. He must make it clarify itself. This is his liability. If a fiction does not show cause for whatever happens in it, that is, if it does not reveal why it is so and not otherwise, then it is not worth the reader's effort. The true test of a fiction is its *necessity*. We are not expected to believe that a fictional episode either did happen or might happen. The fiction is a *supposed* system of events. Given his supposition, the author must persuade us that if these events *were* to happen they would convincingly happen the way they do in his system. His readers are his auditors. The author is always liable to our sense of the way things are. Given whatever we know about ourselves or others, he must persuade us that his supposed relationships between motive and action and between action and response are necessary, or he loses us. The better he conveys a sense of necessity, the more his fiction adds to our knowledge.

Fiction is a strategy of gaining and conveying knowledge. It is a means of theorizing about events, a means of provisionally clarifying what cannot otherwise be explained. As a process of supposing relationships that yield some theory of cause and effect, fiction is a discipline of the mind in the same sense that other reasoning processes are disciplines of the mind. Fiction is different from philosophical reasoning, which is a process of arriving at a conclusive statement by refining abstract concepts. Fiction is different from the empirical process of observing data for the purpose of measuring or describing whatever is observed. Fiction is different from mathematical reasoning, which is a process of describing the value of unknown entities by equating them in combinations with other entities that are known and constant.

All these disciplines of the mind are valid ways of discovering relationships between one's self and whatever is outside and beyond one's self. But, like the other disciplines, the process of fiction yields knowledge in proportion to a person's ability to use it: to recognize why it exists, how it works, and what its limitations are.

Every fiction is a process of selecting details of actuality and ordering them into some metaphorical scheme to show cause and effect. I do not know how I came by this statement, but I suspect a lot of it is based on George Santayana's essay, "The Elements and Function of Poetry." Santayana's title reveals the historical habit of calling all fiction by the name of poetry, and the title of the book in which it appears, *Interpretations of Poetry and Religion* (1900), accurately suggests the romantic philosophy of art that Santayana superbly states.

Santayana begins with the familiar assumption that poetry is a process. He describes two principal aspects of this process which occur more or less at the same time. He explains that the poet "disintegrates" whatever he perceives into its "sensuous elements, and gathers these together" into new combinations. Poetry is a process of disintegrating the particulars of one order and fusing them again into another order. Santayana also describes the nature of this fusion. This new order, he says, provides "appropriate occasions," or "dramatic situations," which localize feelings that cannot otherwise be stated. The function of these "occasions" is not to offer a new entity for its own sake, but rather to clarify the relationships that already exist in actual experience. "Poetry is not at its best when it depicts a further possible experience; but when it initiates us . . . into the meaning of the experience which we have actually had."

Santayana's essay argues that the function of poetry is to turn back to actuality, to inform us of our own experience and clarify it. In the course of developing this argument Santayana states two characteristics about the poetic process that bear especially on the cosmologies and on the fictions related to them (the stories of James and Faulkner). I have been talking about one of these characteristics since the beginning of my study, and that is the peculiar originality of the act of expression. "Expression is a misleading term which suggests that something previously known is rendered or imitated; whereas the expression is itself an original fact. . . ." The other characteristic is somewhat more paradoxical. It has to do with the fact that complexity generates clarity. Santayana says: "The function of poetry, like that of science, can only be fulfilled by the conception of harmonies that become clearer as they grow richer." This bold idea of a clarifying complexity helps to anticipate Henry James's conviction that an artist must always strive to represent the whole density of his subject.

In his novels and tales and in his literary criticism James developed the technique of narrative fiction as few other writers ever have. James wrote fiction, and about fiction, for more than fifty years, and the largest edition of his novels and stories, thirty-six volumes, is incomplete. There is no collected edition of his criticism or his plays or his essays in autobiography or biography or travel. Prefaces to his novels, written late in his life, comprise the longest sustained work of literary criticism written in the English language; these were based on extensive notebooks, now published, and on dictated notes which no longer exist. He wrote thousands of letters about his life and about his art, and the entire canon is not yet published. Piecemeal collections of his fictions, his essays, and his letters continue to appear. From all of this writing it is clear that he believed fiction to be a special kind of knowledge and a special way of knowing.

James was preoccupied with the poetic process. No criticism of his work can ignore either his technique or his preoccupation with the process of writing. James's fiction is preponderantly about the nature of fiction, and the more of it you read the more you are likely to see it reflect its author's intense involvement. The problem of finding a whole view of James's work begins by acknowledging what his extraordinary technique served. James believed that his technique served morality in the broadest sense, meaning an acute awareness of one's relation to one's limiting circumstance. He used the term "appreciation," meaning the morality of the highly developed consciousness.

James believed that he could represent moral awareness only by dramatizing the dense, intense complexity of the consciousness. His struggle was his joy and his despair. "As soon as I begin to appreciate," he said, "simplification is imperilled." [1] He insisted that a fiction could offer the "irresistible illusion" of experience only in proportion to the attention it demands of the reader. "It is greatest," he said, "when we feel the surface, like the thick ice of the skater's pond, bear without cracking the strongest pressure we throw upon it." [2] The consciousness was James's subject; but it was also his medium, which is why his fiction is so complex.

Curiously, James's preoccupation with aesthetic distance deeply involved him in his own fiction. Over the course of many years he worked out ways of representing the illusion of a point of view within the story that appears to build the story by the way it reports events. James was so committed to objectifying the drama of his fictional point of view that his commitment drew him excitedly into the drama, in spite of himself.

The prefaces to his novels and tales frequently allude to this sense of involvement. "The teller of the story . . . is primarily the listener to it," he says in one place.[3] It excited James to be the player and the spectator and the referee all at once in his own fictions; but the real game, the writer's game, was how to build the game that the reader sees. The object of the game for James, as he said, was to get the most meaning out of the least material. The game that James played was a dialectic with his own material. He saw it as a continuous conflict that generates new meaning: "The general sense of the expansive, the explosive principle in one's material . . . but with its other appetites and treacheries, its characteristic space-hunger and space-cunning kept down." [4]

The need to compress, the crisis of "Amount and Number" that made Thomas Wolfe despair, was precisely the problem that James celebrated. He spoke of the adventure of making an adventure, and he spoke of it as though it were a roller-coaster ride: "the thrilling ups and downs, the intricate ins and outs of the compositional problem, made after such a fashion admirably objective, becoming the question at issue and keeping the author's heart in his mouth." [5]

Having said this much in general of the drama of the author's consciousness, and about Henry James in particular, I can state an idea about reading fiction that is more specific than what I have been able to say so far. This idea is simply that the reader's experience approximates what the writer's experience was. Although the reader's experience is less intense, his problem is also comparable to what the writer's problem was. At any given time the reader does not know exactly where he is going. Neither did the writer. But the writer's attempts to find out where he was going are the most reliable guidelines for the reader.

What the reader sees in any fiction is a sense of approximate statement, because the writer has had no other way of getting his idea across to himself. The writer has had some conflict in mind; trying to define and evaluate it he has made repeated attempts to say what he could not quite comprehend at any given time until he said it. He has made overstatements and understatements and fragmentary allusions. Pondering his idea, he might even have made mirror statements. All of these are *various repetitions* of the idea he has had in mind.

The important thing is to realize how these approximate statements occurred in the first place. A good analogy might be the experience of listening to a series of variations on a musical theme without having first heard the theme. After a while the listener's ear can recognize in the variations those repetitions that form the theme. Theme occurs differently in fiction and in music. In fiction it evolves through a series of approximate statements. In the process of building his fiction the writer necessarily repeats himself, not literally but variously; each repetition qualifies what has already occurred.

Such *qualifying repetitions* are the common denominator of the writer's experience and the reader's. The strategy of reading fiction is to let the variations go without worrying over their explicit significance, and to listen, instead, for the repetitions a variation may contain of any other statements (or episodes or metaphors or characters).

You can test this way of reading with William Faulkner's fiction, where sometimes the repetition—the fact of it—is the only meaning there is at the moment. Like Melville and James before him, Faulkner used the subject of the mind finding what would suffice. He tested the validity of a subjective ideal when it collides with the facts. His fiction is a series of statements whose sequence and repetition correlate the realization of the character that appears to be uttering them. The sequence of repeated recollections or sensations or impressions is often all we ever see of a character. The statements themselves do not constitute the meaning, but the series of statements does. In "The Bear," for example, Ike McCaslin's apprehension of his heritage *is* his heritage; and *Absalom, Absalom!* is a fiction about the making of a fiction. These stories represent uneven, spastic dialogues between a character and whatever it is he cannot understand except by saying. The form is its own argument.

CHAPTER SEVEN

The Dense Totality
of Henry James

The possibilities of subjective reality fascinated Henry James. His famous statement to H. G. Wells—"It is art that *makes* life"—attests to this. Wells had been arguing that literature is properly a means and not an end, that its function is to serve experience. And James emphatically disagreed. "It is art that *makes* life, makes interest, makes importance, for our consideration and application of these things, and I know of no substitute whatever for the force and beauty of its process." [1] He wrote this in the knowledge of all the idealisms he had pondered, from the visitors to his remarkable home, from his travels and studies in Europe, from his friendships with dozens of painters and writers. He spent most of his writing years, in fact, speculating over the possibilities of his subjective reality.

Judging by his most famous characters—Christopher Newman, Daisy Miller, Isabel Archer, and Lambert Strether—the possibilities of subjective reality are enormous but, in the end, always limited by circumstance. Placed in a cosmopolitan European society, these characters are all the more insistently American. They all overstate a bold innocence in contrast to the social manners of their environments, and the sharp contrasts provided James with the conflicts of his early international stories. Daisy Miller is apparently unaware of her shocking trespass on European manners of courtship. Christopher Newman's deliberate display of his commercial credentials destroys any hope of his marrying his French fiancée; and his narrow honesty precludes any revenge, or even justice, for the trespasses of her family. Isabel Archer's grand concept of being freely herself imprisons her in a marriage which denies everything about her. With many more ironies, Lambert Strether's brave new morality constricts him as much as the old one he has outgrown. These characters range enormously from Daisy Miller's apparent innocence of herself to Strether's acute self-consciousness, but they all dramatize the same parable. By their own standards each of them is splendidly right, yet each of them illustrates that the world does not equal one's own image of it.

James quarreled with Emerson's idealism precisely because of its moral innocence. During a diatribe over the lack of cultural development in the United States, his biography, *Hawthorne* (1879), mentions Emerson in this connection. Such a provincial and limited society, James thought, would naturally relish the "utterances of a writer who would help one to take a picturesque view of one's internal responsibilities, and to find in the landscape of the soul all sorts of fine sunrise and moonlight effects." [2] James politely belittled Emerson's intoxicating rhapsodies on the intuition, and in a later essay on Emerson, which appeared in *Partial Portraits* (1888), James observed "a certain inadequacy and thinness in his enumerations." Emerson had "a special capacity for moral experience—always that and only that." Yet this in itself is limiting. "We have the impression, somehow, that life had never bribed him to look at anything but the soul. . . ." James's essay delicately gives and takes away: thus, Emerson "knows the nature of man and the long tradition of its dangers," but "He has only a kind of hearsay, uninformed acquaintance with the disorders." [3] Emerson had a strangely limited conception of right, "because he had no great sense of wrong . . . no sense of the dark, the foul, the base."

One of James's early tales, "The Madonna of the Future" (1873), pointedly demonstrates the limitations of idealism. It dramatizes the fate of an idealist named Theobald, an American expatriate living in Florence. Theobald has spent twenty years preparing to paint the consummate Madonna in the manner of the Italian school. During all this time the image of his beautiful model, Serafina, has become his reality, until he abruptly discovers that his image no longer conforms to the facts. She has grown old and gross, and he has only an empty canvas to show for the great work of art to which he has been so faithful.

The fable both ridicules and pities this self-styled idealist. In the moonlight he appears a heroic, fantastic genius, but by daylight he is haggard, threadbare, and looking altogether like a painter who has never sold a painting. Having reported all the evidence against Theobald, the story concludes with a final contradiction of his ideal. During all the years of his uncompromising, pure illusion the beautiful Serafina has been kept by a prosperous man who manufactures obscene statuary—cats and monkeys—"of an indestructible plastic material."

The story is a judgment against excessive idealism. But James had no quarrel with the validity of subjective impressions—far from it. Another of his fables, "The Real Thing" (1893), tells of a painter who attempts to draw some aristocratic persons by using genuine aristocrats as his models. Posed in front of him, his models leave nothing to imagine; and his illustrations are flat and dull because they are literal. "The Real Thing" insists that mere actuality is not sufficient. Its inadequacy, in fact, is what properly excites the painter to construct a more perfect reality. The fable anticipates James's later statement to H. G. Wells: "It is art that *makes* life, makes interest, makes importance . . . and I know of no substitute whatever for the force and beauty of its process."

James understood subjective reality. It was his donnée. The reciprocity of mind and circumstance is really the subject of all of his fiction. Each story fixes a subjective order in conflict with circumstance and tests its validity. Such was James's preoccupation.

James passionately believed that a fiction is an order of reality. One of his early critical essays, a review of Anthony Trollope's novels, states the imperative premise that the fictive world is a real one, an assumption from which the reader must never be allowed to escape. James was amazed and dismayed at Trollope's "suicidal satisfaction in reminding the reader that the story he was telling was only, after all, a make-believe." [4] This would never do. "It is impossible to imagine what a novelist takes himself to be unless he regards himself as an historian and his narrative as a history." Only as a historian does the novelist have any place or standing. "As a narrator of fictitious events he is nowhere; to insert in his attempt a backbone of logic, he must relate events that are assumed to be real."

The nature of this reality James defined a few years later in his formative essay, "The Art of Fiction." Reality lies not in actuality, he asserted, but in the impression of actuality; it lies not in the fact but in the experience of it. On this principle he defined the novel. "A novel is in its broadest definition a personal, a direct impression of life: that, to begin with, constitutes its value, which is greater or less according to the intensity of the impression." [5] Impressions, he said, *are* experience; and the sense of reality, which every novelist must have, is the sensitivity to experience.

James defined the sense of reality as "the power to guess the unseen from the seen, to trace the implication of things, to judge the whole piece by the pattern, the condition of feeling life in general so completely that you are well on your way to knowing any particular corner of it. . . ."

In defining the sense of reality as sensitivity to experience, James was being precise about that quality of the artist that had so excited Emerson. But he was more interested in establishing the precise nature of the fictive reality as nothing less than the consciousness itself. His novels progressively illustrated this fact; and his prefaces, written late in his career, confirm it.

James's perspective of his subject has an analogy close at

hand. In his biography of Hawthorne he discussed Hawthorne's inheritance of the Puritan conscience. This fanciful novelist had surely received the legacy of his ancestors. "To him, as to them," said James, "the consciousness of *sin* was the most importunate fact of life. . . ." [6] But James strongly qualified it, quoting from another biographer—Emile Montégut—to make his point.

Montégut had catalogued the particulars of Hawthorne's Puritan inheritance: the taciturn, scornful, mournful cast of mind; the habit of gazing upon a damned world and seeing hell everywhere; the lonely conversations between the imagination and the conscience; the pitiless analysis and perpetual examination of one's self—"all these elements of the Puritan character have passed into Mr. Hawthorne, or, to speak more justly, have *filtered* into him, through a long succession of generations." Yes and no, said James. "It is all true indeed, but with a difference; Hawthorne was all that M. Montégut says, *minus* the conviction." As James saw it, all these elements have "lodged in the mind of a man of Fancy, whose fancy had straightway begun to take liberties and play tricks with them—to judge them (Heaven forgive him!) from the poetic and aesthetic point of view, the point of view of entertainment and irony."

Here was the distinction on which James insisted. Hawthorne had inherited the Puritan world view *minus* the conviction. "This absence of conviction makes the difference; but the difference is great." The difference was the objectivity Hawthorne gained thereby, the perspective of his material. Ultimately it becomes the difference between believing a doctrine and representing it. James absorbed and incorporated idealism precisely the way Hawthorne absorbed and incorporated the Puritan metaphysics. The donnée of each was a particular metaphysical view, subject to the transaction of fiction. The transaction was an appraisal which each author worked out by involving his metaphysical view in conflict. This is substantially what James did with what he inher-

ited. The rest of this chapter is about how he did it, and
what he achieved thereby.

To explain how James dramatized subjective reality first
requires a few generalities. Using these, it will be possible to
construct a theoretical model from all his fictions, a kind of
typical or normal narrative. Later, the model can illustrate
specific fictions. To begin, the conflict in James's fiction characteristically occurs in the original consciousness, in the mind
of an individual who has complete freedom of choice, and
whose motive, whatever it may be, has helped to create the
circumstances which confound him. So far this does not distinguish James's protagonist, or this protagonist's world, from
a great many others—except in degree. James nearly always
constructed a closed system, impervious to all doctrines or
ideologies that might lie outside of it. Nothing whatever determines the character except his own action and its consequences. "What is character but the determination of
incident?" James asked in "The Art of Fiction." "What is
incident but the illustration of character?" [7]

The singularity of James's fiction lies in the relation of
character to incident. The typical or normal narrative can
usefully explain this relationship. Such a narrative would
begin with a character's intention; only that, and usually not
a very clear one. At the outset all we know about him is his
intention. Incident begins in response to this intention, usually an adverse response, in the other persons around him;
and incident continues with his awareness of these reactions
to his intention. This awareness precipitates his struggle,
which is an attempt to discover simultaneously the nature of
his opposition and a more precise understanding of himself.
He proceeds by doubt and conjecture; as James said, the
whole thing depends on the quality of bewilderment. At any
given point in the character's struggle, his bewilderment
goads him on, subtly increasing and enforcing his intention
to the point of preoccupation and sometimes to obsession.
The more he discovers, the more complex the refinements of
his predicament become.

The reciprocity of character and incident in James's fiction is startlingly like Emerson's idea of the relation between the person and the event. In "Fate" Emerson said, ". . . the secret of the world is the tie between the person and the event." Emerson had a determinism in mind ("person makes event, and event person") which necessarily develops the person and makes him more complete; he intended an ethical progression from one state of awareness to another. This same progression of a character in James's fiction also has a *literal* significance. The interaction of character and incident is literally the means of developing and determining a character. Simply by the process of becoming aware the character grows: not merely grows up, in the colloquial sense, but takes dimensions, solidity and form, and evolves into being. He appears to create himself by the process of fixing and certifying the circumstances around him. The more of his struggle he confirms, the more circumscribed and the more defined he becomes.

This process of prescribing both his own nature and his circumstances gradually burdens him with a realization to acknowledge, and sometimes with a choice to make. It is characteristically a moral choice or recognition; it involves rights and obligations: his own and those of adversaries. He has unquestionable freedom to choose, and either way there is a maximum of consequence. It is a moral recognition, and very often shocking. James used melodrama to emphasize the shock of recognition. The melodramatic quality is excessiveness: thus, an action is not logically prepared for, or a character's response to a situation exceeds what is expected.

James exploited this disproportion between cause and consequence, contradicting the reader's sense of probability: the sudden turn of events against a character, or a serious, unanticipated consequence. Such disproportion evokes a matching recognition in the character; he finally gets the point; he sees the occult logic of events. In the earlier stories the hero is not always likely to see his own complicity in the sudden turn of events, but as James's fiction continued over the years, the denouement of a story progressively involved the character's recognition of its significance. The end of a story (more abruptly in a tale than in a novel, but essentially the same) reveals that the perceiving character had somehow been an accessory before the fact. His recognition of his complicity is the more shocking, because he has considered himself innocent. His initiation has been the discovery of his reciprocity with his circumstances, and therefore his responsibility for what has happened.

The significance of the choice or recognition lies in the ordeal that has caused it, in the confusion and distress and sometimes the passion of slowly defining what the dilemma really is. It has been a mental ordeal, and the character's chief feeling has been anxiety, at times intense anxiety. When he has clearly perceived his relation to his circumstances, and the significance of his situation, his dilemma is resolved, and James's drama of the consciousness concludes. There is no more story, nothing more to write, except James's characteristic signature, which is a final, ironic realization (sometimes in the character and always in the reader) of how clearly this character has determined what he gets. It has all been a version of Pandora's box.

Such is the typical narrative of James. There are variations, of course, but even this much reveals the extraordinary quality of his fiction. As he continued to write over the years his stories became apparently all consciousness and nothing else. James took a long step in this direction with *The Portrait of a Lady* (1881), and the fiction after 1895 consistently emphasizes the consciousness. Everything that happens in these later stories seems to develop in the mind of the same character who is emotionally committed to evaluating the action. Virtually all the detail appears to be subjective, and it is usually registered under stress. The entire construction extends the character struggling within it, and the only facts are impressions, recollections, or surmises. The whole burden of subjective realization is what this fictional world is all about.

James's fiction over the years increasingly insisted on the fact that one's impressions of occurrences are themselves the events. His prefaces are a long and loving exegesis of this refinement. Written for the New York edition of *The Novels and Tales of Henry James* (1907–1917), these eighteen prefaces are stories of how he wrote his stories. They are contemporary with his later, intricate fictions in which the conflict and the mind that contain it are reciprocal and interdependent. This mind, for James, had become the center of composition; he called it that. Reminiscing in these later years, he re-examined his earlier fictions, and he defined his aesthetic, which concerns the morality of awareness. James had several synonyms for this mind, this center of composition; he called it "the intense perceiver" or "the register" or "the reflector."

The essence of this consciousness was its freedom to observe, to speculate, and to explore its own possibilities, unlike the other characters in the fiction. In his preface to *The Spoils of Poynton* (1897) James distinguished between this "free spirit" and the fools around him; ". . . the fixed constituents of almost any reproducible action are the fools who minister, at a particular crisis, to the intensity of the free spirit engaged with them." The fools have all the best of it; they are fixed in their situation and satisfied that they know what they want or do not want. But the free spirit is uncertain; it is his nature to quest for what he wants without knowing what it is. He is "free" only by the fact that he continues to explore his own possibilities; "and the free spirit, always much tormented, and by no means always triumphant, is heroic, ironic, pathetic, or whatever, and . . . 'successful' only through having remained free." [8]

The famous statement in *The Ambassadors* (1903), which James said was the germ of his novel, is a preachment of this ideal of being free to explore one's possibilities. It is Lambert Strether's new realization that he passes on to his young friend: "Live all you can; it's a mistake not to. It doesn't so much matter what you do in particular so long as you have your life. If you haven't had that, what *have* you had?" The notion of right and trespasses is closely related to this singular ideal of freedom. Any act that hinders a person from realizing the full possibilities of his own character is a trespass.

To inflict the abuse of limitation on one's self is even worse. This is what happens, for example, in "The Beast in the Jungle" (1903), in which a man so strongly fears that an unknown something or someone will poach on his freedom that his fear itself destroys what he might have been. Another late story, "The Jolly Corner" (1909), dramatizes a man's intense preoccupation with what he might have been. He conjures an image of himself, a retrospective vision that is plausible but contrary to fact, a kind of subjunctive alter ego, so monstrous as to shock himself senseless.

In these two tales and in *The Ambassadors,* James's notion of the "intense perceiver" fused with his concept of conflict. But this organic joining of perception and conflict was a later development. In his earlier fiction James employed the perceiving mind not as a subject but as a device to record a conflict occurring elsewhere. The events in "Daisy Miller" (1879), for example, are reported largely by Winterbourne, a young American bachelor who has been accustomed to the mores of European courtship. His eyes select the details, and his awareness of the rules Daisy breaks intensifies the conflict between Daisy, a free spirit, if you will, and the women who conform to the rules of social conduct in the American colony in Rome. Winterbourne is bewildered by Daisy, and he indulges in grave, academic speculation in his attempt to categorize her. Like a lens, he focuses and magnifies the conflict.

Another early tale, "Madame De Mauves" (1875), employs the same device of a narrator who feels a conflict beyond his knowledge of it. It dramatizes the disagreement of a Frenchman and his American wife over the license which he takes in sexual indulgence, and which she understands to be nothing but adultery. This conflict between two unalterable attitudes is ordered and evaluated primarily by Longmore, an American young man who innocently admires Madame de Mauves. The selection of details from the point of view of this wholesome youth who is partial to the suffering wife provides James with a means of rendering shock, when it turns out that this righteous woman has driven her husband to suicide.

In his preface to *Roderick Hudson* (1875) James discussed the strategy of refracting a conflict through another consciousness. This novel is named for its hero, but the consciousness possessed by the hero's friend and patron is what enables the story. "The centre of interest throughout 'Roderick' is in Rowland Mallet's consciousness, and the drama is the very drama of that consciousness. . . ." What "happened" to Rowland, said James, "was above all to feel certain things happening to others. . . ." [9] Elsewhere James referred to such centers of consciousness as his "registers or 'single reflectors' "; and the preface to *The Princess Casamassima* (1886) catalogues them all, from *Roderick Hudson* (1875) to *The Golden Bowl* (1904). The preface to *The Princess Casamassima* is James's great argument for complexity in fiction. And complexity has everything to do with what he meant by awareness.

The relationship is this: Characters both do and feel, James observed, but their actions impart interest only in terms of their feelings; to represent the wholeness of the character, therefore—one's actions *through* one's feelings—is necessarily complex. The fools play their parts but have nothing essential to reveal; but only the *sensitive* person (who is committed, who has something to lose, and who cares about it) can convey the whole ambience of the action. "I confess I never see the *leading* interest of any human hazard but in a consciousness . . . subject to the fine intensification and wide enlargement." [10]

A fine awareness and a necessary complexity. These two

ideas were interdependent to James, whether he was talking
about his own fiction or the fiction of other writers. He chas-
tised Zola for the naturalistic theory that prevented him from
making a full and representative collection of human qualities, and which was therefore scarcely natural. He disagreed
with the simplistic fictional theory of Guy De Maupassant.
He scorned De Maupassant's disdain for the analysis of character and his preference for illustration. James thought there
could be no sharp distinctions. "It is as difficult to describe
an action without glancing at its motives, its moral history, as
it is to describe a motive without glancing at its practical
consequence." [11] Our history and our fiction, he said, are
what we do. Determining where "what we do" begins or
leaves off is notoriously hopeless, but this does not relieve the
artist from being faithfully comprehensive.

James celebrated Balzac's fiction, because it came so close
to representing "completeness" and with such intensity. Despite his faults of pedantry and bad taste, James said, Balzac's
breadth and depth, his penetration into his subject, his "sat-
uration with his idea," his negotiating as completely as possible "the complicated human creature or human condition"
really accomplished the function of art. But there must be
proportion. The dense consciousness must match the intricacy of the complications it experiences. James commented
of *Middlemarch* (1871–1872) that George Eliot's heroine
was too complex to be wasted on the narrow moral question
of whether she should marry and thereby forfeit her legacy.
With its abundant and massive ingredients, James argued,
Middlemarch should have represented a weightier drama.
James found the opposite fault in two of Flaubert's characters, Emma Bovary and Frédéric Moreau, each of whom he
thought inadequate to the complexity of their subject, which
he considered to be nothing less than the nature of the romantic imagination.

James practiced what he preached. He strove for complexity
in his own work, but also for a means of controlling it. His

subject was the consciousness ("subject to the fine intensification and wide enlargement"); but the conscious—which he called the "reflector"—must be its own lens and provide its own focus on itself. It took James years to develop a technique of generating and controlling the intensity that he wanted. His first major breakthrough was in *The Portrait of a Lady*, when he discovered the precise relation between his subject and his means of representing it.

In *The Portrait of a Lady* both the conflict and the consciousness of the conflict inhere in the same character. The preface tells how "a certain young woman confronting her destiny" is both the germ and the subject of this novel. What would her destiny be? His first problem, "organizing an 'ado' about Isabel Archer," he would solve by seeing that she insisted on "mattering" in the world. But how to do this?

> "Place the centre of the subject in the young woman's own consciousness," I said to myself, "and you get as interesting and as beautiful difficulty as you could wish. Stick to *that*— for the centre; put the heaviest weight into *that* scale, which will be so largely the scale of her relation to herself." [12]

In the development of a *compositional center* (that is, a single consciousness attempting to organize the terms of the very conflict in which it is involved), *The Portrait of a Lady* anticipated most of James's fiction thereafter.

The step-by-step reasoning by which James evolved an Isabel Archer anticipated his development of the heroine of *What Maisie Knew* (1897). The preface to his novel is an epitome; it is the most complete, compact, and self-sufficient illustration of James's reasoning about the compositional center of a novel. It tells about how he began by recognizing a germ of fiction in an actual situation; how he singled out the central character; and then, by way of solving certain mechanical problems, how he discovered the real subject to be this character's consciousness of the conflict, from which consciousness the whole of the character would evolve.

The actual situation concerned a little girl, the child of divorced parents, one of whom had remarried. James's transformation into fiction began by marrying off the other partner as well, and establishing, with this symmetry, an even conflict for possession of the child's affections. The little girl, Maisie, would be not only the center of contention but also the "register" or "reflector" of all the action. She would be the compositional center of the novel. The sordid refinements of an adult world would ultimately present her with an absolute choice to make.

As the novel proceeds both new marriages founder, largely because of the adulteries of Maisie's parents. Partly as a consequence the step-parents engage each other in a love affair, and thereby make a new claim on the child. Each step-parent genuinely likes her; they are living together, and have asked her to live with them. Throughout the novel Maisie has had a governess, a self-appointed protectress; but there is clearly no place for her in the proposed new living arrangement. So the parties for the contention of Maisie change once more. She must choose between her step-parents and the governess.

To make a child the compositional center of this jaundiced, sophisticated world was indeed a *tour de force*. How to render the whole situation intelligibly through her consciousness and yet keep her believable? James pondered this in his preface, deciding that he would exploit the possibility that children comprehend more than they can articulate. Maisie's awareness would be innocent and unselective, and the adult reader would necessarily see significances in whatever Maisie might contemplate. Above all, Maisie would be credible. The child would exist at that fleeting moment in life of really knowing; yet, because all of her would not be ready for that much knowing, she would accept knowledge without wanting to question it.

What did Maisie know? On the face of it she knew that

she could trust no one to put her ahead of himself. This was what she learned. It was everything. It was her salvation. But James arrived at this thematic conclusion only by the way he worked out the technique.

Technique begat theme. As James saw it, the conflict and the means of rendering it would enable and reinforce each other. In the story the child would be the center of contention; in the rendering she would be the center of composition. He would therefore have to "save" Maisie from moral squalor, and keep her uncontaminated for the sake of her role as recorder or register: "The small expanding consciousness would have to be saved, have to become presentable as a register of impressions." [13] But the process of her registering the impressions of her purgatory—for which she was salvaged—makes her, as a character, finely and richly aware. The process of her small consciousness expanding is what saves her.

There is the illusion finally that Maisie is aware of everything that could possibly have been revealed. This sense of total awareness was what James was after. His use of the point of view, or the relation between the narrator and the story, was his means. The first problem was how to remove from the fiction the illusion of the author's presence and to focus instead on a consciousness within the story.

One of the earliest and still one of the best critical studies of his work, Percy Lubbock's *The Craft of Fiction* (1921), explains how James manipulated the point of view to make the consciousness within the story seem to function nakedly, without being described. Lubbock pointed out that James alternately displayed two views of a given consciousness, open and closed. Alone and by itself the open consciousness meditates freely for the reader, expressing an interior monologue about whatever concerns it. Then abruptly, in a scene with other characters, this consciousness is closed, sealed off from view; thought is described, not rendered; and the consciousness, through dialogue, is thrust into the plane of the other actors on stage.

This is Lubbock's clarifying analysis of what James in his prefaces called the "picture" and the "scene." By the rhythm of change, from the open, visible thought and feeling (of the "picture") to the sealed-off mind (in the "scene"), the reader helps carry the energy of the consciousness on to its next confrontation. By means of the repeated and interrupted glimpses of the mind in the act of perceiving, at some point in the fiction, the whole character seems to *emerge* at once. Even though details may still elude him, the reader suddenly has a sense of cause and continuity, a sense of the *total* situation.

The whole point of a fiction, to James, was the shared sense of the wholeness it could impart. The experience of reading any of his later stories, the ones after 1895, bears this out. As Lubbock explains, at some undetermined stage in the narrative, without knowing how or where it happened, the reader suddenly realizes that he is aware of the entire situation, with all its nuances and refinements, including the intense perceiver's awareness of it. To use James's word, the reader suddenly has an "appreciation" of it all. It has not really been a reasoning process, rather more of an intuition. But the reader scarcely guesses, until he has experienced an approximate revelation about the self-sufficient wholeness of the fiction. The author's experience, in fact, has become a desperate struggle to control his material, even as it has grown under his pen.

The most complete testimonies of the author's tortuous struggle are his *Notebook* entries about *The Spoils of Poynton* (1897) and *What Maisie Knew* (1897). These were the first two novels he completed after his disastrous apprenticeship at playwriting. He worked on them both at the same time, during 1895 and 1896, and both bear the sign of the new discipline he had acquired so dearly. After adapting a novel to the stage, he had written five plays between 1890 and 1895. The only one produced was a disaster, but the experience of structuring plays had immediate effect on his narrative fiction. He thought of scenes and sequence in terms of the stringent economies that a playwright must observe, and he discovered new possibilities of compression. He continually speculated over how and where his principals should confront one another, working out their motives in terms of these encounters. He could define the particular quality of a scene yet unwritten: "It must be unmitigatedly objective narration—unarrested drama. It must be in a word a close little march of cause and effect." [14] Later in this same *Notebook* entry James issued instructions to himself: "I mustn't interrupt it too much with elucidations or it will be interminable. IT MUST BE AS STRAIGHT AS A PLAY—that is the only way to do."

Speaking of his wasted years in the theatrical experiment, in his notes to *The Spoils,* James thought that he had possibly discovered the key to his narrative fiction: "What I have gathered from it will perhaps have been exactly some such mastery of fundamental statement—or the art and secret of it, of expression, of the sacred mystery of structure." [15] Before long he had come to depend utterly on the notion of "fundamental statement":

> I realise—none too soon—that the *scenic* method is my absolute, my imperative, my *only* salvation. The *march of an action* is the thing for me to, more and more, *attach* myself to: it is the only thing that really, for *me,* at least, will produce L'OEUVRE, and L'OEUVRE is, before God, what I'm going in for.[16]

This "scenic method" was a periodic disciplining of events into a sequence whose logic he could perceive. This sequence was what he called his fundamental statement. It would furnish the motive for a new scene which he could then construct. What he was working out, actually, was the logic of soliloquy (or "picture") and "scene," the sequence of opening and closing the mind of his "intense perceiver." The discipline helped James to isolate and circumscribe the compositional center of a fiction, and to refine the consciousness, and to represent it more completely. He committed himself passionately to this process of analyzing and compressing. His *Notebooks* could scarcely contain him. He strove for the mastery of the art and for the secret of what he called the sacred mystery of structure. The scenario, this intensely structural concept, became a mystique ("Ah, this *divine* conception of one's little masses and periods in the scenic light—as rounded ACTS"), and he was rapturous about it:

> this patient, pious, nobly "vindicating" application of the scenic philosophy and method—I feel as if it still (above *all*, yet) had a great deal to give me, which might carry me as far as I dream! God knows how far—into the flushed and dying day—*that* is! [17]

No wonder his excitement, if "the scenic philosophy and method" could render the entirety of a situation, if it could achieve mass with intensity and manage to sustain it. Certainly the last three novels which he completed did achieve this. *The Wings of the Dove* (1902), *The Ambassadors* (1903), and *The Golden Bowl* (1904) all render the illusion of a dense, intense completeness of the mind. In each of these novels the individual consciousness, under great emotional pressure, is engaged in the process of becoming totally aware of itself and its circumstances. It is a tortuous process. We want it clear, James wrote, but we also want it *thick*; he insisted that thickness inheres in the consciousness that records and amplifies and interprets events. Thickness in order to serve clarity; this was the aim of James's technique, particularly in these three novels.

He continued to experiment with the consciousness as a center of composition. Each of these three novels is a technical achievement beyond its predecessors, although this fact is obscured by the order of their publication. *The Ambassadors* (1903) was published a year after *The Wings of the Dove* (1902), but it was completed earlier. This fact clarifies

James's continuous experimenting, for *The Ambassadors* is told through one consciousness, and the two later novels are told through several.

James considered *The Ambassadors* his finest novel. The mind in it seems exactly to circumscribe the subject of it. The book dramatizes Lambert Strether's mission in Paris, where he has been sent by a wealthy widow to rescue her son from a love affair and fetch him back to New England. Psychologically and dramatically the dominating and sustained event in *The Ambassadors* is Strether's change of mind about his mission, and this is also thematically the novel's subject. Matter and manner are virtually the same thing. The subject of the book is Strether's growing appreciation of a life of self-fulfillment. His imagination responds to the young man whom he has been sent to fetch, and to the young man's mistress, and to all his friends, and to the life of Paris: but the book is the action of his mind.

Every stage of Strether's change of mind is limited in its representation to what Strether is capable of comprehending at that moment. The sum of his responses to the situation is his conception of an ideal of the capacity for full life, which invalidates the commonplace existence he has known, and makes it impossible to complete his mission. The young man does not have the capacity to realize this ideal, and he returns to his home; but this does not alter the reality of the ideal for Strether. In the end the conception itself and the events by which he has arrived at it and tested it have become organic in his appreciation of the irony of his whole situation.

Thickness, to James, was a dimension of clarity. His delineation of a consciousness in *The Ambassadors* has the thickness of a transparent overlay. But he was not yet satisfied. Having achieved this much he continued to experiment with multiple minds. In *The Wings of the Dove* he constructed three compositional centers, attempting a kind of community of consciousness. Like *The Ambassadors* it is a parable about the ethics of sexual acts and commitments. It represents the mutual involvement of an engaged couple and another woman, as a result of the fiancée's scheme to lend her lover to the other woman.

Kate is the fiancée of Merton Densher, and Milly is the other woman. Milly is the quintessence of virtues in the Jamesian world; she has beauty, charm, wealth, and above all an excitement for living, the more urgent because she has an unknown but terminal illness. Kate must be secretly engaged, because Merton Densher has no money and Kate's aunt has ambitious plans for her. In these circumstances, since Milly is already fond of Densher and has not long to live, Kate deliberately reasons that a short marriage, after which Milly would leave her estate to her husband, would then enable Densher to marry Kate in style. Everyone would gain; and it would all be honorable on the face of it, but only if Milly could be kept happily ignorant of the ulterior motive. For their own reasons, Kate's aunt and Milly's chaperone enthusiastically join the conspiracy to marry Milly off to Densher. The crisis occurs when Milly learns of the fraud and, dying, leaves her estate to Densher anyway.

Once again, as so often with James's fiction, a technical problem determined the way the novel turned out. Although Milly's plight was what first engaged James, the growth of Densher's perception is the sustaining event in the novel. The intrigue itself and Milly's beatific response to it cause Densher to develop a conscience. All along Densher is reluctant, loving Kate and pitying Milly and wanting not to dishonor either relationship. His doubts and reappraisals of his agony focus all the conflicts. Although the early notes for the novel, in James's *Notebooks*, are mostly about Milly, they contain the germ of an idea about Densher: he is even-handed; he is in the best sense disinterested, yet there is only sacrifice in it for him, or, as James observed, "some great loss or disaster." Densher began to engage James. As the novel took shape, this character's small dilemma became emphatic;

and still later, after finishing the novel, James felt that he had not sufficiently availed himself of the privilege of seeing it all through Densher's eyes.

James's preface indicates that his developing interest in Densher was really the result of a technical decision over how to represent Milly. James originally saw his subject to be the disintegration of Milly, the ordeal of her consciousness. The conflict would be precisely the young woman facing her catastrophe, her prospect of dying without yet having lived. As James saw it, her whole predicament would have to be prepared for her, ominously defined before she would appear. To accommodate this he would delay her entry, establish successive centers of consciousness—Kate, Densher, and then Milly—through the first half of the novel; and then he would use each of these registers or reflectors by turn in shorter phases to accentuate the complication.

Technically his purpose was to anticipate the "scene" with "pictures" of more than one mind. He wanted to achieve a dense totality of consciousness: "Under certain degrees of pressure, a represented community of vision between several parties to the action where it makes for concentration. . . ." [18] What he achieved in the last half of his novel was the illusion of a continuity of thought from one mind to another, the impression of a collective, expanding consciousness in which individual realizations merge with what is already known. In the intrigue the characters pool their information, each sharing a little to get a little, so that awareness, like some great reservoir, absorbs all soluble responses. It is an eerie medium.

James was not entirely satisfied with the result. Reviewing his accomplishment, in his preface, he still believed in the use of multiple compositional centers, in the complexity of his "elastic but definite system," but he felt he had not given himself enough space to work it all out, with the result that parts of the novel were more extravagant than lucid. So he continued to experiment. *The Wings of the Dove* had posed a new problem in ways and means. He reaffirmed the principle of its structure in *The Golden Bowl* (1904), which also employs more than one center of consciousness; but it employs two instead of three and allows more space for their expansion.

The central situation in *The Golden Bowl* is less complicated than in the previous novel, but it is just as liable to accretion and refinement. A father and a daughter, each newly married, continue their long and loving parent-child relationship while their spouses share a liaison of their own. In his early notes for the novel James talked about a circular movement of the relationships, a "rotary motion" of recriminations and consolations, from one person to another. But he abandoned this concept. Recriminations and consolations are left unsaid. What is pointedly and repeatedly *not* said is what intensifies Maggie Verver's speculations, as she proposes a marriage for her father, as she gropes her way to a knowledge of the intimacy between his wife and her husband, as she comes to understand herself.

The structure James finally employed was a refinement of what he had built in *The Wings of the Dove*. Two intense perceivers, each the object of the other's awareness, render the conflict and its resolution. Less intricate than *The Wings*, this scheme is nevertheless more reflexive. Maggie and her husband each dramatize the story by perceiving the other's situation. As James explained it in his preface, "the thing abides rigidly by its law of showing Maggie Verver at first through her suitor's and her husband's exhibitory vision of her, and of then showing the prince, with at least an equal intensity, through his wife's. . . ." [19]

James explained his use of point of view with a metaphor of opening a door, pointing out that the way it is opened is itself meaningful:

> It is the Prince who opens the door to half our light upon Maggie, just as it is she who opens it to half our light upon

himself; the rest of our impression, in either case, coming straight from the very motion with which that act is performed.

This is the dialectic of the novel; rather, the dialectic *is* the novel. "We see very few persons in 'The Golden Bowl,' but the scheme of the book, to make up for that, is that we shall really see about as much of them as a coherent literary form permits." The illusion of *complete* experience was what he was after: "To play the small handful of values really for all they are worth."

In the aesthetics of Henry James two ideas are bound together: the idea of the rich, fine consciousness of his characters and the idea of the dense complexity necessary to represent this consciousness. In the association of these two ideas his art is of a piece, whole and comprehensive. The evolution of a fine consciousness, dramatically and through conflict, is the fiction's evaluation of the actual world. But a fiction can evaluate the actuality only by explaining itself. By complexity in the whole artifact, by development, by reinforcing and amplifying through indirection, by subtle repetition, the fiction is intended to explain itself. These two ideas together, the presence of a fine awareness in the fiction and the necessary complexity in its evolution, make James's art a moral system.

The moral value of any fiction lies in its clarification of the recognizable, actual world. James held that the proper subject for fiction is not actuality but the *experiencing* of actuality; and experiencing, in his fiction, means recognition of one's own complicity and participation in the turn of events, and therefore his responsibility. This recognition serves no particular moral code. James was emphatic about this. One might as well ask a painter for a moral picture or a sculptor for a moral statue, he said in "The Art of Fiction."

James had no patience with doctrinaire fiction. His preface to *The Portrait* dismisses any "reduction to the inane the dull dispute over the 'immoral' subject and the moral." Rather, he argued, the moral sense of a work of art perfectly depends on the amount of "felt life" in producing it. Complexity is crucial to this intense illusion.

> Here we get exactly the high price of the novel as a literary form—its power not only to . . . range through all the differences of the individual relation to its general subject matter, all the varieties of outlook on life, of disposition to reflect and project, created by conditions that are never the same from man to man . . . but positively to appear more true to its character in proportion as it strains, or tends to burst, with a latent extravagance, its mould.[20]

James was preoccupied with the moral matter of rights and obligations. But he assumed that any given moral system is parochial, limited, intractable, and useless, even dangerous, beyond a certain community of interests. Time and again he dramatized a given consciousness arriving at this particular awareness, of realizing the inadequacy of a moral code assumed to have been durable and ultimate. His fiction therefore involves the conflict of moral codes. "We may strike lights by opposing order to order, one sort to another sort; for in that case we get the correspondences and equivalents that make differences mean something; we get the interest and the tension of disparity where a certain parity may have been in question." [21] Opposing order to order, as he worked it out, inevitably meant juxtaposing different convictions of what constitutes a trespass.

James *used* moral systems to dramatize the experiencing of the individual. *The Ambassadors* precisely illustrates this use. James's preface recalls the germ of his novel to have been in the idea of one man exhorting another to exploit his full capacity for experience ("Live all you can; it's a mistake not to. It doesn't so much matter what you do in particular so long as you have your life."); but James was interested in the development of this germ. What reason might there be for such an exhortation? The reason, he said, would be the false position of the man making this statement according to some basic belief that had become inadequate. What would this false position be? The answer is clear:

> *The* false position, for our belated man of the world . . . was obviously to have presented himself at the gate of that boundless menagerie primed with a moral scheme of the most approved pattern which was yet framed to break down on any approach to vivid facts. . . .[22]

Going back to Strether's passionate advice to "live all you can," James made his point. The moral system to which the hero subscribed has just proven to be inadequate. And Strether's felt sense of inadequacy becomes the core of the novel.

The agents in any drama are interesting, James said, only in proportion to their feeling for their situation. Acute awareness is also an intense emotional state. The person with the capacity to get the most out of what happens to him also conveys the most. So James opted for "the acute, the intense, the complete, in a word—the power to be finely aware and richly responsible." [23] Consciousness in this sense and to this degree is conscience, the highest order of conscience. It is a simultaneous awareness of one's own motives, of some norm by which to evaluate them, and more: the sense that they *ought* to be evaluated.

"Conscience" universally connotes a sense of "oughtness." No matter what authority it invokes, its true nature is substantially what James describes as the power to be finely aware and richly responsible. "Their being finely aware—as Hamlet and Lear, say, are finely aware—*makes* absolutely the intensity of their adventure, gives the maximum sense of what befalls them." In James's fiction, "the maximum sense of what befalls" one is a dramatic value; it is also a moral state of being. In developing an aesthetic principle James also developed a moral corollary.

"The essence of moral energy is to survey the whole field," James said in "The Art of Fiction." So he developed a fiction of intense complexity in the broadest scope. But this caused an excruciating consequence. His whole technique of portraying the true moral awareness produced a continuous system of cerebration which could have no end. "The secret of the world is the tie between the person and the event," Emerson had said; and his system was a dynamic, never-ending reciprocity. James's fictions represent the same condition; refinements of refinements are the necessary consequence of any given situation. ("As soon as I begin to appreciate," he said, "simplification is imperilled.") Given his technique of generating chain reactions of awareness, the only perfect fiction would be a continuum of thought. When we realize that a continuum is a life process we see the special significance of James's preachment, "It is art that *makes* life."

James's work as a whole can be explained by the contagion of subjective reality and how it infected him. Like Hawthorne (who, he said, had inherited a particular world view *minus* the conviction) James began with a particular world view. It was idealism, and he developed a formidable technique to represent it. But in the process he developed this world view *plus* a conviction about it. He discovered the endless possibilities of adapting a playwright's methods to the narrative form (all of which he called "the sacred mystery of structure"); and his technique became, in his later novels, the means of representing his own personal system of reality.

As author he lived exactly with the consciousness he represented, or as close to it as he could manage; and the intensity of that consciousness was his own, as he tried to control and confine its myriad possibilities of awareness. James ended up like the romantic cosmologists, those poets engaged in constructing continuous, organic worlds. "Remember that your first duty is to be as complete as possible—to make as perfect a work," he wrote at the end of "The Art of Fiction," and he spent the rest of his life building the technique to represent a continuum of thought.

CHAPTER EIGHT

The Poetic Dialogues of William Faulkner

The romantic cosmology provides a reference for William Faulkner's major novels. It helps to explain the function of mythology in these novels, and also the fact that they so often proceed like poems. Faulkner wrote his own version of the Emersonian poet, the embattled individual searching for a principle to explain the known world. He *used* the subject of the mind in the act of finding what would suffice and constructing analogies in order to see what scheme of cause and effect—if any—might emerge. The scheme that emerges in Faulkner's major novels is usually a metaphor of an encompassing order which both extends and contains the character who has conceived it, as in the case of the romantic cosmology.

The poetic property of Faulkner's novels is the way they develop an idea primarily by repeating elements of it. The elements are past events which are identified only by sensations and fragmented impressions or recollections; and these sensations or impressions are organized as images in a poem. They are variously repeated; they are agitated into patterns whereby they accumulate symbolic value to the character that identifies them. Faulkner's novels are insistently dramatic, emphasizing the mind laboring to control the elements of some encompassing scheme.

Thanks to a formidable and painstaking body of criticism, the mythology in Faulkner's novels is by now in the public domain. His cosmos is Yoknapatawpha County, a mythical part of Mississippi with a population of three Negroes to every two whites. Yoknapatawpha County is a singular version of a determining force called the South, which is a history, a condition, and a state of mind. The condition is a matter of history: of the Civil War and the era of so-called reconstruction, during which the property and dignity and health and even life itself were taken from the defeated Confederates. The condition of defeat and disorder has bred a pervading state of mind, involving doubt, recrimination, pride, hurt, and shock.

This defeat can be explained by the myth, in its broadest aspect, of a traditional, humanistic society—as George Marion O'Donnell first pointed out. But the terrible extent of this defeat is explained by the myth's aspect of divine retribution—as Malcolm Cowley first explained. This latter aspect of the whole myth (which I will refer to, for convenience, simply as the myth) is a version of the covenant theology of the Old Testament, according to which God repeatedly made firm contracts with mankind which men repeatedly disregarded, thereby necessitating God's punishment. According to the mythical covenant of Faulkner's fictional world, God gave the land to the white men in return for which the white men would work it and harvest its abundance. But the white men broke this contract, importing slaves to work the land, and God punished the white men by cursing them with the enduring consequences of this slavery.

This myth of divine, categorical retribution is an ingenious and constant explanation of cause, but it is also a distorting and determining force to the characters who acknowledge it yet without understanding their own culpability. It is important to remember that this myth has been abstracted from the fictions that generated and considered and evaluated it as some monolithic and extrinsic force in the world. This is the peculiar service that a great deal of Faulkner criticism has rendered, approximating as it does what the characters in the Yoknapatawpha novels and stories seem to believe. In varying degree to these characters—the ones who belong to the traditional, humanistic society—the force of circumstance *is* this massive, intractable myth of divine retribution.

One way or another this myth limits and determines the characters in Faulkner's major novels: *The Sound and the Fury* (1929), *Light in August* (1932), and *Absalom, Absalom!* (1936), and in "The Bear" (1942), as well as the characters in the stories closely related to these. These four titles, and a lesser novel, *Intruder in the Dust* (1948), reveal a typical relation between the character and the myth, which is the attempt to put the myth into one's own words and thereby to explain one's heritage.

The most explicit statement of the myth is the story interpolated in *Light in August*, the story told to Joe Christmas by his white mistress, Joanna Burden. It begins with her whisky-drinking Calvinist grandfather from New England, and it features her father's sermon to her about whites and Negroes when he shows her the anonymous carpetbagger graves of her brother and her grandfather. The sense of her father's sermon is that the black man's presence is God's curse on the white man. It is a white man's myth about a white man's God, since obviously no Negro (any more than a white man) would regard himself as a curse. The myth itself is sick.

This interpolated narrative occurs precisely in the middle of *Light in August;* it is an overstatement of the theme of this novel. A more distorted overstatement occurs in *Intruder in the Dust*, when Gavin Stevens—more spokesman than character—alludes to the Negro as Sambo: the little black boy persecuted by the tigers, who submits so categorically to their wishes that they devour one another, while he survives to butter his pancakes with their remains.

The significance of this myth in most cases is the way the character has to work out his personal version of it. He must relive the particular trauma of his own in order to be able to live with himself. In terms of psychoanalysis he must abreact.

This tortuous cerebral process Faulkner represents poetically, whereby a character painfully recalls the fragments of some shocking event. The poetry lies in the various and distorted repetition of fragments, a process which continues until a new, whole realization of one's self emerges.

In most of Faulkner's fictions three components are apparent and related: one is the character's groping toward some immense understanding; another is the oppressive presence of the past, which the myth represents; and the third is the various repetition of fragments in some reinforcing pattern. In most of his fictions this repetition relates the character's groping to the oppressive presence that he is trying to penetrate and understand. The latest of the fictions that I have mentioned, *Intruder in the Dust*, usefully illustrates the way in which Faulkner made the repeated elements correlate all of a fiction's cause and effect. It will serve to show an organizing principle of his other fictions.

Intruder is a detective story with implications. It begins with a corpse and a murder suspect; the corpse was once a white man and the suspect is a Negro, Lucas Beauchamp, in jail awaiting trial. In order to clear the suspect before he is lynched, a sixteen-year-old boy must unravel the complicated details of a murder, which involve exhuming one corpse and exchanging it with another. *Intruder* is as complicated as any conventional detective story; more so, because it is not always clear about what point of view is reporting the action. Yet this novel can be understood without the conventional re-telling. The repeated images and attitudes reveal everything that is needed to understand the relations between events, the reasons for the events, and their consequent significance.

The crucial event in solving the crime occurs when two boys and an old lady dig up a grave at night to see what is buried there. This occurs in Chapter 4, nearly halfway through the novel, and thereafter is recalled by fragmentary passing allusions. Each new allusion to "two children and an old woman" (Chapter 10) adds new significance to the event: one of the boys is a Negro; the old woman is white, a spinster, the godmother of the suspect's first child; their trespass on the grave, if discovered, would bring violent retaliation from the murder victim's kin; and from the murderer, too, since they discover a corpse which is not supposed to be there. But they are dedicated to the ghoulish chore. "It took an old woman and two children for that, to believe truth for no other reason than that it was true. . . ." (Chapter 6).

A second group of repeated fragments clarifies the reason why "three amateurs, an old white spinster and a white child and a black one" (Chapter 10), are so dedicated and so involved in the first place. The trouble all along has been Lucas Beauchamp's *"refusing to mean Mister to anybody even when he says it"* (Chapter 3). Eleven references in four chapters repeat variations of this indictment. *"If he would just be a nigger first, just for one second, one little infinitesimal second"* (Chapter 2). He has been asking all his life for the fix he is in: "A damned highnosed impudent Negro who even if he wasn't a murderer had been about to get if not what he deserved at least exactly what he had spent the sixty-odd years of his life asking for. . . ." (Chapter 7).

An overstatement of these allusions to Beauchamp's stubbornness occurs (in Chapter 3) when the speaker says of another white man: "He has nothing against what he calls niggers"; and he continues: "All he requires is that they act like niggers. Which is exactly what Lucas is doing; blew his top and murdered a white man—which Mr. Lilley is probably convinced all Negroes want to do—and now the white people will take him out and burn him, all regular and in order and themselves acting exactly as he is convinced Lucas would wish them to act:

> like white folks; both of them observing implicitly the rules: the nigger acting like a nigger and the white folks acting like white folks and no real hard feelings on either side . . . once the fury is over; in fact Mr. Lilley would probably be one of the first to contribute cash money toward

> Lucas' funeral and the support of his widow and children if he had them."

A third series of allusions intensifies the white boy's motive for trying to save Lucas. *"So this is what that plate of meat and beans is going to cost me"* (Chapter 3). The boy has a past: "Then to be foiled here by the fact that four years ago a child whose presence in the world he was not even aware of fell into a creek in the presence of that same Negro insomnabulist" (Chapter 10); Lucas had taken him home and dried him out and fed him, and then he had disdained the coins the boy had offered for his meal. And now the boy has to keep reconstructing the incident: *"Maybe he will remind me of that goddam plate of collards and side meat"* (Chapter 3).

Just by being himself in these circumstances this boy has arrived at his present predicament. So has Lucas. Each has collaborated with events in such a way as to be responsible for consequences beyond his own complicity with circumstances. These realizations are conveyed by a sustained dialogue, partly between the boy and his uncle, Gavin Stevens, and partly within the boy's consciousness. It holds for everyone: this reciprocity of person and event has tangled the destinies of white men and Negroes, and determined them all. The theme of the dialogue is simply that mutual interdependence of white and Negro is inevitable and bewildering and terrible.

But on this larger subject of white man and Negro the novel becomes merely shrill; the repeated fragments that convey the idea of reciprocity recur less in the boy's mind and progressively more in the uncle's. The fragments grow into monologues; realizations are replaced by concluded opinions, as the uncle sermonizes about whites and Negroes. The more didactic he becomes, the more confusing he sounds. He keeps repeating the same circular argument: the Negro was our fault; we must be allowed to help him ourselves; the righteous Northerners will only divide and destroy the whites; anyway, maybe the Negro does not want freedom; but keeping him in this condition is terrible; the Negro was our fault; but we must be allowed to help him ourselves; and so on and on. Stevens's confusion might have become a dramatic event, but it turns out to be merely unassimilated opinion; and this stunts the book.

Despite its limits, however, *Intruder* has the same properties that enable Faulkner's greater fictions. Its point of view is dynamic. It moves in and out of the boy's mind, continuously changing the focus of his predicament in keeping with his own realizations. This point of view is a scheme that allows several voices to express different awarenesses of the situation: the boy's voice, and the voice of the boy's unspoken apprehensions, and the uncle's public voice, and the voice of another, nameless presence. This nameless voice speaks with the intensity of the boy and the authority of his uncle; and it can even rhapsodize the "ultimate cosmolined doom" of the door of a prison cell.

Until it degenerates, the governing pattern of the shifting point of view is the dialogue between nephew and uncle. Ostensibly educating the nephew, it has all the significance of the primitive tribal relationship between the two closest males related by blood—there being no father in evidence. Faulkner exploited this primitive family relationship in "The Bear," between Ike and his older cousin. And the dialogue between Shreve and Quentin prevails in *Absalom, Absalom!*

In these two fictions, *Absalom, Absalom!* and "The Bear," a dialogue organizes the repeated sensations and recollections of separate minds into a shared and continuing experience in which the reader necessarily participates. But the organizing dialogue was one of Faulkner's later developments. He preceded it, in earlier fictions, by representing separate voices in succession, notably and stunningly in *The Sound and the Fury*. This book is a sequence of impressions of four separate days, refracted by four points of view proceeding by stages from the unrelated impressions of an idiot to the rational narrative of the omniscient author. Two of these separate voices, Benjy the idiot and Quentin his brother, in Parts 1 and 2 of the novel, express fragmented recollections and sensations; and many of the repeated, unrelated images in the mind of the idiot become subjects in the consciousness of Quentin. As these sensations and recollections accumulate, the voice of Brother Jason, in Part 3, and finally of the author, in Part 4, present an increasingly ordered and representational view of the Compson family.

The compelling fact about *The Sound and the Fury* is that its world has no counterpart in actuality. The book begins with impressions of a world like an exploded diagram whose components are held in space, piecemeal and ready for assembly; and successive minds assemble these components into a new order. Some fifteen years after he had finished the novel Faulkner wrote an appendix which is like a rational set of directions for assembling these parts thematically.

The appendix is all about the myth of the degenerating dynasty. Its brief biographies of the Compson ancestors, over a period of nearly two hundred and fifty years, trace the disposition of the land from the first purchase of a square mile of territory to the present time, when there is nothing left but a house lot and a cemetery plot. But the book does not need this appendix (which is another fiction, anyway) to convey a felt sense of the way things are in this particular world. There is no rational theme, no evolving statement of attitude; instead, there is a developing sense of the *end* of things. Fragmented images refracted by separate minds accrete and confirm the absurdity of logical consequence. And there is no stop to it; time and duration are the same. This closed and separate world is a continuum of degeneration.

A continuum of some sort is the only inference we can draw from the images in the idiot's mind. His sensations of present experience and recollections of the past are interchangeable and of equal value or nonvalue. Looking for a quarter in the grass, listening to the golfers in the pasture hail a caddy, burning his finger on the candle of a birthday cake, walking in the cold to deliver a letter, swimming in the brook, smelling the burning leaves, and seeing the mourners at a funeral are not discrete units of experience in this particular consciousness. "I begin to cry" and "Caddie smelled like leaves" have the same significance.

The repeated images in Part 2, in Quentin's consciousness, insist on a continuum, explicitly denying any value of time: the college bells announcing hourly obligations, unheeded; the smashing of a watch which goes on ticking; a shop full of clocks all telling different times at once. The narrative that contains these images is simple enough. Quentin Compson leaves his college dormitory, rides a trolley to the end of the line, and spends most of the day walking on his shadow. His state of mind is totally disconnected from the present. Quentin's recollections are so intense that he relives a past episode without even realizing that he has imposed it on the present, and this confusion involves him in a series of absurd misunderstandings. Quentin conceived of incest with his sister Caddie, and so he reconstructs a past experience, of losing a fight with Caddie's lover, in order to validate the incest which never happened but which he has always wanted to claim. Meanwhile, in the narrative present, the father of a little girl, thinking that Quentin wants to rape her, has him arrested; and Quentin discovers himself fighting, and being beaten by, an acquaintance whom he has happened to meet. The present episodes parody the past which Quentin, at the time, is intensely reliving.

There are fewer repeated images in Parts 3 and 4, but even these emphasize the sense of frustration and degeneration. Part 3 begins and ends "once a bitch always a bitch," and reviews the failure of Jason Compson to cope with his niece, his mother, or the Negress who has always run the household. "Once a bitch always a bitch" sums up his attitude. "I know I am just a burden to you," his mother says over and over and over, as he uses her to build a neat, mean tyranny over his niece and her income. "Once a bitch always a bitch." Benjy cries continuously, and Jason's indictment stands.

Part 4 continues the narrative, in which Jason pursues his niece to retrieve the money that she has stolen back from him. "I've seed de first en de last," says the timeless Negress in the kitchen where the crazy clock is perched. It strikes five times at eight o'clock and its ticktocking is likened to the dry pulse of the decaying house itself. "I seed de beginnin', en now I sees de endin'," says Dilsey. It is surprising how clearly this ambience of a closed world is conveyed without logical connectives. Here are simply four versions of the dissipation of consequence. Each has supplied local substance to the same recurring idea, which is the destroying presence of the past in a community of minds no longer capable of proportioning events.

The Sound and the Fury represents a real world of its own. The process of *creating* such a subjective and self-consistent world is the subject of *Absalom, Absalom!* and of "The Bear." These two fictions deliberately and explicitly represent the experience of a character's creating a new, separate world by abreacting, by reliving under great pressure what he thinks was his own past. Of all Faulkner's fictions, *Absalom, Absalom!* (1936) most closely resembles the romantic cosmology, and can be understood in these terms. It is about the desperate labor of Quentin Compson and his Harvard roommate Shreve—a Southerner and a Canadian—trying to construct an order of history which will explain itself and show cause for all the tangled events that happened or might have happened or might never have happened.

Quentin and Shreve finally manage to create a fictional world, a closed system of cause and effect which for them becomes a reality. The substance of their fictional world is a series of events which occurred two generations before them in the life of Thomas Sutpen, who had attempted and failed to found a dynasty. Both Quentin and Shreve assume that reconstructing the Sutpen saga will explain the South, which is Quentin's heritage. Their struggle to build a theory of events occurs in the form of a dialogue, and the dialogue creates the illusion of a single consciousness at work. Although their attitudes sharply differ, their awarenesses have somehow fused under the tremendous emotional pressure.

This illusion of Quentin and Shreve as a single identity grows as the dialogue proceeds, and later in the novel (Chapter 8) the illusion becomes explicit. "They stared—glared—at one another. It was Shreve speaking, though for the slight difference which the intervening degrees of latitude had inculcated in them (differences not in tone or pitch but of turns of phrase and usage of words), it might have been either of them and was in a sense both:

> both thinking as one, the voice which happened to be speaking the thought only the thinking becomes audible, vocal; the two of them creating between them, out of the rag-tag and bob-ends of old tales and talking, people who perhaps had never existed at all anywhere, who, shadows, were shadows not of flesh and blood which had lived and died but shadows in turn of what were (to one of them at least, to Shreve) shades too, quiet as the visible murmur of their vaporizing breath."

This statement has authority partly because Quentin is already convinced of it. Earlier in the dialogue (in Chapter 7), with Quentin straining to piece together some of his father's evidence about Sutpen, we find this realization: " 'Yes,' Quentin said. 'The two children' thinking *Yes. Maybe we are both Father. Maybe nothing happens once and is finished.*"

Quentin begins to see that there is more than just the identity of two present minds. He sees a continuity of Shreve's mind and his own with the minds of his father and grandfather, and he develops an elaborate metaphor to express this continuity of awareness. It is a metaphor of two pools of water joined by a channel, so that a disturbance in one pool causes a continuous agitation that reaches the other pool. It is an apt metaphor of the whole book.

> *Maybe happen is never once but like ripples maybe on water after the pebble sinks, the ripples moving on, spreading, the pool attached by a narrow umbilical water-cord to the next pool which the first pool feeds, has fed, did feed, let this second pool contain a different temperature of water, a different molecularity of having seen, felt, remembered, reflect in a different tone the infinite unchanging sky, it doesn't matter: that pebble's watery echo whose fall it did not even see moves across its surface too at the original ripple-space, to the old ineradicable rhythm* thinking *Yes, we are both Father.*

Quentin sees even more implication in this continuous identity of minds, past and present: "Or *maybe Father and I are both Shreve, maybe it took Father and me both to make Shreve or Shreve and me both to make Father or maybe Thomas Sutpen to make all of us.*"

The shared consciousness of the past is what joins Shreve and Quentin as they build a fictional world. The substance of their world is a series of eight events that occurred between 1833 and 1869. Thomas Sutpen arrived in Yoknapatawpha County in 1833 with a deed to a hundred acres of land traded from the Chickasaw Indians, and he began to build a mansion with the labor of Negro slaves. In 1838 he married Ellen Coldfield against her wishes but according to the wishes of her father. In 1839 the marriage yielded a son, Henry, and in 1840 a daughter, Judith. In 1860 Sutpen forbade his daughter's marriage to Charles Bon, his son by another marriage; and Henry Sutpen renounced his birthright in favor of Bon. In 1865, at the gates of Sutpen's Hundred, Henry killed his half brother because of Bon's intention to marry Judith. In 1869 Sutpen was killed by the grandfather of a common white girl on whom he had sired a female child.

These events mark Sutpen's abortive design to found a dynasty. Their significance is partly determined by two pieces of evidence. One of them is doubtful: Sutpen's discovery that Bon, the child of his first marriage, was part Negro. If so, this would explain why Sutpen had forbidden him to marry Judith. An incestuous marriage was no problem at all compared with miscegenation, which would also explain why Henry had killed his half brother. The other piece of evidence concerns Rosa Coldfield, who was Sutpen's sister-in-law. Sutpen had proposed to sire a child upon Rosa and to marry her if the child were male, which outraged and mortified her. Rosa has been the primary source of information about Sutpen, but this unfortunate event has undoubtedly distorted her testimony. Along with these major events in Sutpen's saga, other fragmented episodes come to light, about Sutpen before his arrival in Yoknapatawpha County, and about his progeny after his death, some thirty episodes over a period of seventy-seven years.

The sequence in which all this evidence comes to light is eccentric and distorted. New fragments of evidence continually interrupt chronology and modify whatever Quentin and Shreve have already found out. The first five sections, roughly the first half of the novel, present the testimony of Rosa Coldfield, now an old woman, in a sequence determined not by chronology but by her own agitation. In the last four sections of the novel Quentin and Shreve piece out this testimony by hearsay evidence, and try to evaluate it all by analysis, surmise, deduction, and outright invention.

This hearsay evidence comes from Quentin's father who is objective but limited to the occasional observations made over the years by Quentin's grandfather. And Quentin already knows from Rosa more about some aspects of Sutpen than his grandfather did. Anyway, even without Rosa this knowledge of the South is already bone deep in Quentin:

> because you knew it all already, had learned, absorbed it already without the medium of speech, somehow from hav-

ing been born and living beside it, with it, as children will
and do: so that what your father was saying did not tell you
anything so much as it struck, word by word, the resonant
strings of remembering.

(This occurs in a long interior monologue in Chapter 6.) But
this instinctive remembering is not enough and too much—
both. Everything Quentin knows or learns about Sutpen is
subject to amendment. He and Shreve cannot evaluate Sutpen's "design" and its disastrous consequences without having the whole story, and the whole story is what they must re-
create—and even create—for themselves.

The fragmented narrative past is contained within the dialogue between Quentin and Shreve which occurs in the narrative present. This dialogue governs the entire situation of
Quentin's attempt to reconstruct or create a plausible order
of events. He labors desperately to understand all this in
order to understand himself. Nothing less will suffice.

Here is the problem of the typical character in Henry
James's fiction, who can discover what he is only by knowing
his circumstances; but the problem in this case is compounded, for the circumstances are in the past, not in the
present, and they are knowable—if at all—only through distorted evidence. For Quentin the past tense is ever-present
tension. And not just for Quentin, but for Shreve as well.
Throughout the novel neither character exists apart from the
past which they jointly conjure up.

Shreve shapes the dialogue. He asks the questions that
force Quentin to retell what he knows, what he has somehow
always known about the South. Quentin's labored repetition
accretes new meaning. And Shreve sums up, overstates, and
oversimplifies. "So he just wanted a grandson," Shreve says
(in Chapter 7). "That was all he was after. Jesus, the South
is fine, isn't it. It's better than the theatre, isn't it. It's better
than Ben Hur, isn't it. No wonder you have to come away
now and then, isn't it." And his distortions force Quentin to
rebut. Time and again Shreve gets it all wrong or too pain-

fully right, and so they plunge into the history once more. Shreve's astonishment and disbelief turn to commitment, and he leads the way in elaborating and refining the Sutpen fiction. He devises a motive for Charles Bon (a mission to blackmail or torture his father and half brother for their renunciations of him). Bon really loved Judith, Shreve reasons, but would have renounced her if his father would only have recognized him. As Shreve devises Bon's strategy, he begins to identify with Bon, and Quentin takes Henry's part. The extent of their fiction is apparent in that neither Quentin nor Shreve can substantiate the fact that Bon ever knew he was a Negro in the first place. But no matter, the present dialogue between Shreve and Quentin becomes a concentric repetition of the conflict between Bon and Henry. ("Maybe nothing ever happens once and is finished. Maybe happen is never once but like ripples maybe on the water after the pebble sinks, the ripples moving on. . . .")

The dialogue is irresolvable; it settles nothing. Quentin knows too much, Shreve knows too quickly; and the reciprocity of Quentin's paralyzing knowledge and Shreve's tabloid judgment is the only reality that they can build. Shreve concludes with an inventory of Sutpen's dynasty, ending up with only one survivor, an idiot Negro, Jim Bond; and he prophesies that the Jim Bonds are going to conquer the Western Hemisphere. But this definitive statement defines nothing more than a new beginning, for Shreve goes on to say, "Now I want you to tell me just one thing more. Why do you hate the South?" His impossible question guarantees an interminable dialogue.

Faulkner's other poetic dialogue is in "The Bear." This five-part fiction is an episodic narrative interrupted by the dialogue which also contains episodes. This dialogue obliquely comments on the narrative it interrupts by furnishing a history to explain it. The narrative, contained in the first three parts and the last part of "The Bear," concerns the ritual of the hunt and Ike McCaslin's initiation into the ritual. These episodes begin when Ike is ten years old and first joins the hunting party of Major de Spain and General Compson which travels to the woods every November and every June to hunt the bear. The narrative (like *Intruder in the Dust*) explains its own significance by the various repetition of a few images, mostly as they would occur to Ike.

Alone, the boy tracks and finds the bear; he begins to learn what the rules are; he learns from the bear and an old Indian-Negro. The episodes of the hunt and Ike's novitiate continue for six more years until Boon Hogganbeck finally kills the bear without any rules at all.

By a process of *qualifying repetition,* and with the passage of time, the images become symbolic: in Part 1, a crooked paw print of the bear; and the assertion that the dog has not yet been found that can stop Old Ben. Then a series of encounters with the bear, in Part 2, occur after Sam Fathers has trapped a wild dog and trained him to hunt. They name the dog Lion. "So he should have hated and feared Lion" is one repeated element. The dog has yellow eyes, "a cold and almost impersonal malignance like some natural force." Boy and bear have some mysterious affinity. "So he should have hated and feared Lion." Boon says, "He's the dog that's going to stop Old Ben and hold him." But not yet. Boon Hogganbeck shoots at the bear point-blank five times and misses. In Part 3 the bear with the crooked print is still waiting for them. Meanwhile, in Memphis, Boon gets drunk and shoots at a Negro; shoots five times and misses him. The bear is still in the woods. Hunting for him, Boon shoots at a buck; shoots five times and misses. In the last encounter Lion, "blinking his sleepy topaz eyes," is taken into the woods to find "the head bear." He does; but Boon kills the bear, climbs up on his back, and kills him with a knife.

The dialogue begins at this point. It dramatizes a situation that is almost the same as in *Absalom, Absalom!*: two characters, two minds in the narrative present, both laboring to understand the dense confusion of past events, trying to discover some plausible cause or sequence by which to explain it all. They are Ike McCaslin and his older cousin McCaslin Edmonds. Here is another version of that primitive tribal relationship which approximates the bond between father and son. Ike creates the occasion for the dialogue because of his intention to repudiate his heritage. "You can't repudiate," says McCaslin, and this sets off a tortuous process of recollection and appraisal of the South, that continuing state of mind which extends and contains them both.

Ike McCaslin and McCaslin Edmonds share a dramatic relationship comparable to Shreve and Quentin. They seem to comprise a continuous unseparated consciousness: one with the other, and both together with the persons and events of the past. The dialogue occurs in the commissary of the McCaslin plantation. As it proceeds, speech and thought are not always clearly separated, and one speaker often answers the other's thoughts. The drama correlates a spastic continuity of impressions and chantlike recollections which seem to be imagined and could be claimed by either speaker. It could be a dialogue between the ego and the alter ego. Ike and his cousin share the name McCaslin, and in the paragraphs which designate a change of speakers, Faulkner exploits this identical name to reinforce the impression that the whole dialogue is a single, shared developing awareness.

The primary documents of the South, the metaphorical world that contains Ike and that he wants to repudiate, are the commissary ledgers of the McCaslin plantation (described at the beginning of the dialogue), recording

> the slow outward trickle of food and supplies and equipment which returned each fall as cotton made and ginned and sold (two threads frail as truth and impalpable as equators yet cable-strong to bind for life them who made the cotton to the land their sweat fell on). . . .

The ledgers were begun before the Civil War, and they record the trespasses of old Carothers McCaslin on his slaves:

> . . . the older ledgers clumsy and archaic in size and shape,
> on the yellowed pages of which were recorded in the faded
> hand of his father Theophilus and his uncle Amodeus dur-
> ing the two decades before the Civil War, the manumission
> in title at least of Carothers McCaslin's slaves.

Ike is the direct male descendant of old Carothers McCaslin,
and the trespasses of the old man are what he really wants to
repudiate.

These old ledgers reveal that Carothers McCaslin sired
a daughter on one of his slaves and then sired another child
on his daughter. The child of his child has had three more
children, and these were Carothers' grandchildren and also
his great-grandchildren. By way of acknowledgment he be-
queathed a thousand-dollar legacy on each of the three which
has never been paid. Ike wants to repay it and thereby relinquish his inherited responsibility. But this is only part of the
legacy which Ike wants to relinquish. The whole of it is the
complex state of mind, the metaphorical South.

Organized like a poem, this dialogue repeats and amplifies
the evidence of the inheritance and its burden. The argument between Ike and McCaslin involves the entries in the
old ledgers which are the fragmented images of the past, and
it crisscrosses these images with present events and with the
other recollections of the hunt for the bear. The argument in
the ledger entries between Ike's father and his uncle over
what to do with the free slaves points up the present disagreement between Ike and his cousin over what to do about
his heritage.

The dialogue juxtaposes the impressions of different
epochs in the past, for example, the images of Uncle Hubert
Beauchamp's legacy to Ike. They are nothing but I.O.U.'s
which Uncle Hubert put in a tin cup to acknowledge the
money that he had put aside for Ike in a silver cup, and
then borrowed back for himself (including the silver cup).
Scattered images are all concentrated into the argument that
ranges back and forth in time from the pluperfect past of

Yoknapatawpha County to the present moment of imperfect awareness.

Chronology means nothing in this search for sense. The logic of events is in the repetition of the images. Their repetition amplifies and intensifies the ludicrous, terrifying breach of faith with self and land and God which is Ike's legacy. The repetition clarifies the impossibility of his ever renouncing, since his awareness of all that has happened makes him a part of it. By degrees he learns how much it takes to compound a man, how complex and refined the circumstances of his past which make him what he is. "And it took Him a bear and an old man and four years just for you," McCaslin says. "And it took you fourteen years to reach that point and about that many, maybe more, for Old Ben, and more than seventy for Sam Fathers, and you are just one. How long then? How long?" The unanswerable question recalls Quentin Compson's realization: *"maybe it took Father and me both to make Shreve or Shreve and me both to make Father or maybe Thomas Sutpen to make all of us."*

To sum up. These fictions all represent a characteristic emotional crisis: the extremity of a person who cannot tolerate his situation and who cannot even define what it is he cannot tolerate. He is desperate, possibly hysterical. In order to be able to live, to relate himself to the world around him, he must recognize and acknowledge whatever it is or was in his life that has caused his paralyzing extremity, but he must first discover what it is he has to acknowledge. As his crisis becomes more intense, sooner or later some present event forces him to act or react; and he sees in what he does a connection of sorts with his past. He sees it in spite of himself; and in spite of himself he tries to work out some cause or explanation of events. He participates vicariously in the past until some seizure forces him to live through it all again. This is the crisis of his crisis, and if he survives the shock he becomes a different person.

This shocking confrontation with one's past has a particular relation, in Faulkner's fiction, to the intractable myth of divine retribution. From his fragmentary and distorted knowledge of his past the character is aware that he is somehow responsible for events that have occurred, but without knowing why or how he has been to blame. Working out some plausible relation between responsibility and culpability involves him in trying to put the pervasive myth into his own terms.

He must get it into his own words, and this is how the poetry occurs: the agitation of images in the mind, repeating them again and again, developing a meaning and developing intensity with every variation. This agitating of fragments into a whole pattern, in Faulkner's fiction, is a particular instance of the romantic cosmologies in general. The problem that really organizes the cosmologies is a ceaseless search for a way to say what would be an idea if it could only be said. Only to the extent that he can understand how the past has determined him can the character be free of it. But only to the extent that he can say it can he understand it.

Whether or not a given character accomplishes the entire process of reliving an experience, and some of them do not, the process itself is nevertheless one way for the reader to understand him. This is because it is so prevalent in Faulkner's fictional world. There is an analogy here to Hawthorne's novels and tales. The progress from a state of sin to confession and penitence and then to regeneration is such a common reference in Hawthorne's fiction that it is a measure of almost any one of his characters, no matter how far along in the progression he gets. So, too, in Faulkner's stories. Ike McCaslin, for example, manages to purge his obsession. At the beginning of his dialogue with his cousin, Ike must renounce his heritage, without clearly knowing what it is. He has to relive the ludicrous experience of having tried to pay Carothers's debt to Fonsiba and her husband, which would not change their lives or his obligation. But by virtue of his having tried to buy them off, as he now sees it, Ike has somehow made the old man's burden his own as well; and so now he can live with it.

Later in the dialogue Ike relives another commitment he has made. While being seduced by his wife he has promised to return to the land; being male and husband, he could not repudiate his heritage. The final episode in "The Bear" (Part 5) is revealing (it occurred before the dialogue took place, but Ike could not have understood it until afterward); and this final episode measures Ike's change. He discovers Boon Hogganbeck in a clearing in the woods with squirrels all around him and his rifle on the ground in pieces; and Boon, hammering on some broken part of his rifle, ludicrously screams, "Get out of here! Don't touch them! Don't touch a one of them! They're mine!" Boon's concept of ownership owns him; he is not even capable of beginning to know what has happened to him or what is wrong. But Ike, having harrowed himself, does know and can understand. Boon is one measure of Ike's development.

The two versions of Quentin Compson in two different novels represent the same harrowing process. Although the precise nature of the resolution is less decisive in either case than in Ike's, the process nonetheless occurs. Quentin in *Absalom, Absalom!* cannot relive the actual events, since he did not experience them in the first place, and since they may not have happened anyway. So he creates a fiction, makes the situation his and lives it through, to exorcise a nameless terror. But the book records no resolution of his trauma. The Quentin of *The Sound and the Fury* also struggles with the burden of a guilt which he cannot identify until he re-experiences the beating that his sister's lover gave him. The book records no resolution; he dies by circumstantial evidence. Only when they are considered together do these two versions of Quentin present a resolution, and then only with the reader's help.

The exorcising of the past explains still other characters in these novels. Goodhue Coldfield, in *Absalom, Absalom!* never progressed beyond his paralyzing awareness. He nailed himself up in the attic and died. But the harrowing process does occur, in *Light in August*, in the character of the minister, Gail Hightower. He has withdrawn from the world because his grandfather was shot, not, as supposed, in leading a cavalry charge but while robbing a hen house. Not until Hightower can conjure up this humiliating contradiction of his ideal can he return to reality and commit himself to the present. His attempt to save Joe Christmas is too little, too late, and ludicrous; but it *is* a commitment.

I began by saying that Faulkner wrote his own versions of the Emersonian poet. This typically harrowed character in Faulkner's fiction is the Emersonian poet in spite of himself. His situation corresponds to Emerson's later doctrine of the determinism in which the individual is bound to try to think his way through "unpenetrated cause." But Emerson's earlier theory also clarifies the miseries of this character. Emerson believed that the poet's ideal reality is ineffable until and unless it is acted out; the poet could unfix the land and the sea, rearrange actuality into a new order only by somehow experiencing this new order. The idea is not real until the poet perceives it, but to perceive it is to live it. Here is the dreadful plight of the practical idealist. The ideal is not a reality at all until it is workable in the actual world in which the poet finds himself. It is a harrowing situation.

Paradigm Five

As Santayana explained it, poetry is a strategy of escape and return, the idea being to suppose a new environment, to illuminate and clarify actual experience. But some poems insist on the new environment to such an extent that their clarifying purpose is obscure.

By its nature, any poem (or any fiction) is a theory of events, but when the events themselves are theories of events the poem is already once removed from the experience it is attempting to clarify. Such a poem or fiction may turn out to reveal something other than what its author intended. Such is the case with two cosmologies: E. A. Poe's *Eureka* (1848), which he called a poem, and *The Education of Henry Adams* (1907), an autobiography. Both works propose a definitive relation between mankind and his total environment. They are both intensely cerebral, and superficially they are alike.

Eureka and *The Education* are both theories of theories. Each one appropriates certain mathematical explanations of the physical universe to its own use, and incorporates these theories into a supertheory of the universe involving mankind. The supertheory is of course metaphorical. Specifically each cosmology proposes a dynamic system that relates the human being to the physical universe in terms of motion: the motion of thought and the motion of natural energy. *The Education* dramatizes the making of a metaphor, but the most convincing aspect of *Eureka* is that Poe had to write it.

Poe spent much of his life trying to construct an imaginary world around himself. He finally created such a world in *Eureka*, which is almost unreadable. It epitomizes dozens of murky pieces by Poe that do not justify all the criticism that has been lavished on them. Part of the fascination of his writing is that many parts of it are apparently unrelated; his work eludes any comprehensive and convincing explanation of why it is what it is. But *Eureka* provides a convincing overview of the man and his work, once you see it is the culmination of many experiments. This explanation attracts me because it can afford to admit Poe's poor writing and his limitations as well as his skills; it acknowledges the fact that he often did not know how to say what he wanted to say.

Eureka is dense, obtuse, and precious. It has almost no relation to fact—other than the fact that Poe finally managed to write it, yet it explains a great deal about most of the other things Poe wrote, and why he wrote them. They are what they are because he was trying to work out an organic cosmos that would extend and contain E. A. Poe. Many of his fictions are abstruse and self-indulgent because he could not often dramatize his idea. Some of these fictions were actually fragmentary sketches of the organic theory of being that he was finally able to state in *Eureka*, and his poems, his tales, and his critical theory all variously anticipated it. They are characteristically about a man trying and failing to make the actual world serve his vision of it. Poe composed *Eureka* the year before he died, and it was his final sublimation of himself. *Eureka* was Poe's exorcising of the intolerable world of actuality.

The Education of Henry Adams is a different kind of culmination. It is self-sufficient. It contains its own explanation of the theory it proposes by the way it evolves this theory. Starting with false assumptions and proceeding through a maze of contradictions, Adams devised a strategy of turning experience into evidence and then abstracting a principle from this evidence. This principle is the continuous interaction of mind and matter. Testing it by what he called a dynamic theory of history, Adams explained the development of Western civilization. His dynamic theory is a version of the process by which he discovered it. This process he called his "education."

The chronology of Adams's search occurs approximately in halves. The first twenty chapters describe his formal schooling and his self-styled careers in law, diplomacy, journalism, and teaching—all a failure according to his definition of education; and the next sixteen chapters put the experience of these failures to use in his search. But even as he reassesses his principles, events overtake him. His orderly account of how the nineteenth century has invalidated the a priori assumptions of the eighteenth century becomes, instead, a desperate attempt to understand the twentieth century.

The third cosmology in the next cluster of chapters is William Carlos Williams's *Paterson* (1946–1958). Like *Eureka,* it culminates a lifelong endeavor to build a comprehensive system of cause and effect, and, like *The Education,* it is also a self-sufficient system. Like the other two cosmologies, *Paterson* deliberately presents the apparently causeless, formless elements of the condition of actuality, and it appropriates theories of relationships from other sources to build a clarifying statement of the order inherent in this condition.

But the theories that *Paterson* appropriates are not mathematical; they are aesthetic. The actual and universal condition it acknowledges is the condition of language. It evolves a theory of the relationship of art and actuality by borrowing theories of technique in one medium and adapting them to another. It appropriates a theory of painting and collage to explain how language means. But *Paterson* does not explain; it dramatizes a mind searching for order. By the way it confronts the chaotic condition of language it discovers the order that the poet protests does not exist.

Paterson is about words and the succession of sounds that make meaning. In its broadest terms it is a large scrapbook of borrowed public prose, punctuated by lyric verse that worries what it borrows into larger meaning. Most of the public writings are newspaper stories, faithful records of mere actuality which make sense without significance. The verse is all subjective, probing the undisclosed and deeper reason in events. The poet borrows fragments of public records, of letters he has received, of speeches and sermons and legends and recollections, all of which echo the discrepancy between what he sees around him and what he knows must be there. *Paterson* probes the nature of meaning by countless variations of related patterns in these documents. It juxtaposes the words in chaotic disarrangement or in superficial order with new patterns of those same words. The poem is a vast and intricate collage of lyric verse and fragmentary facts which interrupt each other. It is a continuum of shattering and fusing substances.

These three cosmologies, like all the others, confront the same dual realities of mind and matter; and they all allege or assert or dramatize an organic cosmos on the premise that mind and matter are components of the same reality. Significantly, with the exception of Poe's *Eureka*, they all work out some system of determinism; they all devise some version of a dynamic reciprocity between the individual mind and universal matter. Significantly, with the exception of *Eureka*, they arrive at a doctrine that approximates Emerson's determinism by enabling or even causing the individual to collaborate with his environment. The accent is always on reciprocity, or, as Emerson said, on the tie between the person and the event.

The process of discovering a deterministic system is particularly schematic and obvious in Emerson's successive essays. In *Nature*, he first proposed a cosmos in which the mind paradoxically contains the world beyond itself. It does so through its impression of the totality of all things. But his system showed no cause. It was organic but it was arbitrary. There was no reason why the condition of a world within a mind should necessarily exist for any other person. So Emerson amended his system over the years until he arrived at exactly the opposite relation of these two entities, the mind and the world around it. In "Fate" he proposed a system in which the mind is contained within the world by means of a reciprocal relationship. He proposed a dynamic system in which the reciprocity of world and mind continuously and forever necessitates the mind's trying to overcome the limitations of being contained by what it does not know or understand.

All these cosmologies propose some dynamic relationship between the mind and its environment. They all devise a strategy, like Emerson's, of revising terms in order to incorporate contradictions. Adams called this strategy "the larger synthesis." He worked with the concept of Unity and Chaos. But before he could express his dynamic theory of history he had to abandon the idea that Unity is a given absolute, and to redefine it as a sequence of many alleged absolutes. Adams finally worked out a determinism extraordinarily like Emerson's "Fate," based on the interaction of men's minds and the forces extrinsic to them.

The other cosmologies devise the same reciprocity of mind and matter, terms which they identify differently. Thoreau, in *Walden*, worked with the concepts of the self and its natural environment. The organizing force of his whole system is the repeated recognition, wherever he looked, of reflections of himself. The mind's continuous analogizing is what incorporates the self and the environment in a great organic whole.

The duality that Whitman saw in *Leaves of Grass* was the simple-separate self and the society of mankind, or "the ensemble," as he called it. The self, he asserted, is equivocal, being separate and yet part of humanity at the same time. Whitman defined the United States of America as a political entity incorporating a contradiction of majority rule and minority rights, and he could see this equivocal society as an extension of the equivocal self. Later, when he tried to extend this political concept of society to all mankind, he became less convincing about the organic unity of the world. But his struggle to make his assertions convincing is the organizing principle in *Leaves of Grass*.

Hart Crane tried to incorporate two different, irreconcilable Americas. One was the actual, historical civilization in which he lived, and the other was a visionary world in which past and present, thing and idea, material and spiritual, the self and the mass of men were inseparably one. He tried to idealize the actual but indefinable civilization into an undifferentiated unity which he called America. His poem was his attempt to join two orders of being by a metaphorical bridge, or rather his poem is all his multiple attempts to buttress and support this primary metaphor with piers of others. He managed to suggest what such a unity might be if it ever could be. He did so by making a metaphor of himself searching for a metaphor and by personifying other voices echoing his search.

Paterson is less expansive and less visionary than Whitman's structure and far less lyrical than Crane's. But it is more developed than either; and it is more convincingly comprehensive because it is more precise about the duality it attempts to resolve. *Paterson* dramatizes a mind preoccupied with merging separate orders of art and actuality, and with agitating its materials into a structure. It finally proves his argument that art and actuality must be symbiotic. The proof lies in its creating the medium for its own argument.

Poe's *Eureka* is an exception to these deterministic cosmologies. It denies any reciprocity of self and environment. It incorporates mind and matter in a fatalistic, continuous cycle of change, whereby matter is simply a temporary phase of the spirit. *Eureka* is different from the other American cosmologies by the fact that it has no program. Because its scheme of unity of God and matter is fatalistic, no ethic is possible. In this sense, Poe least of all presents the evangelical strain of American idealism. He is the most unworldly.

But even Poe lived his poem; *Eureka* was largely about his trying to write it. It is a gigantic rationalization of his need to justify himself and to express the undifferentiated unity of Poe and God. Poe lived his poem during all the years in all the fictions in which he tried to comprehend his final cosmic system. In this peculiar sense *Eureka*, too, is evangelical.

Evangelism is the singular and pervasive quality of these cosmologies. This fact expands the perimeter of my subject. Evangelism is apparent in the poet's attitude: in his sense of urgency, in his self-conscious feeling of involvement. It is audible in his tone: in the lyrical agitation of his words or his didactic overstatements. But evangelism is more than an attitude or a tone of voice; it is a form of behavior. To try to explain evangelism in literary terms is to confuse action with verbal communication. The confusion enormously expands the concept of literary expression, to the point of mistaking it for any form of expressive action. The only reason to court such a confusion of meaning is that the poets themselves wilfully did.

CHAPTER NINE

The Theories of Adams and Poe

Henry Adams and E. A. Poe were engaged in the same tremendous task. Each attempted to explain himself to himself in the largest possible way, to discover the nature of the system that contained him. But the search for order engaged them differently. From the evidence in *The Education* it is clear that Adams had to learn how to redefine the concept of "Unity" that he had inherited and to discover a larger concept to incorporate it. From the evidence in *Eureka* it is apparent that Poe had to find a way to rationalize what he wanted to believe anyway; namely, an inevitable sense of belonging.

These cosmologies are something like Poe's ratiocinative tales; they pose a puzzle which the detective brilliantly solves by a reasoning that is not wholly apparent until later. Poe's tale "The Gold-Bug" is a good analogy. Reading these two cosmologies is like deciphering two maps that lead to buried treasure. Each poet finally discovers the super system that he has been searching for. En route to the treasure there are repetitions in each map: the author returns to his evidence, checks the direction he is going in, and paces off his distance again. The reader can make use of these repetitions in order to stay with the author on the author's strenuous journey; they are clues to the author's search as well as his goal. But the maps are different; one is self-sufficient and the other is a fragment. The clues to Adams's treasure are in *The*

Education, but the clues to Poe's treasure are scattered throughout his other, earlier writings.

The key to the mystery that Adams confronts is his own concept of education. By "education" he means an inquiring process: a continuous act of assimilating and organizing data (thereby developing the mind's capacity for more of the same). His first chapter states that the purpose of education is "running order through chaos, direction through space, discipline through freedom, unity through multiplicity"; and when Adams speaks of his own failures in education, which is often, he means the failure to inquire sufficiently or to assimilate and organize the elements of a particular experience—in sum, his failure at "running order through chaos." The twenty-first chapter of the book ("Twenty Years After") begins with a stern reminder: "Once more! This is the story of education, not of adventure! It is meant to help young men—or such as have intelligence enough to seek help—but it is not meant to amuse them."

This severity determines the whole rhetoric of *The Education*, the whole pattern of what Adams chooses to represent and emphasize. In describing his schooling and his several careers the book omits twenty years of Adams's life during which he happened to write a nine-volume political history, two biographies, and two novels. It fails to mention his marriage or the shocking experience of his wife's death; and it virtually leaves out his seven years as a teacher and his editorial direction of the *North American Review*. Yet Adams insists on the exact calendar dates of his return from a journey to Washington or London or Rome, as if those were immensely important in documenting clues or in trying to evaluate them. He insists that what he describes is exclusively a process of education. "What one did—or did not do—with one's education, after getting it, need trouble the inquirer in no way; it is a personal matter only which would confuse him."

The author's severity establishes the tone of the book, too.

The onstage Adams is ironic, testy, evasive; he puts you on edge by masquerading as a failure in the face of his obvious accomplishments. He takes the pose that the world exists to educate Adams; he speaks of world events in terms of dollars and millions of lives being wasted on *his* education, yet he always manages to salvage some "amusement" from the spectacle. All these apparent disproportions emphasize the process that Adams really means to be talking about, the process of finding unity in multiplicity.

Adams's statement of the true function of education (in the pivotal chapter "Twenty Years After") explains the strategy of his book without at first seeming to. Grant the rare fact of "a mind capable of reacting to any purpose on the forces that surround him," Adams says, and the rest follows. "The object of education for that mind should be the teaching itself how to react with vigor and economy." No doubt the world will lag behind this active mind, as history continually illustrates. But no matter; the inquiring act of this mind has a purpose, which is to increase the control of events and reduce chaos: "Education should try to lessen the obstacles, diminish the friction, invigorate the energy, and should train minds to react, not at haphazard, but by choice, on the lines of force that attract their world."

Adams invented his own formula of reciprocity. The interaction of the consciousness and its affecting circumstances is the essence of Adams's concept of education. It is a dynamic relation between the mind and "the forces that surround it," a dialectic of force and reaction that causes realizations. This constant reciprocity *is* education; and it is what *The Education* is all about.

From this point on in the book where Adams begins to make new assaults on the unknown, the narrative illustrates its own argument. He sets a high standard for the act of inquiry, and as his own education develops, he spends enormous energies in hypothesizing and appraising and rejecting and qualifying the relations between natural facts, always to synthesize from the facts themselves, straining to build a larger picture of the world from any available fragments. Newly observed facts compound and qualify his notions of evolution, of force, of natural resources and politics and reproduction. In his strange, intense cerebral dialogue he reasons inductively or intuitively, however he can at the moment.

Adams invokes Hegel's concept of dialectic: a process of reasoning which merges contradictions into a larger proposition that comprehends them. "The larger synthesis" is what he calls this organizing strategy. One of his syntheses involves a concept of human energy, another involves the concept of natural energies; but these are undercut by other syntheses, about the idea of anarchy and the idea of order, which are mutually exclusive. His great struggle is to incorporate these two abstractions, anarchy and order, into some still larger synthesis about energy. The persona of Adams is a questing consciousness: avid and hungry and restless. He deals with vast abstractions as though they were solid facts, and he finally evolves a massive theory from them. This, in general, is the course of the desperate business to which Adams is committed in the last fifteen chapters of *The Education*.

Having stated the task of education, he describes his own trial-and-error search through its course of clarifying decisions. After gathering more information about human energy he decides that history will be the method and the discipline of his synthesis. Choosing to conduct his search in terms of history is his first decision. The evidence he finds in history is political and economic: the morality of party politics in 1893; the panic following the passage of the Silver Act; the fallibility of banks. To test his observations about human energy he travels to Normandy, Cuba, to Yellowstone and the Rockies, to Mexico and London and Paris, to Washington and Egypt. It seems fruitless, as though he were looking in all the closets of an old house for something he has lost and finding only empty closets. In retrospect, only in Normandy did he discover some sign of what he was looking for, some evidence of organized human energies, in the cathedrals of the twelfth and thirteenth centuries.

Adams's second decision (some years after choosing history as his discipline) is that his history must be a *sequence of force* in the universe. Trial and error has led to this decision. He has experimented with history as a method of organizing various sequences, and tried to accommodate the fact of omnipresent energy in the world. He has studied physics and mathematics, and discovered a shocking thing, a basic disparity between history, which depends on continuity, and the kind of evidence that the physical sciences yield, which seems to have nothing to do with continuity.

The famous chapter, "The Dynamo and the Virgin," records the crisis that has led to his decision to consider history as a sequence of force. Confronted with the evidence of immense energy in the Gallery of Machines at the Great Exposition in Paris in the year 1900, Adams suddenly realizes that the sequence of men, of society, of time, or of thought—all of which were possibilities until now—will lead him nowhere. His decision to study the sequence of force is his great breakthrough. Force is the pervasive fact of the universe! The human mind and natural energy are simply aspects of force. And here is the continuity for which he has been searching: *the measurement of any force extrinsic to the mind must be the mind's attraction to it.*

> Clearly if he was bound to reduce all these forces to a common value, this common value could have no measure but that of their attraction on his own mind. He must treat them as they had been felt; as convertible, reversible, interchangeable attractions on thought.

To explain any sequence at all Adams must first discover a pattern in the mind's attraction to force at large. He must test his principle, to see how much it might explain. But the search reveals, instead, a shocking denial of any order whatever. His quest seems to lead to a dead end. Looking for evidence of a continuity of human energy and natural energy, Adams has tried to relate natural resources and national politics, trying to see any influence of one on the other. Traveling in Russia, he has contemplated the subject of political anarchy, and of various anarchies. Reviewing the China policy of his old friend John Hay, and the consequence of Hay's diplomacy, he has next wondered if the law of inertia can also apply to human energies.

Adams then begins to metaphorize the human aspects of energy in terms of politics and then in terms of sex and reproduction. He recalls the symbolic value of the Virgin. And he observes the contemporary woman, whose one natural force of attraction is now somehow denied by the male's attraction to a new life force of natural energy transformed by machines. In all these ponderings Adams finds contradiction instead of order, interruptions instead of continuity, as he states in "Twilight" (Chapter 26):

> Evolution was becoming change of form broken by freaks of force, and warped at times by attractions affecting intelligence, twisted and tortured at other times by sheer violence, cosmic, chemical, solar, supersensual, electrolytic—who knew what?—defying science, if not denying known law. . . .

Having decided on a history, and then on a history of force, he faces a new crisis, which is the apparent anarchy of forces; and this crisis provokes his third major decision. The solution lies in the problem: "The wisest of men could but imitate the Church, and invoke a 'larger synthesis' to unify the anarchy again."

This strategy of incorporating contradictions in some broader concept is consistent with Adams's purpose, which is always to triangulate from the widest possible base to the farthest point he can see. He has already appropriated principles of mechanical physics to explain human energies. But the larger synthesis in this case has still yielded only interruption and discontinuity. As far as Adams can see, according to his authorities, Karl Pearson and Ernst Mach, physics posits only disorder. "The Grammar of Science" (Chapter 31) describes the shock. Pearson has asserted that a multiverse exists, not a universe; the kinetic theory of gas is an assertion of chaos; Mach has denied that matter is substance. And the implications have become clear to Adams: the existence of chance, anarchy, and disorder deny the historian's assumption of unity. "In plain words, Chaos was the law of nature; Order was the dream of man."

Any new synthesis must now incorporate two contradictory concepts: order and anarchy. The "larger synthesis" is a device of the comparative order, but now he must somehow construct a superlative. "To the tired student, the idea that he must give it up seemed sheer senility. As long as he could whisper, he would go on as he had begun, "bluntly refusing to meet his creator with the admission that the creation had taught him nothing except that the square of the hypotenuse of a right-angled triangle might for convenience be taken as equal to something else." Adams wrote this in "Vis Nova" (Chapter 32). Here, in his own words, is the Emersonian poet a generation after Emerson, explaining himself in terms of his reciprocity with the world:

> Every man with self-respect enough to become effective, if only as a machine, has had to account to himself for himself somehow, and to invent a formula of his own for his universe, if the standard formulas failed. There, whether finished or not, education stopped.

Once more and finally the problem yields up its own solution. Ever since the book of Genesis, and probably before, the concept of the Absolute ("Unity, Continuity, Purpose, Order, Law, Truth, the Universe, God") has in fact been only relative. Adams had pondered this in his chapter, "The Grammar of Science":

To Thomas Aquinas, the universe was still a person; to Spinoza, a substance; to Kant, Truth was the essence of the "I"; an innate conviction, a categorical imperative; to Poincaré, it was a convenience; and to Karl Pearson, a medium of exchange.

There is in fact no absolute; the only unity in human history is the *concept* of the absolute. The premise for a theory of history could not lie in the particular concepts themselves, as the differences among Aquinas, Spinoza, Kant, Poincaré, and Pearson testify, but rather in the fact that the mind conceptualizes the absolute.

Here was the synthesis he had sought for so long ("a spool on which to wind the thread of history without breaking it," as he said in "Vis Nova"). His history of force must be based on the fact that the mind continually conceptualizes unity or truth or whatever the absolute might be called. But Adams was old; there would not be time to verify the formula he sought; just getting it stated would have to suffice. The last three chapters of the book describe his dynamic theory of history, and suggest its implications.

"A Dynamic Theory of History" (Chapter 33) describes a determinism in which the individual collaborates with forces outside himself. It assumes two concepts or abstractions. One is a force called the mind, individually or collectively. The other is a greater force, extrinsic to the mind yet which the mind comprehends. The relationship between these two forces is analogous to Isaac Newton's concept of the attraction of unequal masses. According to Adams, the extrinsic force controls the mind by attracting it. But there is an interacting relationship between mind and force by which the mind somehow assimilates force. The theory stresses a dynamic relationship. There is a reciprocity between the human mind and the natural forces, and this interchange of unequal forces produces the events of history.

The mind's attraction to the natural force is an act or a condition of faith. Adams explains this attraction in terms of religion: the belief in some unity or other—Sometimes called God—which the mind perceives to exist. ("To the highest attractive energy, man gave the name of divine, and for its control he invented the science called Religion. . . .") To the perceiving mind this alleged unity is the sum and essence of countless forces in the universe. (Religion "meant, and still means, cultivation of occult force whether in detail or mass.") Since the beginning of recorded time this dynamic relationship has caused a series of events which have determined history. At certain times a preponderant number of minds have believed in the same unity or god. ("Unable to define Force as a unity, man symbolized and pursued it, both in himself, and in the infinite, as philosophy and theology. . . .") The dynamic theory might therefore be called a theory of the sequence of faiths, or a theory of the concepts of unity.

Adams delineates this sequence of faiths or beliefs. From time to time some preponderant faith has determined a distinctive kind of human activity, and the dynamic theory of history describes four such phases of human activity in the Western world, covering a period of some five thousand years to the present. The first phase occurred from about 3000 B.C. to about A.D. 300. It marks a preponderant belief in the supreme authority of an organized human society. It might be called the phase of the city of man. A second phase of Western history occurred from about 400 to about 1400, with the gradual decay of the Roman Empire, and marked a growing faith in the authority of what Augustine called the City of God. The Virgin and the Cross became symbols of this preponderant belief. But this faith was displaced by another faith, which marked a third phase of Western history, from about 1400 to 1800. This new preponderant belief placed ultimate authority in the forces of nature. Bacon's *Novum Organum* (1620) is a gospel of this faith. The fourth phase which occurred from about 1800 to about 1900, was essentially an extension of the third. It marked a faith in the *oc-*

cult forces of nature, in the molecular motion of electricity and radioactivity.

This sequence is Henry Adams's dynamic theory of history. Four phases of faith explain the major events of the history of the Western world, based on the proposition that faith is a reciprocity of mind and extrinsic force.

But my description of Adams's theory is too tidy. It fails to convey the heady sense of discovery; it misses the presence of Adams in his own theory, his excited mind ranging back and forth across centuries of time. His chronology confuses. As he narrates and describes and reasons his way to a whole statement, he keeps interrupting himself and changing directions. The pressure of the events he records accelerates his pace. By turns of inspired confusion he discovers as he goes. The dynamic theory, in fact, reveals Henry Adams more clearly than it reveals the events of history.

The style of his statement projects the author, and his theory itself illustrates its own evolving. Eclectic plundering of theories in physics and mathematics repeatedly reveals Adams's purpose, which was to explain a metaphysical idea in physical terms. But each new "larger synthesis" is subjective. One example of this subjectivity is the duration of the successive phases of history in Adams's dynamic theory. These phases get progressively shorter as they approach that moment in time in which Adams conceives his theory, to the point where he has no perspective on events. The last two chapters of *The Education* elaborate on this phenomenon that Adams calls "a law of acceleration."

Adams later worked out the rationale for these accelerating phases of faith in an essay that was posthumously published (part of *The Degradation of the Democratic Dogma*, 1919). This later essay applies to history the rule of phase which Josiah Gibbs had brilliantly conceived in the field of physical chemistry. Gibbs had worked out a mathematical relationship of variables to explain the change of homogeneous chemical substances from one phase to another. To these physical variables (temperature, pressure, and volume) Adams made arbitrary analogies in his own abstract terms, to explain the change of phases in human events. Thus he equated "attraction" with pressure, he equated "acceleration" with temperature, and he equated the quantity or sum of minds with the physical term, volume.

Subjectivity is really Adams's subject. His book is about the crisis of his own perceiving. The way in which Adams comes upon his dynamic theory of history is the vital principle of *The Education*. The separate elements of metaphors whirl around in Adams's mind, forming new associations and breaking apart, as he tries to fuse them into some larger synthesis: unity, anarchy, multiplicity, magnetic force, natural resources, sex, woman, politics, coal, the dynamo, the Virgin, the Cross. As they recur in new associations, they accumulate metaphorical meaning.

Adams develops a sense of metaphor as he goes along. During the first half of the book the ever-present concept of Unity is a fixed value, an end in itself which Adams tries to impose on his own experience. When the facts do not fit the assumption and his attempts to judge events by this a priori Unity yield only discrepancies his attitudes remain passive, inert, and he feels separated from his own experience. He finally becomes aware of this in the chapters "Chaos" and "Failure," and he starts all over again, examining events by analogy to others which he cannot understand either. Making metaphors becomes a strategy of discovery. His concept of unity begins to change. Because he can recognize unity as a concept, he can use it as a means of relating himself to his experience. "Unity" becomes a metaphor of an organic, inseparable condition, no longer to be assumed, but, if possible, discovered.

Adams—the persona—strongly resembles the intense perceiver in Henry James's fictions, the characteristic, disembodied mind that James called the "center of composition" and the "register of opinions." This fictional Adams is the center of his own composition. His theory of history assumes the existence of reciprocity of mind and extrinsic force. His own education is the reciprocity between his mind and the empirical material of his theory of history. Both his theory and his own education are aspects of the same dialectic, the same discovery of relationship between the self and its environment.

The relationship of a mind and force interacting, which Adams's theory posits and which Adams himself illustrates, is remarkably similar to the determinism that Emerson finally worked out in "Fate." According to Emerson, Fate ("unpenetrated cause") contains mankind; it is the sum of limiting events that determine the man and to which he is antagonistic. But Fate is also thereby a system that, containing mankind, contains the energy to overcome these limiting events. The very fact of "unpenetrated cause" goads the man to probe what he does not know, to clarify cause, to increase his awareness and therefore his moral understanding. Emerson's ingenious determinism necessitates a man's moral improvement, whereby one's self works with and against one's circumstances in order to overcome them.

Adams also builds a determinism that necessitates an interaction between two unequal forces: the vital energy of man and the natural energy of the universe; and this interaction causes man to perceive order and to react by choice instead of by chance on the forces that impinge on him. "A Dynamic Theory of History" describes the process: "The sum of force attracts; the feeble atom or molecule called man is attracted; he suffers education or growth. . . ." Adams, like Emerson, celebrates the individual consciousness in the act of perceiving. As Adams says, in "The Grammar of Science": "Thought alone was Form. Mind and Unity flourished or perished together."

Poe might have uttered these same words, but he would have meant something entirely different by them. He would have meant that "Thought," being the essence of God, is the only substance of the universe, and that if "Thought" were to perish there would indeed be no unity—and no universe —because there would be no substance. The mystery of the universe that *Eureka* finally reveals is a complete and literal pantheism. The key to this mystery, like the key in Adams's cosmology, is the energy of thought; but the two systems are utterly different. Mind and matter are one and the same in *Eureka*; although they appear to be discrete they are merely successive manifestations of "Divine Volition" in a cyclical universe. All human activity, therefore, is simply an aspect of a fatalistic cosmos. This was the treasure that Poe searched for.

Eureka begins with this statement: "I design to speak of the *Physical, Metaphysical and Mathematical—of the Material and Spiritual Universe:—of its Essence, its Origin, its Creation, its Present Condition, and its Destiny.*" In proportion to its enormous scope *Eureka* is enormously simple. It proposes that matter and spirit are one and the same. Stripped of all its proofs and rationalizations, the argument can be briefly stated. *Eureka* argues that what is commonly regarded as material is none other than God in a present and temporary state of diffusion. Spirit and matter are phases in a continuously pulsing cycle of energy, and the universe is a continuum of repulsion and attraction, in which each phase in turn causes the other. Life as we know it is approaching the end of the material phase; the diffused particles are about to respond to the attractive force of their sum, and return to a state of undifferentiated unity.

Poe's cosmology is an immense tour de force, a hair-raising scheme of intuitive hypotheses that are "proven" by empirical observations. Poe gravely cites Newton's law of gravity, Laplace's nebular theory of the universe, and the cosmos of Alexander von Humboldt (to whom the work is dedicated). Appropriating the authority of these natural scientists, *Eureka* claims to lead the reader inductively from premise to inevitable conclusion. But this peculiar induction reveals nothing so much as the author struggling with his own material. It ranges back and forth between hypothesis and empirical fact, emphatically accompanied by italics and capitalized nouns.

Laplace's nebular theory of the sun's explosion of gases (which condensed and contracted to the solid masses of the planets) and Newton's law of gravity (describing a mathematical relation between attracting masses) complement each other for Poe's purpose. Newton's law defines the process of attraction, and Laplace's theory offers a sequence of events. *Eureka* alleges some principle beyond these theories that causes them to be related; namely, that the attracting process is a reaction to the "Divine Act of diffusion" in the first place.

Eureka begins by promising to define the ultimate principle of the universe, but Poe did not discover the precise relation that he wanted between these borrowed theories until the middle of his essay. Only at this point does Poe apparently come upon a way to relate the fact of gravity and what he calls the act of irradiation or diffusion: gravity must be a reaction to "irradiation." At this point also the poetic structure of the essay, the organization of analogies, begins to be apparent. Poe sought analogies to his continuum wherever he could find them, in terms of philosophy, of physics, of astronomy, of geometry, and of mathematical reasoning in general. These analogies to the argument reveal some stress in the arguer. There is an excited confusion of terms. The counterforces, "repulsion" and "attraction," are synonymous to "electricity" and "condensation," to "irradiation" and "concentralization"; and significantly to "Soul" and "Body."

Eureka asserts that in the beginning was "the absolute Unity in the primordial Particle," also the "Divine Volition," that is, "the Divine Act of Diffusion." Accordingly, therefore, "Soul" must be either matter or some derivative of matter. One way around this snarl is to assume a dynamic system as Poe did. Only in motion could the wholeness of the whole be understood. Matter is motion; motion is thought; thought is force (either diffusion or attraction). The "Oneness" Poe asserted is the perpetual motion of "a novel Universe swelling into existence, and then subsiding into nothingness, at every throb of the Heart Divine." The climax of *Eureka* is the excited revelation of the true nature of this "Heart Divine."

Like Monsieur C. August Dupin in one of Poe's detective stories, Poe finally clears up the mystery. "And now—this Heart Divine—what is it? *It is our own.*" There is but one "conscious Intelligence," one Divinity; and the individual is part and parcel of it. Suddenly the equations all balance. Motion is thought; thought is force; force is consciousness; consciousness is one. And the conscious self is the center and the substance of the universe.

The clues to the mystery of the universe that *Eureka* finally reveals lie in Poe's other writings: in his literary criticism and his verse and his narrative prose. And these writings reflect a pattern in his life that has already been explained many times. Poe's short life was full of false starts. It is a record of illness and poverty and loneliness and despair and the repeated experience of being rejected both personally and professionally.

Apparently from these experiences Poe's dream of a substitute world took shape. Under pressure of staying alive, under the tyranny of printers' deadlines, he set down his dream as best he could. He recorded it in fits and starts, in his tales and poems; and he rationalized it in his criticism. Finally he pieced out his theory of the universe as an ordered whole, rationalizing a mystical union in mechanistic terms. His lecture on this metaphysical system, "Eureka," was delivered in February, 1848, at the Society Library in New York City and on subsequent occasions until his death in 1849. This final record of his fantastic cosmos was also a testament to his war with the actual world, and his other writings anticipated it.

Poe's literary criticism, for example, helps to explain his colossal claim for *Eureka*. In a short preface to *Eureka*, with fantastic logic, Poe states that this cosmology is a Book of Truths; an Art-Product, a Romance. In fact, it is a Poem whose permanence abides in the Beauty of Truth; and therefore it cannot die. This extraordinary preface contains all the assumptions of Poe's theory of art. By "Poem" he meant nothing less than total religious revelation. But since Poe was a churchless Antinomian, his terms are peculiar to him, and their definition is crucial to his meaning.

Poe tried to define his own terms over and over again in his critical essays, from the preface to his *Poems by Edgar A. Poe* (1831) to his final lecture on aesthetics, "The Poetic Principle" (1848–1849). His magazine journalism and the *ad hoc* nature of so much of his criticism, in reviews of other writings, prevented him from making a single definitive statement of his aesthetics; he was always revising, qualifying, and borrowing from himself. His various pronouncements, however, piece out a theory according to which there are stages in the value of literary expression. At the bottom of a hierarchy of literature is the presentation of the actual—produced by what Poe called the evil genius of mere matter of fact; next higher is prose fiction, including the species known as the tale conceived to dramatize some particular effect; and at the top is the poem, which stimulates all human responses to a contemplation of Beauty. But this hierarchy has meaning only insofar as it reflects Poe's religious vision, his overview of God and man.

Poe's poems offer obvious clues to the composition of *Eureka*. They assert the existence of another world than the here and now, and his poetic theory rationalized them. A poem, he said, must excite the Soul by directing its attention to Beauty; it must construct an ideal world, although philosophical ideas have no place in a poem. His own poems deny any dimensional world; they assert a condition. Metaphors of space and time connote the absence of space and time; familiar scenic details are transposed into immaterial landscapes. His poems are gauzy dioramas with indirect lighting. In "The

City in the Sea" a domain is doomed to exist in its own pallor until it is swallowed up. "Dream-Land" is a dismal region out of space and time, drearier because it has no horizons. In "The Sleeper" an opiate vapor shrouds a moonlit mountaintop. "To One in Paradise" acknowledges the eternity of another world; so does "Eldorado." "Al Aaraaf" celebrates unearthly beauty in some other realm between heaven and hell. The poet Israfel is in heaven. "Ulalume" is a setting for a requiem. "Dreams" and "A Dream within a Dream" are two poems whose titles would fit any of these others.

These poems are surrealistic. An anonymous point of view indulges in its own fabrications, and the indulgence is a restless continuum of shifting attention. Poe was exploiting the convention of any lyric poem, which makes the voice that speaks it a presence in a dramatic situation. The vitality is in the point of view. But Poe exploited the convention in a singular way. The listener in his poems is almost always an apparition in the mind of the fictional speaker. No corporeal being, although her corpse is usually onstage, the listener is spiritual, sometimes allegorical, but dead in any case and surviving only in the speaker's recollection. One exception is "The Raven," in which the speaker's apparition is not his listener but his subject. And the speaker in "The Raven," as in Poe's other poems, is lost, abandoned, derelict. His restless self-indulgence is what the poem dramatizes.

Poe wrote most of his poems early in his career and rationalized them later. Beauty is their subject, and Beauty is their aim. This ambiguity he tried to specify in two of his later essays, "The Philosophy of Composition" (1846), and "The Poetic Principle" (1848–1849). The point of any poem, accordingly, is something called the "poetic moment," the instant at which the reader in a highly excited state of mind perceives the attributes of Beauty.

From Poe's remarks, however, the locus of the poem is not entirely certain. Apparently the poem proper is not the structure on a page but the *revelation* caused by the printed words. It is an apocalyptic moment in the consciousness of the reader. Poe makes it sound so square and rational because the terms he uses at different times mutually imply each other: "single effect," "unity," "elevation of the Soul," "poetic principle," and "Beauty." His theory is circular. The poem is the rhythmical creation of Beauty, he says; that is, the poem excites the Soul, and this excitation is Beauty. But since Beauty thereby exists in the reader's excited Soul, Beauty is what we get when we apprehend Beauty. The theory chases its own tail.

Another clue to the mystery that *Eureka* reveals is the nature of the narrator in Poe's prose tales. It is precisely in the narrator that his prose tales are most compatible to his poems and to his whole theory of fiction, although not all the tales, of course, have narrators. Poe's early tales parody the conventions of the gothic romance, the sentimental horror story located in some exotic time and place. In the gothic tale the clanking chains and bleeding statues and other apparently supernatural events are finally explained away, but Poe began to use these conventions to convey causality, motive, and consequence. In his best stories the sensations and the apparitions explain some extreme state of mind. His principal characters are all extraordinary in this respect. They have an acute sensitivity. They are excitable, intensely responsive, and either manic or depressed. These characters probe into their circumstances in a way that causes them difficulties. The horror or perversity or sensationalism of a given tale usually reflects the extraordinary sensitivity of its hero.

From this kind of character Poe developed his narrator. In some of the early tales the narrator accomplishes nothing that the omniscient author could not accomplish; he merely reports the actions and the foggy, ominous atmosphere of the sentimental horror story. He is simply there. But in later and more developed tales the narrator's acutely sensitive and responsive mind really becomes the center of the story. "The

Fall of the House of Usher," "Ligeia," "The Pit and the Pendulum," and "The Oval Portrait" all depend on the narrator's singular responsiveness in order to carry out what Poe determined would be the "effect" of each story. Without the responsive narrator the "effect" would be entirely different.

All these tales are about the drama of *apprehending* something or other. "The Man of the Crowd" is as much about the narrator as it is about the restless, solitary fugitive he has decided to follow. More so, in fact; the tension in this story exists almost entirely in the narrator's impressions, and it has grown in the first place from his assumption that there *must* be something to discover. The confessional tales, of course, depend entirely on the narrator, obviously so in "The Tell-Tale Heart," "The Black Cat," and "The Imp of the Perverse," more subtly in "The Cask of Amontillado," and consummately in "William Wilson."

The narrators of the tales and the speaking voice in the poems are fictional relatives. They are out of joint with the world, unable to reconcile themselves to the material environment, fearful of being buried alive. Poe's personas are versions of a sensitive, acute, responsive, lonely consciousness expressing its *Weltschmerz*. In this emotional state the speaker fabricates an immaterial world animated only by his own apprehensions. The forming of the fantasy is the whole value of the fiction.

Still other clues are more explicit. They concern the doctrine of *Eureka* (the proposition that the original will, having dispersed itself into matter, recalls its parts into essence). Poe had to work out some way of expressing a physical rationale for spiritual being. Over the years he experimented with fragments of such a theory, and these fragments help to clarify *Eureka*. His most explicit experiments are four dialogues, three of which are similar. Each of these three dialogues is a conversation between two spirits who have died and departed from this world and who are engaged in contemplating the immense implications of what has happened.

Poe published the three dialogues over a period of six years: "The Conversation between Eiros and Charmion" (1839), "The Colloquy of Monos and Una" (1841), and "The Power of Words" (1845). They all express the continuity of thought and matter.

In part and together the dialogues are discursive. They deal with the personal consequence of individual death and with the cosmic consequence of the end of the planet Earth. The speakers are conventionally spirits of heaven, alluding to the Biblical prophecy of the end of the world, to the myth of innocence, and to the process of the soul leaving the body; but this is no doctrinal heaven, and certainly no Christian one. The spirits exist in a condition called Aidenn. They have no particular individuality except in the relative time each has spent in this condition of eternal life. In each dialogue a novice spirit has just arrived in Aidenn and requires an explanation of this new existence from a veteran spirit who in turn craves news from Earth. By this simple dramatic situation Poe used each dialogue to make a formal exposition of an ideal world and its imperfect earthly counterpart. These are fragments, each hypothesizing something later incorporated in *Eureka*.

"The Conversation between Eiros and Charmion" explains the violent end of the world by fire, after an approaching comet has vastly increased the proportion of oxygen in the earth's atmosphere. This astronomical event is expressed in mechanistic language. Poe's specious scheme is scientistic.

The second dialogue, "The Colloquy of Monos and Una," makes two different attempts to explain the relationship between material and immaterial existence. First, Una recalls the general disintegration of the human condition before the destruction of the world took place. In terms of facultative psychology, which fascinated Poe, Una describes how mankind's will perverted his taste, dissociated it from his moral sense and his intellect, and therefore separated him from the natural law of order and proportion in all things. The second part of the dialogue contains Monos's description of the physical sensations of dying. It is a loving and detailed account of funereal rites, burial, and decomposition, all reported as if they were sensations of a corpse relinquishing its sense of identity.

Poe's third dialogue, "The Power of Words," sounds like a justification of the *Eureka* which he had not yet written. It specifies the creative power of words. It proposes that the Deity created only in the beginning; that subsequent creation comes of motion; that thought is motion. Hence the creative power of words, which express thought.

These three heavenly dialogues anticipated obvious qualities in Poe's cosmology: the existence of an ideal world; the concept of thought or will as motion; a process of the loss of self-identity in the divine merger; and the scientistic language to explain it all. The sequence of ideas in these dialogues, moreover, indicates that Poe was working toward an organic cosmos: the destruction of the physical world (in the first dialogue); the dissociation of man's moral faculty from his will, his physical destruction, and a process of rebirth after death (in the second dialogue); and the conviction that the individual's thought continues to be the creating power, capable of bringing worlds into existence (in the third dialogue). But the fragmentary nature of these dialogues is even more revealing. They assert ideas without developing them. The first two dialogues are dramatically incomplete; the third is only tentatively resolved, as though Poe were talking to himself and struggling to discover the possibilities of his own material.

Between the last two of these dialogues he published yet another, "Mesmeric Revelation" (1844–1845), in which he worked out the essentials of the ontology that *Eureka* defines. "Mesmeric Revelation" is Poe's most explicit anticipation of his vast cosmology, an attempt to explain the mystery of what he later called "the primordial Particle." This is a dialogue between a mesmerist and his subject who is presumed to perceive far more in his trance than is possible in the waking state. The mesmerized man reports that he is now in a state approximating death, that with his normal organs of sense now sleeping he has a heightened sensitivity; and from this vantage he reports his perceptions of the ultimate nature of things.

These are the essentials of the ontology that Poe was working out in "Mesmeric Revelation": spirit does not exist, ("immateriality" is a mere word); God exists and is therefore no spirit; neither is God material in the normal sense of the word, but rather an infinite extension of materiality. These assumptions, of course, beget an explanation. Grant the atomic theory of matter, with the tiniest particles in mutual relation, and then imagine matter so dense that all "interspace" vanishes, so dense as to be "unparticled—without particles—indivisible—one. . . ." God is mass absolutely coalesced. This "unparticled" matter is God. It is defined as the universal thought of the universal mind. It creates all things and permeates all things.

This theory states virtually the same nature of being that Poe finally stated in *Eureka*: God is thought; thought is matter in motion. And on this basis *Eureka* proceeds to argue the annihilation of the present material world. Divested of its body, each man's thought will be one with God. But the next and last subject of "Mesmeric Revelation" does not proceed to this conclusion at all; on the contrary, it posits the eternal individualization of all men. Accordingly, the body discarded in death is merely the shell of an inner form of individualized self or thought that will always remain. The individual after death comprehends all things except the nature of the volition of God, that is, the motion of the unparticled matter.

This distinction concerning the nature of individuality indicates Poe's final step in defining a cosmos. The earlier work, "Mesmeric Revelation," provides for individuality abiding; it preserves the mystery of God. But *Eureka* annihilates individuality, as it annihilates the personality of God. It is an advance or a retreat, depending on how you look at it. What Poe finally worked out, in any case, was an encyclopedic rationalization of a continuing, unseparated cosmos.

Eureka, you might say, is the last word in cosmologies. It was certainly the last word in every sense for Poe. A biographer might speculate on the events in Poe's life between 1844 and 1848, on the accumulating frustrations and denials and rejections he suffered during his last years, and on his losing struggle to preserve his personal identity or even the idea of identity. What is certain, however, is that *Eureka* presents a cosmos in which the mystery of God has been displaced in a vast democracy of thought, an ingenious cosmos of which the annihilated self becomes the center. Given the possibility of annihilation in the first place, Poe's repeated attempts to formulate his cosmos testify to his obsession with finding a rational victory.

His rational victory was just that, purely that. His cosmos has no ethical program. On the contrary, its ethical implication is a vague antinomian exemption from moral law. In the inexorable process of matter in motion, in Poe's fatalistic cosmos, individuality is a transient state of being. Since the total scheme is a cycle of phases there is no such thing as melioration or progress. In this sense Poe's romanticism is squarely opposite Emerson's. Each man constructed an idealized universe in order to cope with living, but Poe's was no stratagem for improving one's present self or present circumstances. It is Emerson, not Poe, who has represented the main preoccupation of the American visionaries.

But Adams's determinism is Emersonian, as Emerson wrote it in "Fate": two forces, mind and nature, continually interact in such a way as to make the mind develop. This determinism encouraged Adams, like Emerson, to be evangelical. Both men clung to the tempting notion that progress is inherent in evolution. Despite the way events disabused him, Adams, like Emerson, continued to believe in the idea of

moral perfectibility. "To evolutionists may be left the processes of evolution," Adams wrote (in "A Law of Acceleration"); "to historians the single interest is the law of reaction
between force and force—between mind and nature—the
law of progress." And so he continued the ethical legacy of
the Emersonian poem: the idea that the poem exists only in
the living of it, that the struggle to synthesize is inherently
moral, that the reciprocity with Nature which this struggle
involves is a matter of progress.

This sense of responsibility to an ethical ideal appears to
be an American parochialism. The great synthesis must
somehow be lived. But keeping up with the world in the
twentieth century—as Adams had to—necessarily grounds
the poet to the revelations of science, that is to empirical evidence that contradicts his vision with undeniable authority.
Finding—and living—his own synthesis, the poet necessarily
begins with the problem that Henry Adams had to face: "in
plain words, Chaos was the law of nature; Order was the
dream of man." To the extent that the contemporary cosmologist respects the bristling evidence of multiplicity and
chaotic energy his struggle desperately grows.

CHAPTER TEN

The Lay of Paterson

Paterson (1946-1958) is the most developed of all the American cosmologies. It builds a simple, comprehensive theory of events; it is convincingly pragmatic; and it succeeds in its own difficult terms. William Carlos Williams developed a bold strategy for perceiving order and meaning in all unorganized actuality. *Paterson* is both the statement of that strategy and the example of its own statement. It is also the drama of its author's desperate enterprise. This work *is* the reality that it talks about. *Paterson* saturates actual details and fragments of a historical civilization into a new entity that is like nothing else in existence.

Paterson is all of a piece because it dramatizes the poet's dialogue with his material. In his pre-preface Williams calls it a plan for action, or rather "a plan for action to supplant a plan for action." Having denied the validity of the consummate fiction in *The Great American Novel* (1923) he continued to brood over how to bring into being, into form, just such a comprehensive theory of events. He brooded and wrote. This pediatrician from Rutherford, New Jersey, published twenty-seven titles of poetry; two long, impressionistic excursions in prose; a play; three volumes of short stories; four novels; a volume of essays; and an autobiography.

Then in 1946 he published the first of four "Books" of *Paterson*, about a city and a man with the same name. Williams mapped out an area of his imagination, defined its topography (abstracting a roar from an actual waterfall and
228

amplifying it); he populated the area, caricatured into promi-
nence a few names and nameless persons (both), and generated a history to help explain it all. He published three
more books by 1951. Although by this time *Paterson* was a
whole entity, Williams decided that it was not yet finished.

Seven years later, in 1958, after reinhabiting his fiction,
Williams published *Paterson* V. The curious thing is that the
first four books of *Paterson* are a totality, yet—with a different meaning—so are all five books. The struggle to build an
organic world of the mind resolves, at the end of *Paterson*
IV, into a despairing resignation at the limited achievement
of the poet. But in *Paterson* V the poet named Paterson becomes William Carlos Williams, who reviews the evidence
of love and death and art in the extant symbols of *Paterson*
I–IV, and amends despair to ironic celebration of the
cloven-footed human. *Paterson* *IV* ends with these lines:

> This is the blast
> the eternal close
> the spiral
> the final somersault
> the end.

And *Paterson* V, which Williams began after "the final
somersault / the end," concludes with this amendment:

> Yo ho! ta ho!
> We know nothing and can know nothing
> but
> the dance, to dance to a measure
> contrapuntally,
>   Satyrically, the tragic foot.

The Autobiography of William Carlos Williams (1951)
only briefly mentions *Paterson*, which was then presumably
finished. But in talking about the beginning of *Paterson* Williams does recall its plan of action, which is to make "things"
generate "ideas." The idea of a city as a correlation of
"things" had occurred to him as early as 1941; in particular a

city identified with a man, a consciousness. This was to be
the strategy: the man and the city as one, generating ideas
out of things, as *Paterson I* insists:

> Say it! No ideas but in things. Mr.
> Paterson has gone away
> to rest and write. Inside the bus one sees
> his thoughts sitting and standing. His
> thoughts alight and scatter—   (I, 1)

Williams's search for a city to begin with is now familiar.
He finally chose Paterson, New Jersey, with its colonial history and a wealth of antiquarian lore, with the Passaic River
and its spectacular and vocal falls running through its center.
Each book of the poem would follow the flow of this river,
from its beginnings above the city to the sea beyond it; and
Paterson-the-man would perceive the implications of its continuity. The poet and the city, one and the same: this identity would correlate a new world. "No ideas but in things."
For this purpose Williams needed a new poetic form. "It
called for a poetry such as I did not know," he says in his autobiography. The new structure would assimilate a local
idiom in such a way as to symbolize a whole world exactly
like it.

> To *make* a poem, fulfilling the requirements of the art, and
> yet new, in the sense that in the very lay of the syllables
> Paterson as Paterson would be discovered, perfect . . . in
> the special sense of the poem . . . as itself locally, and so
> like every other place in the world. For it is in that, that it
> be particular to its own idiom, that it lives.

Here was Williams's strategy of form: "in the very lay of the
syllables" the actual particulars would supersede themselves
into a new order of being. The lay of the syllables makes the
collage.

Williams worked out his prosody as he went along; he discovered what he had only after he had begun to construct it.
And in the same way the reader is forced to discover it as he

comes upon it. You discover many fragmented versions of Paterson-the-man and Paterson-the-place: discrete surfaces which obscure some edges and reveal others as they fuse into a new and visual reality, a sort of Greater Paterson.

Once you see from the poem itself that *Paterson* is constructed like a collage, you can recall many reasons for it. Given the fact that for years Williams sought a new poetic form, these reasons are compelling: William's friendship over the years with dozens of painters in Europe and America; his early experiments with the idiom of verse called Imagism, and the idea of building static metaphors with the visual impact of Impressionistic paintings. His enthusiasm for the bold representations of the "Ash Can" school of art; his response to the paintings of Post-Impressionism: Fauvism, Futurism, and Cubism, which he began to study seriously after the Armory Show in 1913. Williams clearly understood the revolution of Analytical Cubism, which anatomized forms and rearranged the parts into new schemes or orders.

Paterson is a configuration of interrupted planes, an area of surfaces delineated into shapes by one another, by the way the mind has laid them together—by "the lay of the syllables." What you see are bits and pieces of one language denoting actuality, which interrupt another language of sustained attempt to make a pattern of them. *Paterson* is about language and meaning. But since "language" and "meaning" are only abstractions, Williams had to make them sensory in order to talk about them. So he built a collage of words which would exploit two ways in which words mean. They are conventionally images of things and ideas, but they are also insistently things in themselves; and they work both ways at once.

The sequences of syllables are like so many surfaces in a visual area. But the surfaces present patterns, and the area becomes an accumulation of events. These sequences of syllables direct the eye to planes, but the way they are plaited (weaving in and out, and promising perspective only to contradict it) causes these patterned planes to convey a sense of solidity, of depth and scope, of personality and duration. The pattern, "the lay of the syllables," conveys a presence, an entity. The totality of plaited surfaces is more intensely actual than actuality.

The method of association is the same in all five books. Surfaces of different textures, different shapes, as in a visual collage, are juxtaposed in ways which force the edges to delineate still other shapes of other textures. The substances are words; the various textures are provided by prose and verse, and by description and narration; the shapes are past events, present recollections, apprehended sights. But the poem, unlike a painter's collage, can exploit the fact of duration, so that delineated shapes imply the continuity of a mind realizing new significances. Each of the five books contains three parts; these are large areas of repeated fragments which amplify the same continuous process of discovery and realization. Delineated shapes appear, then change significance as other shapes redefine them.

Any one book of *Paterson* demonstrates the way of them all. Here are the obtuse surfaces, for example, in *Paterson I*, 1: a letter from a woman poet ("more the woman than the poet"); the indiscriminate harvest of the mussels in Notch Brook, in 1857, in the rush for pearls; Paterson-the-man; a population report of 1870; a monster dwarf who was a tourist attraction, visited by clergymen and even by George Washington; the great sturgeon caught below the falls in 1817; an episode of Jackson's Whites: a motley mixture of women (Indian, Negro, White), and deserters from the British army, in the Appalachian woods; a picture from the *Geographic* of nine wives of an African chief, sitting astride a log ("an official log / to be presumed") in the order of their marriages; Mrs. Sarah Cumming, the wife of a minister, who plunged to her death from the top of the Passaic Falls; and Sam Patch, the town character, alias N. F. Paterson:

THE GRRRREAT HISTORY of that
old time Jersey Patriot
N. F. PATERSON!
(N for Noah; F for Faitoute; P for short)
"Jersey Lightning" to the boys.   (*I*, 1)

This character (Patch-Paterson) made a career of jumping from the tops of falls, until one day in 1826 when he jumped from the falls of the Genesee River (making his customary speech), but got confused; he landed clumsily and disappeared until the following spring, when his body was discovered in a cake of ice. "No ideas but in things."

By the way they touch one another these fragmentary shapes or bits of information delineate still other and more allusive shapes suggesting certain concepts: marriage, death, life, language, divorce, incoherence—paired and grouped in shifting connotations. As *Paterson I* continues, a dense and agitated pattern of these illusions begins to form within a given single consciousness. The richer the pattern the clearer it becomes. *Paterson II* fixes Paterson-the-poet in the park on a Sunday afternoon; he ponders the possibilities of organizing these myriad, extraneous impressions and all their implications. A pastoral world of blouses, shirt sleeves, and suspenders interrupts and reinforces his recollections of a deep, historical past.

Paterson III is the poet's crisis. It is an interior monologue about language and the limits of a poem, and about the spuriousness of actuality that is reflected in images of earth, air, fire, and water. What can art ever do about it? is the desperate question. "Give it up. Quit it. Stop writing" is the desperate answer. Exploded images of living and writing fuse. Facts and consciousness of facts mix and melt together in the heat of thought. *Paterson IV* is the lay of the old minstrel. It parodies pastoral love poetry with an absurd sexual situation, and then ponders the image of Eve Curie and the energy of woman and fertility and matter. Episodes of death and violence counterpoint each other, and terminate the whole affair of language. ("Kill the explicit sentence, don't you think?") Actuality has been intractable.

Paterson V amends this despair. Thoughts about death and disorder and the efficacy of art still preoccupy the poet, who is now an old man; but they are interrupted with images of spring and the bride and the unicorn. All the images are now symbolic because they exist in a medieval tapestry—a work of art—at which the old man is looking. He begins to see that violence and death are part of an ordered view of experience in the tapestry. Love and imagination have begot a work of art which *is* a total scheme of events.

Paterson V permutes the surfaces of *Paterson* I–IV, working with the relationships already established. In the lay of its syllables the broad, inherited subjects are fixed into a simple, governing overview of actuality. The marriage of things and the divorce of things, order and confusion, unity and separation are all aspects of life and death, but these are all components of a larger order. And art is the process of organizing separated and confused things into an order that is in itself alive. There is nothing new about these relationships. It is just that in re-examining them *Paterson* V settles for a fair compromise.

The poet has changed his mind about the limits of art and actuality, but the grounds for his new realization have been there all along. The tapestry merely presents to him again the images of male and female; like all the images of *Paterson* it is a record of the passions. Art appears to be the ordering of that dialogue between male and female by which life continues. The lay of the syllables, dramatizing the life process, begets an understanding of it. Art is a process of understanding. The consequence of this process, the work of art, *is* a reality, whether it happens to be a medieval Flemish tapestry or a modern action painting.

This poet's change of mind reflects a distinct change in the evolving philosophy of modern art. The collage is a medium, and *Paterson* I–IV uses the collage of words in the way of

Analytical Cubism, as a dialogue between the actual world and the form of the poem. In both cases the newspaper fragments counteract the abstractness of the subject. Because they are actual, they enable a dialogue between the actual world and the containing form.

From the works of Braque and Picasso and Gris, Williams understood the concept of a work of art as an entity itself, not an imitation of something else. But he was eclectic, and by the time he began *Paterson* V he could also appropriate ideas from a later generation of artists—from Pollack and deKooning and Rothko and Kline and Motherwell—who were developing what historians call Abstract Expressionism. Although Abstract Expressionism was not all that homogeneous, these later artists did exploit the idea that the painting itself is the only reality. In their collages the newsprint was no longer a sign of the outside world; it became merely part of the pattern, one of the textures in the work of art. The analogue in terms of *Paterson* is that the rhetoric of the poem itself is real. In fact, *Paterson III* closes with this explicit idea. At this point in the poem, dramatically speaking, it comes as a desperate statement. Not until later, in *Paterson* V, does Williams really celebrate the reality of his own rhetoric. The poem does so by calling attention to the analogue in action painting:

> Pollock's blobs of paint squeezed out
> with design!
> pure from the tube. Nothing else
> is real . . .   (V, 1)

So far I have been discussing various aspects of the fact that *Paterson* is about its own medium. The governing attitude of this cosmology is that language ought to correlate a state of order and a larger meaning to life as a whole, despite the fact that it continuously conveys only disarrangement and superficiality. Granting the attitude, the whole subject is so abstract that Williams had to find a tangible way to convey it, to make the words demonstrate their own arguments. The need to make language sensory was sufficient reason for Williams to build a collage; and the poet's later realization about the reality of his own rhetoric, or his own collage, corresponded to the evolving philosophy of art which enabled his collage in the first place. But a poem is thematic in a different way from a painting, and Williams *used* his collage to develop a concept or theory. Specifically, the form of the poetic lines in *Paterson* is a continuous experiment in *Paterson*'s theme about the need for an ordering of the language. The manner of *Paterson* insists on the matter. The poem's prosody clinches the argument.

Williams's strategy was to stay with actuality and intensify it, to insist on the literal to some extreme degree at which actuality would reveal pattern and order and therefore meaning. ("No ideas but in things!") To Williams, language meant what people speak. For years he experimented with prosody to find a verse form that could exploit the literal quality of contemporary speech and yet reveal that fruitful repetition which generates meaning.

After his early imitations of Keats he had embraced Whitman's idea of the need for autochthonous song, insisting on the poet's special task of constructing an indigenous verse. Williams had experimented with Imagism, with impressionistic images of visual clarity and concentrated attention, and he had found ways to incorporate Imagistic images in larger patterns. His purpose was to make the images seem to flow together in surprising mergers. He experimented with quantitative verse, with lines measured by duration instead of stress. He studied the adaptations of Latin hexameters to English speech, the unsuccessful attempts of poets from Edmund Spenser to Ezra Pound to accommodate quantitative units of syllables in the Latin language to colloquial English with its normal stress or accent.

Williams was looking for a poetic line that would intrinsically indicate tone of voice. He finally found a line, more properly a unit of measuring syllables, which could ac-

commodate the variations in tone and the colloquial authen-
ticity. He called it "the variable foot." It is one of the important inventions in the history of English prosody, and for
Williams's purpose it was a tremendous breakthrough in
poetic form. He later discovered this formal construction
while rereading *Paterson II*, 3. It was a series of stepped-
down lines, beginning

> The descent beckons
> > as the ascent beckoned
> > > Memory is a kind
> of accomplishment
> > a sort of renewal
> > > even
> an initiation, since the spaces it opens are new
> places
> > inhabited by hordes
> > > heretofore unrealized,
> of new kinds—
> > since their movements
> > > are toward new objectives
> (even though formerly they were abandoned).

These stepped-down lines are simply a series of variable units
of syllables. Each unit (or foot) of varying duration contains
its own stress pattern; and each line (each sum of three variable feet) has approximately the same duration (that is, it
takes the same amount of time to say it or to apprehend it)
as the other lines.

> No defeat is made up entirely of defeat—since
> the world it opens is always a place
> > formerly
> > > unsuspected. A
> world lost,
> > a world unsuspected
> > > beckons to new places
> and no whiteness (lost) is so white as the memory
> of whiteness.

In this construction a sentence—if there were any sentence at all—might begin in any one of the three parts of a line. Moreover, partial lines—or lines of short duration—by contradicting the ear's expectation thereby emphasize whatever they might say.

> With evening, love wakens
> though its shadows
> which are alive by reason
> of the sun shining—
> grow sleepy now and drop away
> from desire.
> Love without shadows stirs now
> beginning to waken
> as night
> advances.

The effect is to achieve a continuity which enforces pauses, isolating certain words, and thereby emphasizing whatever concept they might convey.

> The descent
> made up of despairs
> and without accomplishment
> realizes a new awakening:
> which is a reversal
> of despair.
> For what we cannot accomplish, what
> is denied to love,
> what we have lost in the anticipation—
> a descent follows,
> endless and indestructible   .

These lines slow down speech so that the realization that occurs can be apprehended. At the same time the lines also dramatize the poet's process of realizing. This passage which Williams later recognized as being so important to him, for example, expresses the argument that recollections of any sort (even in defeat) initiate the mind to new possibilities. The words which advance this argument occur in variable feet which slow down the argument and even interrupt it. The effect is that of limited, tentative advances upon a new realization. The significance of this realization, therefore, appears to lie in the manner in which it has occurred.

Prosody and theme reinforce each other. Thematically in *Paterson* the search for language is really the search for a governing order which most of the dramatis personae lack.

> The language, the language
> fails them
> They do not know the words
> or have not
> the courage to use them   .   (*I*, 1)

Sam Patch is accustomed to complete what he has to say by leaping from the tops of waterfalls, and his death is represented (at the end of *Paterson I*, 1) as a failure of language. "Speech had failed him. He was confused. The word had been drained of its meaning. There's no mistake in Sam Patch. He struck the water on his side and disappeared." Mrs. Cumming is another one who plunges over the falls, and her death is similarly represented as a failure of words. In fact, the words about the words that married her to Mr. Cumming cascade down the page, carrying her to annihilation.

> She was married with empty words:
> better to
> stumble at
> the edge
> to fall
> fall
> and be
> —divorced.   (*II*, 3)

Words and woman tumble down together. The conventional marrying words are powerless to save her from the divorce that is death. Since divorce in *Paterson* also signifies the annihilation of meaning, the implication is that conventional words cannot permanently marry anything to anything.

Paterson argues that the sheer volume of words obscures the order which inheres in words.

> Texts mount and complicate themselves, lead to further texts and those to synopses, digests and emendations. So be it. Until the words break loose or—sadly hold, unshaken. Unshaken! So be it.   (*III, 3*)

The trouble is that words cannot be separated from the events themselves ("no ideas but in things!"), and so the strategy of perceiving order must always begin with this limiting fact. In *Paterson IV, 3,* among the episodes of unexplainable, violent death, one finds this proposition: "Kill the explicit sentence, don't you think? and expand our meaning—by verbal sequences." The violent deaths, defying cause or order in the world, underscore—perhaps provoke—the poet's strategy of annihilating the customary confinements of words, to free the words to make a meaning, to make an order that he seeks. The form is the idea. In *Paterson* the longing for a language and the liberating of words to fashion such a language simultaneously occur.

As the search for a language becomes more and more localized in the poet's consciousness, it accumulates a broad significance; it becomes a dialectic between the poet and the materials of the actual world. He sees it as a great debate between art and actuality, which at first seem to him to be irreconcilable conditions; art has meaning, actuality has none. Yet one must somehow be the key to the other. "No ideas but in things!" is itself, of course, an idea. When he insists on it he commits himself to the urgent problem of finding the means by which art means.

One episode will suffice to show how the prosody of the poem and the drama of the search for language reinforce each other. It occurs in *Paterson III,* in the poet's intense debate with his material. At this point he has already admitted that the province of the poem is the world; he has railed over the fact that a poem should ever have to be composed of such debased substance; and he has realized that the poet must draw on some inner, personal vitality in order to transpose this deadening substance into a condition that will survive itself. And then he discovers an absolutely intractable mass, which is the earth itself. Entitled "SUBSTRATUM," it is a list of the kinds of stone and minerals discovered in the boring of an artesian well at the Passaic Rolling Mill in Paterson, New Jersey, from September, 1879, to November, 1880.

This tabular record of the inert material world is irreducible, utterly uncongenial to the function of art. "SUBSTRATUM" is a list of the geological specimens ("Red sandstone, fine"; "Red sandstone, coarse"; "Red sandstone, and a little shale"; "Soft shale"; "Selenite, 2 x 1 1/16 in."; "Pyrites"; "Red shale"; and twenty-three other stone formations) discovered at thirty separate random samplings, to a depth of 2,100 feet. What could be more intractable or more antithetical to poetry than this? Layers of rock that have been covered by mud. Mud: "If it were only fertile. Rather a sort of muck, a detritus, / . . . a pustular scum, a decay, a choking / lifelessness. . . ." Here is the ultimate impossibility for the poet.

What ever can be done with this primordial actuality? How to construct a living entity out of inert substance?

> How to begin to find a shape—to begin to begin again,
> turning the inside out: to find one phrase that will
> lie married beside another for delight   .   ?
> —seems beyond attainment   ."   (III, 3)

No wonder, the emphatic shrug that follows next. (*"American poetry is a very easy subject to discuss for the / simple reason that it does not exist"*).

And yet precisely in this crisis his denial that there is life in the inert matter is itself a vital awareness. Even in the organizing of his evidence that no poetry can exist in material actuality he generates a metaphor. The decayed and lifeless mud becomes a metaphor by the way he describes it. The mud becomes an active stimulus upon the consciousness. Its acrid stench, "almost one / might say a granular stench— fouls the mind." The awareness is all, is everything; the stench of inert matter "fouls the mind," and thereby comes alive with meaning.

In fact, this unremitting poet has already responded to "SUBSTRATUM." Even before recording it he has already discovered an analogy to layered earth in terms of words on a page. By the time he gets around to asking "How to begin to find a shape—to begin to begin again, / turning the inside out," he has already shaped a page of comparable surfaces. It has occurred three pages earlier. It is a typographical tour de force of unrelated phrases (signs and dates and slogans) stratified in broken, cockeyed lines from top to bottom of a page. The last two cockeyed lines assert: "—the association / is indefensible."

Despite the assertion, however, these jumbled lines do yield a pattern. The juxtaposition of unrelated phrases forces a continuity of thought, a something out of nothing. Even random, fragmented shards of actuality contain a pattern; and this page of stratified phrases has already accomplished what, three pages later, seems to be beyond attainment: "to find one phrase that will / lie married beside another for delight." In many ways *Paterson III* repeats a contradiction by which pattern exists in the very means of denying that pattern exists. The lay of the syllables amends the proposition that mere actual syllables are inert.

The final lyric in *Paterson III* states the poet's awesome commitment to discover an ordering principle. The roar of language in the world sounds to him like the falls cascading into ineffable vapor; and he must organize the energy of it all. "Not until I have made of it a replica / will my sins be forgiven and my / disease cured. . . ." The past is no help to him, and the future holds no answer.

> I must
> find my meaning and lay it, white,
> beside the sliding water: myself—
> comb out the language—or succumb   (III, 3)

The burden of expression is almost more than the poet can bear. This is partly because of his firm resolve, "No ideas but in things!" The things of this world must be the substance of the poem ("Be reconciled, poet, with your world, it is / the only truth," he says in *Paterson II, 3*). This substance is inert, and the poet has to bring it alive out of his own consciousness. But the poet's burden really lies in his concept of expression, which he understands to be an act of total commitment. In order to build a poem he must live it, and this means living through the experience of trying to comprehend the total order in mere actuality. Living and writing are inseparable.

The poet's crisis is precisely his realization of this terrifying commitment. He finally manages to say it in *Paterson III, 2.* "The writing is nothing, the being / in a position to write (that's / where they get you) is nine tenths / of the difficulty. . . . So that / to write, nine tenths of the problem / is to live."

It takes the poet twenty lines to say this much; and in the course of this strenuous attempt, even as he tries to separate living from writing for the sake of argument, he innocently uses a metaphor—the heat of fire—which fuses the very things he tries to separate. "Fire burns," he says, "that is the first law"; and the wind fans the flames. The world is a burning substance, and the poet's talk fans the flames into a holocaust which consumes everything in the world, including the poem about it—especially the poem. An interpolated news story about a fire in the car barns of the street railway company adds fuel to the poet's metaphor of a fire raging out of control, until "the person / passed into the flame, becomes the flame— / the flame taking over the person"; and again, "The person submerged / in wonder, the fire become the person ." (*III, 2*)

In the smoke of his own metaphor he has tried to see, clearly see, the relationship between the poet and the poem:

> What more clear than that of all things
> nothing is so unclear, between man and
> his writing, as to which is the man and
> which the thing and of them both which
> is the more to be valued. (*III, 2*)

This crisis has been intensifying since *Paterson I*, and every book in the poem variously repeats it. The longest prose passage in the poem, for example, a letter from the woman poet ("more the woman than the poet") spells out the dilemma. In terms of her own relationship with Paterson-the-poet she berates him for separating literature from life. She says, in effect, you love me only for my ideas; you are thrilled by my ideas for poetry, particularly for your poetry, but you deny *me*. She demands response from the whole man, not merely from the writer. Williams placed this long letter at the end of *Paterson I, 2*, without any rebuttal. It stands as testimony of his unconvincing attempt to separate living from writing, and the rest of *Paterson* tries to amend it.

But even the whole of *Paterson* was not enough. Although the poem is a complete entity, Williams was not convinced of it. He introduced *Paterson I* as "a plan for action to supplant a plan for action," that is, in terms suggesting even further amendment, *Paterson V*, for example. The "Author's Note" in the complete *Paterson* (1963) includes an apology for *Paterson V*, which says, "I have been forced to recognize that there can be no end to such a story I have envisioned with the terms which I have laid down for myself." Although *Paterson V* develops the idea that art is a completing process, Williams could not stop his poem even then.

Among his papers when he died were notes and drafts for yet another book of Paterson. Having concluded the argument about the completing process of art, he promptly turned his whole cosmology into a fragment and made the burden of expression a life's work. Williams confirmed the fact—as Whitman, Thoreau, Adams and Crane did before him—that the Emersonian poem really has no end. The lay of *Paterson* continued as long as the poet was able to sing.

Paradigm Six

Paterson is as *Paterson* does. It is an experiment in language that also insists on the need to find a language to convey what it means. As Williams claims, "This rhetoric / is real." The reflexive nature of *Paterson* illustrates what in fact organizes all these cosmologies. Each one is a writer's dialogue with his material or his matter in which he tries to make this matter prove a universe in which thought and things are continuous and unseparated. "No ideas but in things!" *Paterson* insists. But like all religious visions, the organic wholeness of all being is personal and essentially ineffable, so that representing this vision puts a special value and a special burden on the act of expressing. The particular vision has no form until it is expressed; and there is no precedent for expressing it. Neither statement nor description will suffice. The poet can render the felt immediacy of his vision, if at all, only by dramatizing the experience of it. "So that / to write," as Williams says, "nine tenths of the problem / is to live."

Of all these cosmologists it was Emerson who first confused writing with living. He even celebrated the confusion. The cosmic unity that he sought to express depends exactly on the notion that thought is action. At every stage in Emerson's evolving philosophy the action of thought establishes and verifies the continuity of mind and matter. In his original system this notion is the crux of his theory of language. In his later, amended system the action of thinking combines the individual man with his circumstances in a necessary ethic. By developing the idea that thought fuses mind and matter, and by making this fusion an ethical necessity, Emerson finally explained the process of poetry as a struggle to understand the world. In doing so he also anticipated the singular and ethical evangelism of all these American cosmologies.

If we think about verbal expression in terms of action, a curious question comes to mind. When does literary style become a form of behavior? Well, possibly when it duplicates the argument it conveys. Each of these cosmologies duplicates itself; each is an organic model of its own doctrine.

Its evolving form *is* the idea it conveys. Emerson's *ad hoc* use of metaphors, for example: by stating one metaphor and then explaining it with another and then another, Emerson built a tautology in *Nature*. This is confusing, perhaps, but it also confirms the argument that he was trying to express; namely, that the significance of all things lies in their totality; nothing is wholly self-sufficient. Emerson's *ad hoc* style is a strategy of discovery, using one image to reveal another, surprising the mind with possibilities.

Whitman's preface to *Leaves of Grass* models its own doctrine. It argues that America is the poem and that the poet is its Answerer; and the form of the preface is antiphonal: catalogues of the people's qualities are answered by assertions of the poet's qualities. Similarly, *The Education* correlates the realization that it dramatizes; so does *Moby Dick*. Melville's novel becomes a cosmology by evaluating an attempt to build a cosmology. It correlates its meaning by the way it repeats itself. By Ishmael's speculating on the facts and successively contradicting his own conclusions, Melville expresses a faith that is based on the limitation of all doctrines. There are probably many ways to describe the organic quality of these cosmologies. You can call it "innate form" as Coleridge did; you can say that the form *is* the struggle to formulate; or you can say it is the poet's inspired confusion of speaking and doing.

The idea of confusing action and verbal expression gets us into a kind of extra-literary criticism. It helps to explain certain extra-literary ideas that have become part of the history of American literature. One such idea is the mystique of The Great American Novel, that legendary fiction that has vaguely haunted American writers and reviewers for the past hundred years. It is curious, for example, the way the cosmologies become more evangelical the more they invoke the metaphor of America. Thomas Wolfe's passion for living his writing produced a caricature of a cosmology. His vast fragment with its projected table of contents is probably the nearest thing to The Great American Novel. According to the mystique, The Great American Novel would assimilate the myriad details of a geographical and historical America —past, present, and future—into a single record, a single comprehensive order of being. This is nothing more than a parochial version of any writer's endeavor to find out who he is by discovering his relationship to his environment. The Great American Novel is a naïve concept of limitless achievement; yet it has persisted since the 1860s, and the persistence of the mystique is an enlightening fact about American writers in general.

The term connotes some sort of literary superform, as broad in scope as an epic, as intense and concentrated as a poem, as alive and dynamic as its author is in fact. Significantly, this legendary work has always been defined in terms of its impossibility. In fact, its impossibility was expressed even before the concept got its familiar name. Henry Longfellow's *Kavanagh* (1849) spends a chapter admonishing the notion of a literature that would be truly, exclusively, and quintessentially national. John William DeForest's editorial in *The Nation* (January 9, 1868), the first printed mention of the term to gain wide circulation, called the notion impossible. The editorial contains DeForest's conversation with a friend who has proposed to write The Great American Novel; and DeForest points out the impossibility of the task for the reason that this nation has not yet *lived* a good poem. DeForest's argument against the concept is just as revealing as the concept in the first place: the conviction about the inseparability of writing the poem and living it.

This evangelism is part of American history. The preoccupation with American quintessence has been exhaustively documented by Benjamin Spencer's book, *The Quest for Nationality* (1957), that recalls dozens and dozens of writers who anticipated Emerson's declaration of cultural and literary independence in *The American Scholar* (1837). Spencer quotes liberally from the mass of published opinions about native literature and native style and a native language and a native copyright law. His first sentence declares "Almost from the beginning there was a sense of distinctive nationality"; and he documents this parochial attitude from its origins in the seventeenth century, with the Puritan notion of New England as a New Jerusalem, to the year of the death of Whitman, who made "autochthonous song" into a literary philosophy. In this climate of opinion the notion of The Great American Novel has become a familiar synonym for the national epitome.

The notion of the consummate national fiction is still familiar. One theory in the eighties held that The Great American Novel might possibly be accomplished in installments, with an epitomizing fiction of each region contributing to a collected record of the entire national culture. This theory was suggested by Edward Eggleston and later discussed by Mark Twain and by Frank Norris, among others. By 1900 this idea of a cumulative fiction was congenial to the imported theory of literary naturalism and to the growing popularity of journalistic fiction. One result has been the continued production of trilogies and bulky novels with massive American settings. Frank Norris's plan for "The Epic of the Wheat," Theodore Dreiser's Cowperwood trilogy, James T. Farrell's several sagas, John Dos Passos's *U.S.A.* and its sequel *Midcentury* are all public monuments to America. So is Carl Sandburg's *Remembrance Rock*, although Sandburg had already built a better monument to America in his lyrical compendium, *The People, Yes*. Thomas Wolfe's work belongs with these fictions, most of which are attempts to accommodate large public events to some individual or group of private lives, to show somehow the continuity of consciousness and environment.

But the mystique of The Great American Novel is merely an aspect of the subject I began with; it carries to a mythical extremity what I think is a recurring characteristic among American writers: the endeavor to expand the limits of verbal expression. Going back to Emerson again, you can see a sustained attempt to make the processes of apprehending and speaking and doing mutually interchangeable. Emerson's theory of language in *Nature* was a capsule of his theory of the universe: since words are signs of natural facts, and natural facts are symbols of spiritual facts, the naming of a natural fact necessarily interprets that fact symbolically in the largest sense. The act of expressing words, therefore, establishes the continuity of mind and matter.

The process of verbal expression, for Emerson, included both comprehension and behavior. He saw it as a continuous act, from the inception of an idea to the practical application of it; and he insisted on this in a bewildering array of statements. He said in "The Poet" that "words and deeds are quite indifferent modes of divine energy. Words are also actions, and actions are a kind of words." The word, or expression of an image, moreover, is the *essential* act, because it establishes the continuity of mind and matter. "The preamble of thought, the transition through which it passes from the unconscious to the conscious, is action," he wrote in *The American Scholar*; and to this idea he added another: "Only so much do I know, as I have lived."

Emerson kept making these orphic statements about the continuity of thought and behavior. "Thinking is the function. Living is the functionary," he wrote in *The American*

Scholar. The "Divinity School Address" (1838) is a full-length argument for identifying thinking with living. Christ is the case in point. Christ's realization of the harmony of moral laws and natural laws was revelation; and this was no academic matter, for Christ *lived* His revelation. Expressing one's own revelation is what "The Poet" exhorts, and we infer from Emerson that Christ was the true poet because He lived what He revealed.

These statements about the continuity of thought and action do not all say the same thing. Emerson did not always distinguish between the word itself and the process of forming the word, but there is no doubt of his conviction that expression is the most comprehensive action of the consciousness.

Emerson blurred the distinctions between mental action and physical action, and he occasionally contradicted himself. Speaking for all idealists, in "The Transcendentalist," he said, "we are miserable with inaction." He was distinguishing between the essential action of expressing a principle, which people in general do not understand, and the mere application of a principle, which people mistake for action. ("Once possessed of the principle, it is equally easy to make four or forty thousand applications of it.") But he stated a different attitude in his funeral oration on Thoreau. The oration is about the way Thoreau lived: not about what he *did* in his life but about the way he *thought*; yet Emerson decided that Thoreau had not fully expressed himself: Thoreau had lacked ambition, and "instead of engineering for all America, he was the captain of a huckleberry-party."

Emerson insisted that the poem is a continuous process of action. To put it another way, the poem is a continuous extension of the poet; it is the poet's performance. All the romantic cosmologies bear this out. The poet *performs* his poem. To comprehend the grand scheme is necessarily to perform it and enforce it, as Ahab literally tried to do and Ishmael metaphorically did. The actual poets have all committed themselves this way. Whitman, Adams, Crane, Wolfe, and Williams performed their poems, insofar as they symbolized themselves in the act of comprehending. To express the poem was to live it through (and somehow to live through it), to carry one's inner comprehensions to one's outer circumstances, to convert revelation into fact.

So committed, the poet could scarcely escape being an evangelist; even Thoreau, who made a point of belittling doers and reformers. If the reformer has a pain in his bowels, Thoreau said, he is sure that the world has been eating green apples, and forthwith sets about reforming the world. But even Thoreau contradicted himself. He made this remark at the end of "Economy," which is the longest chapter in *Walden*; and he spent most of this chapter preaching an ethic, proselytizing a way of living, a way of behaving. Williams was really speaking for all these poets when he said, "The writing is nothing, the being/in a position to write (that's/ where they get you) is nine tenths/of the difficulty. . . ."

With these cosmologies for my examples, I have been saying that the most intimate and revealing subject of any fiction, when he makes it available to the reader, is the author's dialogue with his material. It is what *makes* the cosmologies, and it explains a great deal about the other fictions that I have described. But the record of the author's struggle is not always available to the reader; it is not always intrinsic in the work of art. There is not likely to be an author's dialogue in those fictions which assume or state a well-defined theory of cause and effect, even when such fictions are ostensibly about a comprehensive idealism. Although most persuasive fictions are records of a writer's exploration of his subject, there is usually no sharp distinction between those that reveal it and those that do not. In this respect the cosmologies are exceptionally clear overstatements of the author's situation.

The cosmologies offer some guidelines in considering both the limitations and the possibilities of understanding a fiction through its author's struggle to express it. A few generalizations illustrate these limitations and these possibilities. Haw-thorne's narratives, for example, are not germane to the cosmologies, even *The Blithedale Romance* (1852), which is about one man's attempt to impose an idealistic system on the world. Although Hollingsworth attempts to decree a single, true, and sufficient social scheme, it is clear that the author condemns the attempt for ethical reasons that are well established in the book. Hawthorne chastises Hollingsworth through the indictments of several principal characters and through the resolution of the conflict. The closed system of God and man which evaluates the hero of this book, as in Hawthorne's other narratives, is very clear.

Another novel which is different in kind from the cosmologies, although ostensibly about a character's attempt to decree an idealism, is Scott Fitzgerald's *The Great Gatsby* (1925). Fitzgerald was so certain about the implications of experience that he could objectively summarize the whole situation of the embattled romantic. Even the book's first chapter contains a caricature of this despairing idealist: the tableau of Gatsby by the dark shore of his rented villa, staring into the night across the harbor, and stretching his arms toward the distant green light on the end of the dock that belongs to Daisy Buchanan.

Nathaniel West's *Miss Lonelyhearts* (1933) is another fiction that judges a questing idealist according to a fixed view of consequences. This book is about the hero's disastrous mistake in trying to live his own idealism; and the plot, which is the author's scheme of cause and effect, makes it clear that the hero's dilemma is not the author's. The point is that Hawthorne and Fitzgerald and West—as different as their fictions are—could each believe in some well-defined theory of events by which to explain human experience. So could J. F. Cooper and W. D. Howells and Stephen Crane and Theodore Dreiser and Edith Wharton and John Steinbeck and John Marquand; and so could W. C. Bryant and H. W. Longfellow and Robinson Jeffers and Benjamin

Franklin—to name a few more writers whose works are not germane to the romantic cosmologies, and for the same reason.

But the distinctive characteristic of the cosmologies, the dialogue between the author and his material, does clarify a common relationship among other fictions as various as Emily Dickinson's poems and *The Adventures of Huckleberry Finn*, for example, and *Death in the Afternoon*. I mention them because they are so apparently different, yet these poems, this novel, and this autobiographical essay all principally dramatize what Wallace Stevens has called the act of the mind finding what will suffice. This act *is* their subject in common.

For Emily Dickinson, as indeed for Wallace Stevens, the true business of the poet is to probe and doubt and discover. Dickinson's poems argue with the dogma of nineteenth-century Calvinism, and they affirm the rightness of the questing self. She raised her questions of doubt and faith largely on the strength of Emerson's early philosophy, although she was also capable of doubting Transcendentalism. Dickinson's relation to Emerson's ideas was something like Henry James's relation to them, in that Emerson's coherence and his confusions both furnished her with a subject. No one poem or even group of poems is a definitive statement of her belief; and doctrine is not really the point of her poetry so much as her incessant return to the subject of some given comprehensive overview, orthodox or otherwise, to develop her own self-sufficient questioning. Her faith was not in any dogma but in the finding out, and this emphasis was peculiarly Emersonian.

The author's dialogue with his material also organizes the structure of *Huckleberry Finn*. Huck's continual attempts to evaluate his own experiences generate a large indictment of the moral system of a slaveholding society and raise still larger questions about the efficacy of mankind. Huck's piecemeal responses to his situation accomplish all this because they are ambivalent; they force the reader to collaborate. Huck's point of view is variously innocent and sophisticated, full of wonder and iconoclasm, and it is not always clear how much he understands himself or how categorically he represents the author's opinion. Nearly every episode in some way repeats this ambivalent point of view with the same effect, which is to express an honest disenchantment with some idealized illusion about human beings.

It is surprising to realize that Huck does not morally improve as the book develops. He is as honestly selfish and expedient in deciding to steal watermelons instead of persimmons at the beginning of his journey down the river as he is in deciding to save Jim from slavery. But his arch-innocent questioning in these dilemmas, as in all his others, dramatizes the process of his realizing just what it is he does believe. Events force him to perceive a moral system which he can express only by living.

The author's struggle to build a comprehensive metaphor of order also organizes *Death in the Afternoon*. In fact, this autobiographical essay has many characteristics of a cosmology. It is an *ars poetica*: it is a primer on bullfighting which assesses the contest as an art form, and discovers analogies in bullfighting to sculpture and painting and writing. But it does not begin with this comprehensive view of bullfighting. Hemingway has to work out the analogies bit by bit as he goes along, narratively and editorially and descriptively by turns. This artist begins with a concept of style that involves his delineating a sequence of nothing but what he calls "motion and fact," in order to convey the emotion inherent in a situation. As the essay proceeds, he evolves the idea that this style is inherent in living as well as in representation. He merges an aesthetic of bullfighting with an ethic that is as personal and subjective as the author. *Death in the Afternoon* does not build a comprehensive overview of God and man; but its similarity to the cosmologies helps to explain the ethical formulations in all of Hemingway's fiction.

The idea that the writer's performance and his expression

are generically alike also helps to explain Hemingway's reluctant disciple, Norman Mailer, particularly in *Advertisements for Myself* (1959) and *Presidential Papers* (1963). Among contemporary writers, in fact, the whole Beat movement as derived from the Hipsters can be partly explained by Emerson's doctrine of total expression. This is a statement of kind and not quality. Their evangelism is one of their distinctive characteristics: the attempt to *perform* a vaguely rebellious doctrine which they cannot otherwise express.

It is difficult to know just where this particular version of romantic expression stopped being literary. The Hippies have now converted the expression of their beatific visions exclusively into a cult of performance. They attempt to relive their narcotic revelations by proselytizing the nonbelievers. Their evangelism is blatant. Emerson wrote a text for their kind of sermon in the first paragraph of "Fate." After listening to other persons talk about the "Spirit of the Times," he said: "To me, however, the question of the times resolved itself into a practical question of the conduct of life. How shall I live?"

In this essay Emerson finally found a way to say that poetry is the necessary and continuing process of *all* men, not just the hypothetical poet; and that poetry—as he meant it —enables and causes *all* moral development. "Fate" was his final rationale of the poetic process; it describes a necessary dialectic between the individual man and whatever he cannot understand. "Fate" is the system which enforces men's continuous endeavor to penetrate unpenetrated cause, "a stupendous antagonism, a dragging together of the poles of the universe"; and it happens to all men, each in his own degree.

Emerson said in his earlier essays that all men would be poets if they would only realize it, and in "Fate" he finally managed to spread the poet's divine affliction among all men by ordaining them in his own religion of practical idealism. His theory of language finally developed into his valedictory: Everyman his own poet.

Notes

CHAPTER ONE   *The Mystique of Expression*

1. To Maxwell Perkins (November 17, 1928), in Elizabeth Nowell, ed., *The Letters of Thomas Wolfe* (New York, 1956), p. 113.
2. To George W. McCoy (March 22, 1932), *Letters*, p. 330.
3. To Horace Williams (September 9, 1921), *Letters*, p. 18.
4. Thomas W. Wolfe, *The Story of a Novel* (New York, 1936), p. 35.
5. To Maxwell Perkins (December 29, 1930), *Letters*, p. 287.
6. To Maxwell Perkins (December 9, 1930), *Letters*, p. 280.
7. Thomas Wolfe, *Of Time and the River* (New York, 1935), p. 660.
8. To Sherwood Anderson (September 22, 1937), *Letters*, p. 654.
9. To Maxwell Perkins (December 15, 1936), *Letters*, p. 587.

CHAPTER FOUR   *Hart Crane's "Span of Consciousness"*

1. To Gorham Munson (February 18, 1923), in Brom Weber, ed., *The Letters of Hart Crane: 1916–1932* (New York, 1952), p. 125. All citations of Crane's correspondence refer to this collection.
2. To Gorham Munson (March 17, 1926), *Letters*, p. 237.
3. To Alfred Stieglitz (April 15, 1923), *Letters*, p. 131.
4. To Otto H. Kahn (March 18, 1926), *Letters*, p. 240.
5. To Otto H. Kahn (December 3, 1925), *Letters*, p. 223.
6. To Seldon Rodman (May 22, 1930), *Letters*, p. 351.
7. To Gorham Munson (March 5, 1926), *Letters*, p. 236.
8. To Allen Tate (June 12, 1922), *Letters*, p. 90.
9. To Gorham Munson (January 5, 1923), *Letters*, p. 114f.
10. Malcolm Cowley, "A Preface to Hart Crane," *New Republic*, 62 (April 23, 1930), pp. 276ff.
11. Allen Tate, "A Distinguished Poet," *Hound and Horn*, 3 (July–September, 1930), p. 581.
12. Yvor Winters, "The Progress of Hart Crane," *Poetry* 36, (June, 1930), p. 157.

13. Tate, p. 581.
14. William James, *The Varieties of Religious Experience: A Study in Human Nature* (New York, 1902), p. 427.
15. To Gorham Munson (ca. June 18, 1922), *Letters*, p. 91f.
16. To Waldo Frank (March 21, 1924), *Letters*, p. 181.
17. To Waldo Frank (July 26, 1926), *Letters*, p. 268.
18. To Allen Tate (May 16, 1922), *Letters*, p. 89.
19. To Sherwood Anderson (January 10, 1922), *Letters*, p. 77.
20. Hart Crane, "Modern Poetry," in Waldo Frank, ed., *The Collected Poems of Hart Crane* (New York, 1933), pp. 175ff. The essay first appeared in Oliver Saylor, ed., *Revolt in the Arts* (New York, 1929).
21. To Otto H. Kahn (September 12, 1927), *Letters*, p. 305.
22. To Waldo Frank (June 20, 1926), *Letters*, p. 261.
23. To Waldo Frank (July 24, 1926), *Letters*, p. 267.
24. Brom Weber, *Hart Crane: A Biographical and Critical Study* (New York, 1948), p. 365f.
25. Karl Shapiro, "The Meaning of the Discarded Poem," in Charles D. Abbott, ed., *Poets at Work* (New York, 1948), pp. 111ff.
26. To Caresse Crosby (September 6, 1929), *Letters*, p. 345.
27. Crane, *Collected Poems*, p. 31ff.

PARADIGM FOUR

1. Henry James, "Preface to *The Princess Casamassima*," in *The Art of the Novel: Critical Prefaces by Henry James*, with an introduction by Richard P. Blackmur (New York, 1948), p. 65.
2. "Preface to *The Wings of the Dove*," *Prefaces*, p. 304.
3. "Preface to *The Princess Casamassima*," *Prefaces*, p. 304.
4. "Preface to *Daisy Miller and Other Stories*," *Prefaces*, p. 278.
5. "Preface to *The Ambassadors*," *Prefaces*, p. 319.

CHAPTER SEVEN   *The Dense Totality of Henry James*

1. To H. G. Wells (July 10, 1915), in Morton Zabel, ed., *The Portable Henry James* (New York, 1961), p. 489.
2. Henry James, *Hawthorne* (1879; Cornell, 1956), p. 67f.
3. Henry James, *Partial Portraits* (1888), p. 9; and following quotations on p. 8 and p. 31.
4. Henry James, "Anthony Trollope," in Leon Edel, ed., *Henry James: The Future of the Novel* and other essays (New York, 1956), p. 247; and following quotations, p. 248.
5. Henry James, "The Art of Fiction," in Edel, p. 9f; and following quotation, p. 13.

6. *Hawthorne*, p. 8; and following quotation, p. 48.

7. Edel, p. 15f.

8. "Preface to *The Spoils of Poynton*," *Prefaces*, p. 129f.

9. "Preface to *Roderick Hudson*," *Prefaces*, p. 16.

10. "Preface to *The Princess Casamassima*," *Prefaces*, p. 67.

11. Henry James, "Guy de Maupassant," in Edel, p. 203. James's essays on Zola, Balzac, George Eliot, and Flaubert are also reprinted in this collection.

12. Preface to *The Portrait of a Lady*, *Prefaces*, p. 51.

13. Preface to *What Maisie Knew*, *Prefaces*, p. 142.

14. F. O. Matthiessen and Kenneth B. Murdock, eds., *The Notebooks of Henry James* (New York, 1947), p. 251.

15. *Notebooks*, p. 208.

16. *Notebooks*, p. 263.

17. *Notebooks*, p. 258.

18. Preface to *The Wings of the Dove*, *Prefaces*, p. 300.

19. Preface to *The Golden Bowl*, *Prefaces*, p. 330.

20. Preface to *The Portrait of a Lady*, *Prefaces*, p. 45f.

21. Preface to *The Spoils of Poynton*, *Prefaces*, p. 132.

22. Preface to *The Ambassadors*, *Prefaces*, p. 315.

23. Preface to *The Princess Casamassima*, *Prefaces*, p. 62.

Index

Dr. A. D. Van Nostrand is Associate Professor of English at Brown University and is on the Fulbright Commission appointed by the State Department to formulate long-range plans for teaching, research and the exchange of information in Brazil and Peru. Dr. Van Nostrand has conducted a television series on NBC, *The American Scene*, a series on the National Educational Television network and is the author of *The Denatured Novel*, an appraisal of the economics of publishing in America. In addition, Dr. Van Nostrand is working on a new book, *The Strategy of Writing*, which will be published by McGraw-Hill in the spring of 1969.